P9-CLH-908

THE MYSTERY OF THE CHILD

RELIGION, MARRIAGE, AND FAMILY

Series Editors

Don S. Browning
John Witte Jr.

THE MYSTERY OF THE CHILD

Martin E. Marty

William B. Eerdmans Publishing Company
Grand Rapids, Michigan / Cambridge, U.K.

Published 2007 by
Wm. B. Eerdmans Publishing Co.
2140 Oak Industrial Drive N.E., Grand Rapids, Michigan 49505 /
P.O. Box 163, Cambridge CB3 9PU U.K.
www.eerdmans.com

Printed in the United States of America

12 11 10 09 08 07 7 6 5 4 3 2 1

Library of Congress Cataloging-in-Publication Data

Marty, Martin E., 1928-
The mystery of the child / Martin E. Marty
p. cm.
ISBN 978-0-8028-1766-2 (cloth: alk. paper)
1. Child care — Religious aspects — Christianity. 2. Parenting — Religious aspects — Christianity. 3. Child rearing — Religious — aspects — Christianity. 4. Mystery. 5. Children. I. Title.

BV4529.M363 2007
261.8′35874 — dc22

2006039450

To the children of Ascension Parish

who have been teaching me for forty-three years

Contents

Series Foreword

The Religion, Marriage, and Family series has a complex history. It is also the product of some synergism. The books in the first phase evolved from a research project located at the University of Chicago and supported by a generous grant from the Division of Religion of the Lilly Endowment. The books in this new phase of the series will come from more recent research projects located in the Center for the Study of Law and Religion in the School of Law of Emory University.

This second phase of the series will include books from two of this Center's projects, both supported by generous grants from the Pew Charitable Trust and Emory University. The first project was called Sex, Marriage, and Family in the Abrahamic Religions and began with an Emory University faculty seminar in 2001. The second project was called The Child in Law, Religion, and Society and also was initiated by a semester-long Emory faculty seminar that met during the autumn of 2003.

Although the first phase of the Religion, Marriage, and Family series primarily examined Christian perspectives on the family, it also included books on theological views of children. In this second phase, family in the broad sense is still in the picture but an even greater emphasis on children will be evident. The Chicago projects and the Emory projects have enjoyed a profitable synergistic relationship. Legal historian John Witte, director of the two Emory projects, worked with practical theologian Don Browning on the Chicago initiatives. Later, Browning worked with Witte on the research at Emory. Historian Martin Marty joined Witte and Browning to lead the 2003 seminar on childhood.

Some of the coming books in the Religion, Marriage, and Family series will be written or edited by Emory faculty members who participated in the two seminars of 2001 and 2003. But authors in this new phase also will come from other universities and academic settings. They will be scholars, however, who have been in conversation with the Emory projects.

This series intends to go beyond the sentimentality, political manipulation, and ungrounded assertions that characterize so much of the contemporary debate over marriage, family, and children. In all cases, they will be books probing the depth of resources in Christianity and the other Abrahamic religions for understanding, renewing, and in some respects redefining current views of marriage, family, and children. The series will continue its investigation of parenthood and children, work and family, responsible fatherhood and motherhood, and equality in the family. It will study the responsibility of the major professions such as law, medicine, and education in promoting and protecting sound families and healthy children. It will analyze the respective roles of church, market, state, legislature, and court in supporting marriages, families, children, and parents.

The editors of this series hope to develop a thoughtful and accessible new literature for colleges, seminaries, churches, other religious institutions, and probing laypersons. In this post-9/11 era, we are all learning that issues pertaining to families, marriage, and children are not just idiosyncratic preoccupations of the United States; they have become worldwide concerns as modernization, globalization, changing values, emerging poverty, changing gender roles, and colliding religious traditions are disrupting families and challenging us to think anew about what it means to be husbands, wives, parents, and children.

The editors of this series are honored to include Martin Marty's profound and engaging *The Mystery of the Child.* We are all used to being informed by Marty's flagship contributions to the history of American Christianity, his insightful editorials for the *Christian Century,* and his groundbreaking research on worldwide fundamentalism. But Martin Marty is a man of many parts. Friends cannot be near Marty when he is interacting with his own children and grandchildren or the offspring of others without realizing that, yes, he had within him a wonderful book on children.

During the autumn of 2003, he helped John Witte lead a faculty seminar at the School of Law of Emory University titled "The Child in Law, Religion, and Society." The idea for this book was born there. And now we have it.

It will constitute a contribution to both scholarship in the emerging field of childhood studies as well as an inspiring meditation on children for parents, grandparents, religious leaders, and anyone who has ever been a child – which includes us all. Be prepared for a great ride through the pathways of childhood guided by one of America's premier scholars and commentators on religion.

Don S. Browning
John Witte Jr.

Acknowledgments

This book would not exist were it not for the invitation of the Center for the Study of Law and Religion at Emory University, where for three years I co-directed a project on "The Child in Religion, Law, and Society." The other, and prime, director was John Witte, director also of the Center itself, who with his colleagues at Emory was the strongest influence on the author. University of Chicago colleague Don Browning, a veteran at the Center, was a regular stimulating conversation-partner on this subject. Nineteen Emory faculty members were important instructors to me in our regular seminars. I acknowledge with thanks the splendid cooperation of the colloquially and appropriately named "Dream Team" staff at the Center, who also contributed more to the substance of the work than they can know.

Beyond the Center sphere, I recognize with thanks the following: Linda Les Nelson, who has been my pastor, co-teacher, and friend, who worked over the manuscript line by line, making substantive contributions along with editorial queries and suggestions. The main work of editing fell to Barbara Hofmeier, my oft-times colleague in editing ventures, in whom I have complete confidence. I am also grateful for the editorial work of Jennifer Hoffman at Eerdmans. My regular assistant at correspondence, Mary Jean Marinier, was a gracious and prompt expediter. As always, proofreader Harriet Julia Marty, with whom I share grand- and great-grandparenthood, provided unmatched existential counsel and support.

M.E.M.

1. The Subject of Care

"One book is about one thing – at least the good ones are." Because I hope to write a good book, I have to follow the advice I have long offered to students and authors whose books I have edited. That means being clear about the thesis of this one.

Here it is: the provision of care for children will proceed on a radically revised and improved basis if instead of seeing the child first as a problem faced with a complex of problems, we see her as a mystery surrounded by mystery. The need to deal with problems will, of course, be pressing in the case of every child, but if this need dominates the thoughts and actions of those who provide care, much of the wonder and joy of relating to children will be shrouded or even lost.

In the clinic, experts offer advice about how to *conceive* a child. But we are interested in a nonclinical question: how to conceive *of* a child. In the schools other experts on childhood offer guidance and advice. We are interested in what might be called meta-guidance or meta-advice, treating issues that are situated behind or beyond those involving practical counsel. Providing care for the child is the business of the whole society, which means that it involves all the citizens – parents and teachers, nurses and doctors, coaches and tutors, pastors and religious educators, attorneys and judges, politicians and artists, entertainers and theorists. They bear various responsibilities for the care of children. Each provider of care will welcome advice by specialists to satisfy a particular curiosity or to promote research in various fields, but some questions and approaches apply to the situation of most children. All of these are cast in a different light when one invokes first of all "mystery" rather than "problem." A new parent will be mindful of the problems of having another mouth to feed, but he will also serve the child well if he is moved to regard her as a wonder, something more and other than the combination of parental genes and the result of scientifically explicable procreating processes.

Because the constant focus will be on the provision of care, it is important to be clear about what exactly *providing* means in this case. Recalling the background and origin of the word will suggest how appropriate it is for describing the activity of those who care for children. The second syllable, *vide,* comes from the Latin *videre,* "to see." A form of it shows up in the English word *vision.* The *pro-* in the first syllable means "forward." To provide, then, entails "seeing forward." The responsible provider is a foreseer who arranges to supply what is needed or will be needed in the future. Such supplying can be, and in the case of the child is, "provisional," because the providing is "for the time being." The child is constantly growing and changing, and so is the way in which adults relate to him. In the short term, a parent may provide lunch for a school-bound child or arrange for a tutor after school, but providing also implies foresight, picturing what the child will need and what he may become through the years.

When people speak, as many do, of God's *providence,* they are referring to divine foresight and supply. When they speak of a person as a *supervisor,* they expect that person to look ahead as if from above, which is what givers of care for children often are called to do. Other terms in the family of the word *supervise* suggest still more. Thus if adults "survey" the scenes of child care, they are "looking over" conditions and values. Even when they "improvise," as everyone who relates to children must do, they are inventing approaches while "seeing ahead."

Care, as in "the provision of care," does not here suggest a sentimental activity – part of the "caring and sharing" often spoken of in days past. Care here instead may involve concern and rigorous action. In my list of typical providers of care, I include attorneys, judges, legislators, politicians. Introducing professionals in fields relating to law is a way of assuring that this book is not "soft," since by nature law is considered to be "hard." Yet representing children who are in foster care or under adoption, reforming penal systems involving children, and ensuring the rights of the young certainly demonstrate that legal agendas are open to the provision of care and that legal professionals can be committed to that endeavor. As the acknowledgments make clear, the project of which this book is a part, sponsored by a center for the study of law and religion, is called "The Child in Religion, Law, and Society."

Further, lest any reader expects a book in which the adults are charged to swarm above and swoop down on the world of the child, let it be noted that I conceive the provision of care to go in two directions. Sensitive and generous adults testify that they learn much from children, so the child is in some cases a teacher and, in her own ways, a provider of care for those older than she. The provision of care does not allow for static adult-child relations; nor does the older person play a role that is condescending or patronizing. Sustained care relies on a constant appraising and revising of situations on the part of providers, who keep on learning through their encounters with each child.

What Does the Book Offer to Providers of Care?

To speak of adults in broad categories like "citizens" or "members of society," or in narrower ones like "parents and teachers," is to leave the writer and readers at an impersonal distance from each other. Here are some imagined readers who, I hope, will find something of interest in this plumbing of the mysterious dimensions of the child:

First among providers of care could be a *senior couple* driving to a family reunion, a man and a woman who are not likely to converse about how an abstraction called society as a whole determines a child's life. They will be more particular, especially if they concentrate on problems. They may spend energy discussing a grandchild who is delinquent, rebellious, or alienated. Upon arriving at the gathering, they will try to talk to her, but, meeting with little success, will become frustrated or even sad. On the way home they might probe some ways of relating to her with new resolve and understanding. They will draw on resources of hope that they have been developing, thanks to their concern and the love that never abandons a child who has or creates problems.

The same couple while at the reunion may also gain a fresh awareness of the dimensions of mystery that surround a child, especially if they have been given a chance to lift into their arms a new great-grandchild. If they allow themselves a tear of joy to accompany their tremors, they will admit that questions crowd their minds. "Who is this child?" It may sound strange to put it this way, but their question might well be "What *is* a child?" They won't ask something like that because they wish to write a dictionary definition. They will ponder it because the tiny miracle they hold offers so many possibilities for good and ill that they are left to wonder over the mystery of the child.

These seniors might read this book in search of *self-understanding*. As they read, they should find some new ways for thinking about what it means to be a child. They might also reflect on what it means for each of them to have been a child. When we connect the "mystery of the child" with the mysteries that are present when one grows old, the search for meaning in all of life can prosper. When those who have been parents someday become great-grandparents, they can still show care by providing for the child in their last will and testament.

Second, and again much less remote than citizenry or society as providers of care, are *parents and other family members.* Societies regard parents as the primary suppliers of attention and concern, though the fortunate child draws as well on other family members, and the unfortunate one hopes for and may find surrogates for these. Wonder over the mystery of the child's gifts will often enthrall two parents whom we picture coming home from a dance recital that featured their four-year-old. We can imagine overhearing in their conversation the question, "Why are children at that age so uninhibited, so eager to show off to their parents, so ready to display what must be a built-in tendency to wiggle to music and put their bodies to work and play?" Later, such parents might ask what happens to so many children who become inhibited as they reach adolescence. What are the sources of the self-consciousness in some children, the emotional defensiveness that kills off art?

Another couple might be jarred because their daughter, from whom they expected so much on stage, had become shy and was sometimes out of step with the other dancers. The psychologist or the ballet teacher can approach that situation practically. The parents might use the occasion to consider a whole set of issues about the human personality, confronting themes that deal with all lives, beginning with their own. Will their child make it on her own in this world of the arts, or does she need help? Because the impulse when dealing with problems is to take practical steps, parents might at first glance find impractical a book on wonder and mystery. They might react to the book's title by saying, "So? So the child is a mystery. If we understand what you mean, we agree. Then what?"

Talk about the wonder and mystery of the child will not license any encouragement of child-worship — anything but that! I will, however, point to some analogies between worshiping and being awakened to wonder. The German theologian Romano Guardini wrote that the *act* of worship is "pointless but significant" *(zwecklos aber doch sinnvoll).* On shelves of books that focus on resolving practical issues, this book on the mystery of the child promotes a different kind of interest. I do not aspire, at least not directly, to present a "how-to" handbook. Instead, my call here for parents to explore the mystery of the child is intended to inspire positive responses that will reach into many aspects of life. Not all of them deal narrowly with childhood and children.

In a third case, as the providers of care see their circle enlarged, not only those in the family line have opportunities and responsibilities in relating to the child. In this larger circle, in a book that encourages envisioning, I see *imaginative people:* artists, writers, readers of poetry, lovers of beauty, busy people of any age. They offer contexts for the development of the child. They can be motivated to deepen their imaginations by contemplating the mystery of the child, the child napping or romping, writing poetry or stumbling, questioning or emoting. In this zone of mystery, what is practical meets with what is theoretical. There are two sides to this meeting.

These poets, artists, and writers will first behold the child as a subject of *intrinsic* worth. They behold the child, and *beholding* in the classical tradition meant "to inspire theory." The Greek word behind *theory* means first "to be a spectator, to look at, observe, perceive" someone or something with physical eyes. The same word also refers to the use of "perception by the mind or spirit – to notice, perceive, observe, find." Readers will not become professional theorists on philosophical terms by reflecting on these chapters, but readers will be theorists – beholders – in the original sense. In an aesthetic vision that can inspire practical consequences, we are simply called to behold the child, to wonder at the mystery that she is and what she represents. To view the provision of care for the child *extrinsically,* for what this means for other relations in society, is a bonus, but it should not obscure the original intrinsic understanding.

Fourth, among the providers of care for the child whom I would like to engage with the concept of mystery are whole clusters of important *professionals* beyond the circle of parents and artists. Here we address those who in various situations and roles are being called to celebrate the mystery. Educators, nurses, pastors, physicians, statisticians, social workers, strategists, and counselors are always among the target readerships of how-to books on the young. Thanks to their professional training or through what they have picked up informally, most of them specialize in facing issues raised by children. Among many of them, what is practical will be more immediately attractive and more demanding than what appears ideal or mysterious.

Teachers stand out among them. Every provider of care is somehow a teacher, but a professional teacher becomes a learner as well, and always in particular ways. Teachers of any age group often see the child as a teacher. Back when he was advising my dissertation fifty years ago, historian Daniel J. Boorstin paraphrased a line by Ralph Waldo Emerson in the dedication of one of his books: "For Paul, Jonathan, and David . . . like Genius, simple: that is why they are the immortal teachers."[1] The line still informs my beholding of children, which means my theorizing about them. Paradoxically, children are also the immortal teachers because they are complex. Their simplicity and their complexity in interplay make them beguiling and promising candidates for research, observation, and care.

Why Care about Children and the Providers of Their Care?

Authors of books like this one often declare in the introduction their reason for writing the book. So let me put myself in the mind of the reader and ask, "Why are *you* writing this book?" Friends and other critics on occasion have sprung that question as a bracing challenge. I could respond, of course, "Because I love children," which is true. These objects of my love are not abstractions. They are real children playing on swings, kicking soccer balls, trying the patience of their parents, or being partners in bedtime prayers. Most people who love children, however, do not translate that love into the making of a manuscript and a book. Some persistent and therefore helpful questioners then go on to say something that is also true: "Nothing in what you have written during the past half century has signaled much direct and focused interest in the topic of the child." Admittedly, little of it has. These probing questions and observations represent two ways of asking about the motives and credentials of an author who took three-quarters of a century of living to get around to writing book-length reflections about childhood and children. So let me explain:

I write this book in an attempt to inspire readers to reflect creatively on what they have inherited and what they still carry from their own earliest years and to do so in order to become better providers themselves of care for children. This aim has to do with my being a rememberer, a historian. Some may expect me to serve as a memoirist who would recall and trade explicitly on the experiences of my own earliest years. But although memories of my childhood will subtly and inevitably color my argument in this book, few will appear in direct support.

I write this book in the hope that readers will be encouraged to apply their reflections on their own childhood to childhood in general, because they are involved

1. Daniel J. Boorstin, *The Genius of American Politics* (Chicago: University of Chicago Press, 1953), dedication.

in the care of children known and unknown to them. For this reason I will usually refrain from offering my own well-remembered experiences as a child or with children as models — good or bad — for dealing with the child. Were the author and the company of readers participating in a workshop or a seminar, where give-and-take is the pattern of discourse, stories of all our experiences could have a prominent place. But a book remains in many ways a monologue, even when the author makes an effort to converse in print with the readers. It is true that the personal experience of family living may give a writer some qualifications to treat "childhood in general" at book length. As a brief orientation I offer just a few details from my own background: I have shared the parenting of four Swiss-German-American children and have learned from having been a foster-adopting parent of two Mexican-American children, stepparent of one child, grandparent of nine, great-grandparent of three Somali-American children, and occasional cohost in our home of foreign students and African-American children who lived in the inner city of Chicago. Family life in this case reached its numerical and noisy climax when two Ugandan boys also crowded the table. Being part of a household that for a year included a foster daughter and seven boys aged nine to fourteen gave me experiences that alone could more than fill this book. However, my grateful awareness of my late wife's far greater investment in them, my respect for the privacy of all these children, and my considerable uneasiness about the limited value of drawing personally on the experience of rearing children as long ago as the 1950s led me to decide against being autobiographical. The gifts that all these children, their friends, and our numerous godchildren brought to the experience of parenting will perhaps color these pages, but they will not be featured.

I write this book in the hope that it can testify to the value of consciously relating childhood to the rest of adults' own longer lives, because such a value will enhance the tasks of supplying care for children and appreciating the world around them. Here the perspective of having lived long can be helpful, but I will make little of that. What follows has to do with conversations and argument about the way the being of the child informs all the passages of life. The ending of the eighth decade of life should inspire an author like me to reflect on how aspects of having been a child — or of keeping alive through the senior years something of the being of the child — should color all the phases of later life about which he writes. Believing that adults should allow some dimensions of childhood to be sustained and used as a guide for both the philosophy and the behavior of older people is an animating reason for writing.

I write also to suggest that each of us can explore how to use the record and testimony of others, as revealed in both fictional and nonfictional narratives, to inform our lives and gain new resources for providing care for the child. This means, then, that I will draw on vocational and professional interests to enlarge the scope of this conversation. Each of us brings a vantage from our professional sphere. Mine is that of a decades-long vocation involving scholarship in the humanities and social sciences, centering in history. Someone once asked the British scholar R. H. Tawney why he was a historian. He found the world very odd, he said, and he wondered how it had gotten to be so. Not only is the world odd, but so are historians, especially when they choose their subjects for research and writing. If the tables of contents and indexes of most historians' works are indicators, children appear only incidentally in narratives, except when a book is devoted to special topics concerning children. That is odd. Stories of the wars, famines, pestilences, catastrophes, and traumas that threaten the existence of children more than other people get overlooked by all but a few specialists. Historians characteristically write narratives about those they picture as the agents, the makers of history and actors in it. Such characters show up in the roles of warriors, planters, physicians, relief workers, counselors, and adult victims. Children make rare appearances.

Most preoccupied parents, busy teachers, and focused technicians will not instinctively turn to works of history to gain insight into the lives of children. If they do read works of popular history, however, they will benefit from the fact that in recent decades, as social-historical disciplines have come into favor, the scene has begun to change. More scholars than in the recent past now choose to write about children even as they also create narratives about women, the poor, the ill, the marginalized, the folk artists and makers of the objects in material culture. All of these people, roles, and topics await more discovery and deserve explicit attention, and they are likely to receive it.

Ironically, children may not have appeared in most stories because they played such obvious roles in ordinary daily life. Historian Jacob Burckhardt in the nineteenth century sagely noticed that "everywhere in the past we encounter things which remain unexplained only because they were completely self-understood in their time and, like all daily matters, were not thought necessary to write down."[2] For most of the scholars, the doings of children belonged to such "daily matters." They some-

2. Jacob Burckhardt, *Griechische Kulturgeschichte,* 1:400, quoted in Karl J. Weintraub, *Visions of Culture* (Chicago: University of Chicago Press, 1966), 270.

times showed up in oblique glimpses, as when narrators recorded the mourning and grieving of parents who were burying their dead infants, or their glorying when a healthy one survived. Other occasions that warranted notice were when some Christian parents agonized over whether their unbaptized child would spend eternity in hell. But common and self-understood events like these were slighted in most narratives.

Change has come among some historians who, in effect, are repenting over their past slighting of this subject. Philosopher Max Scheler helpfully illuminated what such personal turning can mean. Quoting Arthur Schopenhauer, he called for deeper repentance than the one suggested by the formula "Alas! What have I done?" The typical historian has "done" history without having given much attention to children. Scheler was not yet content when he read Schopenhauer upping this to the formula "Alas! What kind of person am I?" The historian is a fine scholar who in the depths of her being has shaped her career in such a way that, even when children should be in a story, they usually are not. The expression of mere regret by itself would not suffice as a basis for change, said Scheler, because it is not possible to repent one's own being. So he suggested that the theme in repenting should begin with an "Alas! That I was such a person as *could* do that deed!" In this third case, "doing that deed" meant neglecting to do a better one. The philosopher concluded by saying that demonstrating a new awareness that better things could have been done has its "way of bursting through once we know from present experience our capacity for improvement of conduct."[3]

I should speak only for myself, though I am asking a generic question: What kind of persons are we historians if we always restrict to adults all stories of human success and failure, achievement and disappointment, hope and despair, laughter and tears, while leaving children unmentioned? Although this book is not a work of history, it is designed to serve as a compensatory token that recognizes my own past neglect and that might help quicken some other historians who chance upon it to be more mindful of the young as they make surveys of the past.

And I also write to help readers engage with several thinkers who can embolden them to be explicit about their own reflections on the transcendent dimensions and contexts of children's lives. This book draws on biblical and philosophical resources. One of the points I hope to reinforce is that children

3. Max Scheler, *On the Eternal in Man* (Hamden, CT: Shoe String Press, 1972), 46.

have to be taken with special seriousness by religious and humanist thinkers. Isolating that theme prompts this fifth reason for writing. From a very early age children experience or learn of realities that they must define and with which they must cope. A parent or other gift-giver will ordinarily visit the parents' or children's section of a bookstore for works to provide insight for child care, but not the philosophy and theology section. Occasional books on children as thinkers, however, often now include anecdotes and illustrations that demonstrate how intuitively philosophical they can be. Some children ask many of the questions that senior philosophers ponder and that their own elders try to explicate all their lives. Children also come up with some answers of their own to conundrums. These will serve them better than many answers given by academics who so rarely listen to children. Every religious schoolteacher and most parents can log extensive collections of uninhibited questions posed by the very young. Such bold and artless offerings often get muffled or obscured when the children grow older. By then many have become too timid, insecure, unimaginative, or haughty to voice them clearly. Insofar as this book deals with experienced realities that cry out for definition, it seeks to contribute some fresh angles on the provision of care.

Parents will sometimes publicize questions or assertions by their children, many of them having to do with pondering God. Still others speak of their dread of the day when their children will become old enough to ask unanswerable questions or adolescent enough to turn their questioning into belligerence or revolt. What their bemusements often signal is that adults feel called to play God or at least to be sages or scholars like St. Thomas Aquinas or the Jewish philosopher Maimonides. They may not know or may have forgotten that the second of these two giants wrote a primer for the ages called *Guide for the Perplexed.* If the queries and statements of children clash with doctrines as defined by adults, the best advice is to recall Alfred North Whitehead's observation that a clash of doctrines is an opportunity, not a disaster. Children are then to be treated as inquisitive inquirers, not as candidates for silencing or inquisition.

I write in an effort to draw adult citizens into the zones where providing the care of children is treated urgently and to help motivate them to keep children in the forefront of their concerns. Another part of an adult's vocation is trying to be a cooperative and responsible citizen. Some of my own past assignments have exposed me to the interests of children. Reflecting on what I learned during these assignments provides another reason for this work. Service on one U.S. presidential commission involved engagements with providers of care for children in matters of "health, education, and welfare." Membership on another commission that dealt with arts and the humanities included a call to concentrate on the activities of the very young as they produced visual arts and music or experimented with literature. Participation on still another national commission that dealt with the experiences of teenaged and unmarried mothers meant turning attention to their children. Pastoral ministry for more than ten years kept me close to children, as all such ministry does. In a score of other ventures, including the support of foster care and adoption agencies and causes, my focus has fallen on children.

I also write because I was asked to, which means that I am to transmit something of what I learned after having been given a special opportunity to do that learning. The Center for the Study of Law and Religion, located in the Law School of Emory University in Atlanta, through the person of its director John Witte and his associate and my University of Chicago colleague Don Browning, invited me to codirect the project "The Child in Religion, Law, and Society." Working with Emory faculty colleagues, I had the chance to learn from scholarly experts who deal with problems and then with the provision of care. In our first conversation on the subject, I was asked by Professors Witte and Browning what my own focus in this field would be. Immediately I blurted out that I wanted to address a subject that has been alluring to poets and philosophers and that has long tantalized me: "The Mystery of the Child."

So I write this with a desire that the subject of the mystery *of the child can find more of its place alongside some of the immediately practical advice by others about how to provide care for the child.* Some inspiration for this final element, in my case, came from poets. Whoever reads much poetry from most ages comes across children frequently because many poets have a special regard for them. In fact, it was poets who first stimulated my curiosity about the formal treatments of the mystery of the child. Rainer Maria von Rilke, Walt Whitman, Charles Péguy, and other preferred poets consistently treated the child not as someone to be dominated, controlled, managed, reduced, or used. Instead, they saw the child as a subject of wonder, astonishment, awe, and, yes, mystery.

To illustrate, here are two samples from poets who provide a vocabulary for approaching children in wonder. In a few lines of a short poem from 1865, Walt Whitman startles readers by making a noun out of "amaze." He helps readers celebrate wonder, but he does so in a creatively unsettling way that lets the hard edge of a child's reaction show:

A Child's Amaze

Silent and amazed even when a little boy,
I remember I heard the preacher every Sunday put God
in his statements.
As contending against some being or influence.[4]

French poet, journalist, and activist Charles Péguy elaborated on the relation between childhood and mystery. Decades ago the translation of his *Le Mystère des Saints Innocents* reached my soul because of the imaginative way in which we there hear the poet's God speak about children.[5] There are, to be sure, good reasons to argue with the hyperbolic words uttered by the poet's God concerning infant innocence – are children truly innocents? – but there are also better reasons to affirm Péguy's word about "play" in the mystery of childhood:

Faith is a loyal wife,
Charity is a fervent mother,
But hope is a very little girl. . . .

It is faith who holds fast through century upon century.

It is charity who gives herself through centuries of centuries,
But it is my little hope
Who gets up every morning. . . .

. . . .
You believe that children know nothing.
And that parents and grown-up people know something.
Well, I tell you it is the contrary.
(It is always the contrary).
It is the parents, it is the grown-up people who know nothing.
And it is the children who know
Everything. . . .

For they know first innocence,
Which is everything.

4. *Walt Whitman: Complete Poetry and Selected Prose and Letters,* ed. Emory Holloway (London: Nonesuch, 1971), 253.

5. Charles Péguy, *The Mystery of the Holy Innocents,* trans. Pansy Pakenham (New York: Harper and Brothers, 1956), 69, 135, 165.

The world is always inside out, God says.
And in the contrary sense.
Happy is he who remains like a child
And who like a child keeps
His first innocence. . . .

After the poet draws on the Gospel of Luke with its story of the massacre of the Holy Innocents at Bethlehem following the birth of Jesus, he offers more on mystery:

Such is my Paradise, God says. "My Paradise could not be simpler.
Nothing is less elaborate than my Paradise.
Aram sub ipsam, on the steps of the altar itself
These simple children *play* with their palms and their
martyrs' crowns,"
That is what is going on in my Paradise. Whatever can they play at
With palms and martyrs' crowns.
I believe they play at hoops, God says, and perhaps at quoits
(at least I believe so, for do not think
that they ever ask my permission)
And the palm forever green they use apparently as a hoop-stick.

Péguy thus alerts readers to keep the element of play alive when they deal with the mystery not only of "the holy innocents" of long ago but also of contemporary children.

The fathomlessness, the apparently limitless depth of the child, gives dimension to the mystery, both in the metaphor of an abyss – children are deep! – and, for height and reach, in the image of an apogee – which signals that which is beyond. In cultures where "down" can be associated with evil – hell is down, while "up," referring to heaven, is good – the notion of an abyss often connotes problems, many of which reflect evil. In the opposite analogy, the apogee, because it is the highest point, climax, or culmination of any arc, symbolizes achievement and success. Here the abyss refers to "any unfathomable or apparently unfathomable cavity or void space." In the present context, psychologists who study child abuse regularly refer to its traumatic legacy as one that has created an abyss, a void in the mind of the abused. Educators who celebrate genius among children speak of their reaching a height, as if to the edge of infinity. In the present case, both abyss and apogee suggest the immeasurable. Of course these still refer to what is finite, to dimensions of the relations in which we locate the developing person who is the infant, the child for whom adults are to provide practical care. This will become clearer when we explore some meanings of mystery as it relates to the child. However, from birth and through the years, the child brings problems that need attention, problems that dominate most agendas. These problems can obscure the mystery of the child and diminish the sense of wonder among those who are to provide care. That is a problem about problems.

2. Care as a Problem

Those who are to provide care for a child are often bemused or even enraged when she frustrates them by her words and actions. Examples: A little one creates a problem when he scrawls and scribbles with paint on an inviting but hitherto clean wall. Another child presents a problem when she has climbed a tree and cannot come down on her own. A child afflicted with attention deficit disorder may cause problems in the classroom. A teen experiments with drugs, becomes addicted, and presents a desperate problem to all who love him.

It would be a failure on my part to communicate well if readers came away from this book thinking that I intended to minimize problems and plaguing issues by not beginning all references to the child as being a problem or as having problems. If a child I know is a problem or has a problem, I am among those who are ready with the telephone book's Yellow Pages, the Internet, and lists of clinics or teachers so that we together can seek experts who will address what is causing bewilderment or turmoil. However, whether one begins with an approach to the issue as "problem" or, the contrast being developed here, with an approach to "mystery," the chosen beginning point makes a decisive difference for all that follows.

Although numbers of thinkers have written on the interplay of problem and mystery, the one who has been clearest and most helpful to me as I thought about the child is the French philosopher and playwright Gabriel Marcel. He did not have the child on his agenda when he developed the distinction between the two concepts, but his statement of the contrast helpfully frames our approach. Because he was a philosopher devoted to the experience and analysis of wonder, his thought is especially appropriate.

The fundamental distinction for Marcel and now for us is this: It is at least in principle possible to address and come up with a potential solution when a problem exists. There is no solution, however, to a *mystery* as he conceived it and as it appears here. If a child is troubled with anxiety, a problem solver responsibly faces up to the issue by drawing on appropriate resources to address it. When a child experiences anxiety every night after the parent turns off the lights in his bedroom, one potential solution is to install a night-light. If that does not work, a parent may linger in the room, providing assurance until the child is asleep. If the dying of a grandfather has led an older child to draw some conclusions about death, if she begins to be anxious about her own father's mortality and is concerned about when she herself will die, adults can provide all kinds of counsel, fully aware that they cannot fully solve everything that troubles one child by removing death from the human adventure.

Similarly, if matters of health are urgent, a parent will call the doctor. If the trouble is a sniffle or a stubbed toe, solutions are simple. If the child has cerebral palsy or cystic fibrosis, no responsible adult would pretend that a cure lies just around the corner. At the same time, such an adult would find ways to support research and relief. Now, over against the child as problem or in the face of the problems of the child, we pose mystery.

The Case of *Mystery* in the Provision of Care

To speak of mystery without explaining oneself is to create confusion, so prevalent is a different use of the term. To explain: on the last page of detective stories, one finds a solution – the butler did it, the mystery is solved. But that use of the term is misleading in our context. Whether a person approaches mystery through reference to history, religion, literature, or personal observation, there can be no guarantee that specialists in any particular discipline will be able to offer a solution. In fact, to propose a solution means that one has not been working with genuine mystery. To pursue or advertise a solution would be to make a mistake about categories – it would be as unpromising and unhelpful as advertising a solution to a recipe or saying "'Good morning,' he explained."

Mystery refers to something fathomless. That means that the deeper one goes, the further the reach into that fathomlessness. The higher one probes, as in attempted reaches toward transcendent realms, there is always some thing or some place higher. A scholar would not properly employ the concept of mystery in this context if she could exhaust a search by reaching bottom or by bumping into a ceiling. What is fathomless is open to discovery and revelation without end, but it never finds resolution or conclusion. Perceive the child as a subject of wonder, as mystery, and no combination of approaches to him will permit observers and analysts to say that they have exhausted the possibilities in their search.

In his earlier *Being and Having,* and again in *The Mystery of Being,*[1] Marcel explored the two concepts. "A problem," he wrote, "is something which I meet, which I find complete before me, but which I can lay siege to and reduce." For Marcel, such "laying siege" – a provocative and delightful metaphor to store in mind! – meant amassing all possible mental resources and attacking the specific problem until it was reduced or until it disappeared. Thus if a child is grossly overweight, those who care about this condition see to it that medical authority will provide a changed diet and prescribe physical recreation. Such policies and disciplines will likely lead to some measured weight loss. Those who provide care can then move on and lay siege to another problem that appears to be defined and complete and can then reduce or solve it.

A provider of care for the child will profit from Marcel's contention that "a mystery is something in which I myself am involved, and it can therefore only be thought of as 'a sphere where the distinction between what is in me and what is before me loses its meaning and its initial validity.'" There are many ways to translate and conceive of this theme. A parent, even one who deals with an alienated and distant older child, never is able to draw a clear line between "what is in me and what is before me." That is most certainly the case when the child is a dependent infant. Even the most responsible and attentive physician who is the parent of an ill child will be engaged with him in ways that differ from those she employs with the category of children who have a specific ailment that the physician is analyzing by the use of statistics and tests.

Therefore Marcel can continue: "A genuine problem is subject to an appropriate technique by the exercise of which it is defined; whereas a mystery, by definition, transcends every conceivable technique. It is, no doubt, always possible (logically and psychologically) to degrade a mystery so as to turn it into a problem. But this is a fundamentally vicious proceeding, whose springs might perhaps be discovered in a kind of corruption of the intelligence." His use of words like *vicious* and *corruption* of-

1. Gabriel Marcel, *The Mystery of Being,* vol. 1: *Reflection and Mystery* (Chicago: Gateway, 1960), 260-61. The several quotations from Marcel that follow are on these pages.

fers clues to how seriously he took the issue. The adult who brings a diseased child to a medical professional team that can isolate the medical problem can never walk away from the clinic feeling that these techniques will "take care" of the child. The child needs and welcomes embraces, face-to-face relations, and interactions that include play. I have heard people say something like this: "My doctor cured me, but she did not heal me. She never looked in my face." In face-to-face relations, what is sometimes called "the mystery of 'the other'" is revealed.

The child seen first and fundamentally or even only in the context of her problems is, in Marcel's world, "complete" before us. Who she is and what she represents can be "laid siege to" by physicians, psychologists, ministers, or coaches, or "reduced" by psychological analysts. The adult who conceives of the child as mystery, however, is involved with that child on a different set of terms. Elsewhere Marcel implies that, by analogy between the human and the divine, to be in the face of the divine mystery is to be in that "sphere where the distinction between what is in me and what is before me loses its meaning and its initial validity." A parent or any adult who refuses to become open to wonder and who thus never sees the child as mystery will be deprived of that sense of involvement and interaction between the self of the child and the self of the provider of care.

One way to sharpen the distinction between a problem and mystery is to project it into the sphere of talk about God. Marcel's two paragraphs inspired Kilian McDonnell, OSB, to write a poem that bounces the issue of problem versus mystery off the largest possible screen: talk about God. The priest's work contributes to the definition that provides the background and backbone for this book. If the child as mystery will be related by analogy to the divine mystery, the child as problem as being one made in the image of God will be illumined by the poetic reference to God as mystery, not God as problem.

God Is Not a Problem

(*"A problem is something which I meet,*
which I find complete before me."
— Gabriel Marcel, *The Mystery of Being*)

God is not a problem
I need to solve, not an
algebraic polynomial equation
I find complete before me,

With positive and negative numbers
I can add, subtract, multiply.
God is not a fortress
I can lay siege to and reduce.

God is not a confusion
I can place in order by my logic.
God's boundaries cannot be set,
Like marking trees to fell.

God is the presence in which
I live, where the line between
what is in me and what
before me is real, but only God

can draw it. God is the mystery
I meet on the street, but cannot
lay ahold of from the outside,
For God is my situation,

the condition I cannot stand
beyond, cannot view from a distance,
the presence I cannot make an object,
Only enter on my knees.[2]

Mystery in the Face of Three Limiting Circumstances

The motive for my stressing such a strong distinction between problem and mystery will become clearer when we discuss the issue of control. One of the strongest impulses to deal with the child as problem or to isolate the problems of the child has to do significantly with the adult impulse to control. In all human relations the temptation to seek mastery over and domination of the other is intense, but it is to be resisted most strenuously in the case of the adult as he relates to the child. You cannot control the mysterious; it will always be finally beyond reach. Think of the parent who theorizes and then plots control of the life of the child of four — so that the overprovident and thus foreclosing adult can help him get into a

2. Kilian McDonnell, OSB, *Swift Lord, You Are Not* (Collegeville, MN: Saint John's University Press, 2003), 50-51.

prestigious university when he becomes eighteen. The seeker of control seldom lets the child experience independent adventures but wants him to avoid all risks and is protective as he anticipates and tries to head off problems. Such a parent has "laid siege to" a problem and will be unready to regard the child as mystery.

Those who would provide care for the child face three limits in their own and the child's life, and relating to them is better advanced through the approach to mystery than through recourse to the category of problem. My colleague of many years and next-door office-neighbor David Tracy taught us — or at least taught me, when we co-taught — that before the mysteries of faith and hope and love have their effect, a person has to become aware of three limits. He gave various names to them but favored this trio: finitude, contingency, and transience. Seen as problems, which they also are, they are simply insoluble. Bluntly:

The child someday will die.

The child will be subject to accidents and chance happenings, not all of them positive.

The child's presence and her creations will be transient and will someday disappear without a trace, be this day in a decade or after millennia.

The child at birth cannot be aware of what these mean but will in the course of his early years begin to grow into awareness. Because of them, the mysterious aspect of all human life, especially child life, will emerge clearly and with most force.

First, *finitude.* The adults who would provide care may be tempted to dream of immortality for a child, to see her as eternal or at least as being worth sacrificial investment so long as they can remain unmindful of the limit death places on her as on everyone. Of course, no sentient and intelligent person is truly under the illusion that death is escapable, but some can live with the delusion that they need not deal with its prospect. It is true that in prosperous cultures the shadow of death can be half-dispelled or temporarily almost forgotten. Not many centuries ago that shadow visited the nursery and playroom more ominously than it does in affluent nations today. Yet even if the infant or small child is protected much more than before from death by pestilence or malnutrition, responsible adults will make every effort to diminish the other forces that still can lead to the death of the child. Yet if they seek to do this through the exercise of control over all the child does or all that might happen to her, they will be frustrated because "laying siege" to the problem of death is finally futile.

The child may not, and in the earliest years of life cannot, become conscious of the end of life in order to work through its meanings. At the same time everything the child is and does is marked by signals of the end. Brain cells immediately begin dying. Now and then one hears the flip comment that life is a sexually transmitted disease with a terminal prognosis. Such quips may be amusing and momentarily therapeutic, but they can also trivialize life. At least it has to cross the mind of any serious person that death is the robber of promise, even while one is watching two-year-olds frolic in abandon on the beach, chase butterflies, or mourn a dead cat.

Father John Dunne once asked the question that all sensible people, by the evidence of their activities in the light of their death, ask: "If I must some day die, what can I do to satisfy my desire to live?"[3] The child who grows in awareness, along with all those who care for or learn about her, will be answering that question for herself and vicariously for others. Providers of care for the child conventionally catalog some of the ways adults try to deal with mortality, offering counsels for health and well-being. There are good reasons, of course, for people helped by them to be grateful because of such counsel and stimuli to creativity. Yet whatever counsel people follow, they still have to ponder death as a limit and consider the theological questions that connect it with human sin and the "fall" of all creation.

The linking of the child with death is such a chilling subject that adults work with the best of intentions to come up with reasonable strategies for dealing with it. They contrive environments or distractions that should help a child cope with death. The child, responding to these, might thereupon find his attention steered away from the issue of limits as these appear in the world of fallen sparrows, fallen reputations, and falling protective walls. However, those who offer help will not dispel the terror of death for the way it limits life, or abolish the threat of nonbeing that helps define the being of all. Death remains the abyss of mystery. However, the one who regards the child as mystery and enters her world as much as possible with humility and imagination will begin to find more appropriate and helpful ways to deal with finitude, now without evasion or illusion, through the exercise of empathy and imagination plus the use of play, storytelling, and much more. Pondering death as only a problem

3. John Dunne, CSC, *The City of the Gods: A Study in Myth and Mortality* (New York: Macmillan, 1965), v.

produces nothing but fear; regarding it as mystery brings its reality into the zone where a person experiences freedom.

The second mark of all human life, which also frames the existence of the child, is *contingency*. Contingency in this context refers to "an event (or emergency) that may but is not certain to occur." Or it is "something liable to happen as an adjunct to or a result of something else." Contingency, dealing with "chance" or "unforeseen causes," represents everything that is not foreseen, predictable, or controllable in the life of the child. All those dictionary citations serve a single purpose. They remind us that the child emerging from the womb, though surrounded by parents, professionals, and at some distance a citizenry that exists within an often benign society, is at every moment vulnerable to unforeseen misfortunes. It would be foolish and irresponsible for those charged with care for a single child, or adult fellow-citizens with concern for children everywhere in their scope, not to do what they can to prevent devastating contingencies from occurring.

Because contingency, accident, coincidence, luck good and bad, and, frankly, sin shadow everyone, those who are responsible for children welcome manuals that deal with these. Here is where the reconception of the child as mystery comes into creative play. Many of the positive actions of the infant and very young child are inevitably marked by response to contingencies. The nether side of all this, however, will be destructive if the only approach to the child is to regard him as a problem to be solved or as someone defined by the problems he faces. As a consequence, when what is accidental is at issue, thoughtful adults will take positive action and make plans. They will see to it that poisons are out of reach of the child. They will do what they can to keep bad influences and company at a distance. The responsible provider of care deliberates whether a tetanus shot is needed after the child receives a certain sort of wound. Or he wonders how to ensure that the school bus driver is certified and will drive safely. Another asks, Will this textbook for a second-grader induce the child to be reckless? What if an admired peer taunts the child and challenges him with a dangerous dare? Book titles that address themes of this sort rightfully have a special appeal that will help adults fulfill practical missions. If those who read them can develop concern and know-how so that they can prevent an accident or rescue a child when a misfortune occurs, they deserve a medal. Most of us would take our place in a line to present it or applaud those who receive one.

The simplest conversations, the comforting gestures, the openings for discussion when something unforeseen and terrible occurs help initiate the child and reinforce the thinking of the adult providers of care, so that they can cast contingency into the mold of mystery. These help prepare the child and the provider of care for living in the face of the unforeseen and the uncontrollable better than do problem solvers who seek mastery. Especially among those who want to anticipate and ward off every danger with measures that promise absolute security, which means those who face the responsibilities we have described, many will still be tempted to try to control circumstances, often at expense to the child in his development. Thus, without anticipating the potential of a particular child and while not allowing for a variety of educational outcomes, an overly provident and worried parent may enroll her child in an expensive nursery school with one main purpose in mind: guaranteeing a specific future. Thus, subsequently she may demand the firing of a teacher who in her view has not made a success of her son. This is the case, says the demander, because the child received some low grades that set him on a course that will count against him when he applies to elite colleges. If he fails to be accepted by them, his professional prospects after graduation will be diminished. Someone must suffer for helping him fail early on. The usual candidate is the teacher.

The parents in such cases want to manage every detail related to the destiny of the child, because they consider being privileged to be a birthright for their child. This kind of worrying can lead adults to hover over children at play and to do this so ardently and nervously that the young never learn to become adventurous and responsible themselves. It likely means that they are seeking a "cure" for blights real or imagined in efforts to leave nothing to nature and chance. The controller or manager sees to the injection of growth hormones in the offspring lest he remain too short to make the basketball team years later. Of course, the child who is regarded as mystery, and those who care for him with that regard in mind, cannot be sheltered in an absolutely secure environment or assured a future that excludes all dangers, but with this awareness in mind, they will be freer than otherwise to face whatever comes.

Nothing that comes under the category of mystery will remove contingency from life. Were it to disappear, so would the adventure of life itself. However, practice in approaching the child through the category of mystery can assist young and old alike and together to find ways to deal with the prevention or consequence of accidents, whereas those bound only to the approach through problems will find it difficult to reach for resources to deal with both the shocks and the delights that come with contingency and accidents. Some events seen as accidental do have *positive* outcomes! Some of the best academic work is done by students who found themselves at second-best colleges. Meanwhile, most marriages, often the best among them, occur between people who met each other in wholly unforeseeable ways. They interpret their lives in the light of some transcendent reality, which they grasp through various scriptures, philosophies, or narratives.

Third, those who provide care for the child may be tempted to think that their care is an investment in stability and permanence, but children, like all other people, live under the third sign, the mark of *transience.* According to the first truisms that cross one's mind, everything passes and nothing physical endures. The adult who conceives of the child as having come from an abyss of mystery and who is moving toward another can make more of the moment than those who resort to compiling scrapbooks in order to retain the past or who make all their moves in efforts to ensure lasting outcomes in the future. We shall discuss some of the ways of "making more of the moment" in subsequent chapters. Those for whom the child is essentially a problem or is one who has problems to be solved will not always take such a reality seriously. Those who provide care in such circumstances often give evidence that they are preparing the child in such a way as to ensure that he will make future indestructible marks on history. They often try to pretend away the evanescence of the moments and phases of childhood or try to freeze and enshrine them in memory in an effort to make them lasting.

These thoughts reflect the reading of history and theology; they have to do with the uses of the past for dealing with the contemporary scene. One of the best ways to see how some providers of care would live with the illusion that finitude, contingency, and transience need not mark the life of a child is to study the best-selling child-care manuals. Millions of books in this genre are sold each year. A reader can do her own research in this field by taking a list of best-sellers to a bookstore, where she will find them well displayed for sales. Reading them will reinforce the point that such manuals help adults "lay siege to" particular problems of the child. One can watch cable television to see and hear authors touting their books of solutions to child-care problems to vast audiences.

It is not our agenda to research great numbers of these books in order to produce fresh detail, but a sampling of the more prominent among them is available in an informal history, Ann Hulbert's *Raising America: Experts, Parents, and a Century of Advice about Children.*[4] The author ap-

4. Ann Hulbert, *Raising America: Experts, Parents, and a Century of Advice about Children* (New York: Knopf, 2003).

praises some of the books that had the most apparent influence in the United States in the century past. Many are by experts who became celebrities by creating the impression that they brought so much science to child rearing that parents would be irresponsible if they did not buy into the books' suggestions. The authors and their immediate followers regarded the proposals and commands not only as the best word for the moment, the word that reflected the light of present-day knowledge, but also as the final word. Over against them, Hulbert's perspective helps her show how often these counsels have turned out to be ephemeral. Most of them have been countered almost immediately before being displaced or ruled obsolete. What appeared to be avant-garde prescription soon came to look antique or quaint, and what was designed to be impressive later often turned out to look oppressive.

The books that offer advice can be helpful in many circumstances, but most of them offer in the end little more than a few among millions of often contradictory signals that remind us that the cultural achievements of the past were transient. Seeing the eclipse of the advice and resolutions of the past colored the careers of the great counselors and other therapists for children about whom Hulbert wrote. It should not take much imagination, then, to envision that today's "last words" and permanent counsels about dealing with problems will also soon pass.

To be lost from view within the year or the generation after they were produced or achieved will be the kindergarten drawings, the trophies and certificates, along with the school papers and merit badges of a favored child who has made a mark. Intrinsically valuable in their own moment, all these will become dust as time passes, as one is almost embarrassed to have to remind oneself. Over against all this, the one who reflects on the mystery of the child creatively factors in some inevitable meanings of transience and learns the value of each moment.

In sum, the act of beginning to face the presence of the child as mystery is a way of dispelling the illusions that so easily come with the promises of problem solvers. It also reduces the temptation to manage and control the life of a young person, a temptation that finds expression even in the act of naming problems. That act inspires the question: Who has the credentials and the right to name, define, isolate, and address the specified problems of a child? Often, sad to say, the assessment of those problems comes from someone who does not know and may not care to know any particular child. In such cases there is little motive for anyone to try to assess and penetrate many dimensions of his being. The adult who fails to make an effort to ponder these dimensions will have little empathy for the child who is dealing, as he must, with his own inner world and his relation to his specific environment. The temptation is strong for the definer of the problem or the authorizer of a solution to assert mastery and to seek control over the child.

Hulbert's chronicle of best-selling advice books demonstrates how important the naming of problems and solutions is to authors and readers. This naming is often associated with the futile passion by members of the public to gain the monopoly of control. The odds that after thousands of years of advice-giving someone will find the magic permanent solution to the problems of the child are all but hopeless. By implicitly and sometimes even explicitly claiming possession of a solution to each problem, the experts who make such claims suck up all the moral and intellectual oxygen in the nursery or on the preschool scene.

For a most obvious instance, consider an adult who serves conscientiously by discovering that a child is a victim of abuse. Subsequently, the child labeled victim is not likely to be seen, explained, or dealt with in any other way than as a victim by those very threatening adults who were close to him and may even have violated him. Now the danger is that all the other dimensions of his childhood will also get overlooked and remain underdeveloped. Perhaps the one categorized as abused is also good at writing poetry or using Lego blocks, speaking to frogs or going on hikes, but no one notices or cares. Similarly, when the expert labels a child "mentally deficient" or "hyperactive" or "prone to losing" — all of such terms possibly quite accurate in clinical and laboratory senses — she risks obscuring the other elements of the child's life. Some of these might have provided resources for the child's life beyond therapy and for freedom from being reduced to "nothing but" the subject of existing treatments. This is also the case when, according to labels, a child "*is* a diabetic" or "*is* autistic" because he "has" diabetes or "suffers" autism. After such labeling, the entire universe around the child becomes oriented to one conditioning feature of a name or label — even and especially in the cases where the child is successfully working around or transcending its attendant difficulties.

Categorizing the child as problem instead of mystery can lead to labeling for the sake of matching what the diagnostician recognizes can be accurately addressed. Selecting which problem is the most demanding of immediate attention and which possible solution might best avail narrows the range of elements that define the child and that provide the basis on which one can build new measures of health. Whenever precise definition brings premature and confining limits to the boundless and limitless mystery of childhood, the one who makes the diagnosis and provides a name for its result may be overlooking what has to be applicable to many other children in a community.

A Child's Perspective

Providers of care who can imagine their way into the child's world are more likely to preserve the sense of wonder, possibility, and mystery than are those who remain too soberly adult and prescriptive in all their dealings. After having pointed to some limits that become pressing if problem solving is the first, the dominant, and even sometimes the only approach to raising children, it is time to pause for a reality check and another point of view — that of the child. That task calls for looking in a mirror for self-examination and then using binoculars to survey the larger scene of childhood. It is possible to become so aware of the abyss of possibilities, so awed by what is not and cannot be known about the child, that we neglect what is valuable in the contributions of the salt-of-the-earth souls who offer actual and immediate solutions to what ails children and also to what in the culture is destined to threaten them. Those souls are often the children themselves, who make part of their way through the mazes of life and bring perspectives of their own.

Adults, possessing as they do one kind of memory and one set of diagnostic tools, define problems. The years take their toll. Many of them have forgotten even the basic marks of what it is to be a child. Or they likely lack empathy in dealing with little people who bear those marks. Sympathetic and practical adults ask, or had better ask, the child, "Where does it hurt?" or "Why are you grumpy?" or "Why are you smiling?" or "Why are you trembling?" or "Why are you acting cruelly?" Beginning with the awareness of the mysterious dimensions of the child need in no way diminish curiosity, and it actually should help an adult gain and retain something of the child's perspective.

One does well to think of the perspective of the small child even in physical terms. Although the experience of being tiny gets progressively forgotten by adults of medium size, it is problematic for the child. Those who doubt this might engage in a homely experiment in empathy by visiting a display at any number of sites such as Chicago's Museum of Science and Industry. The exhibit I have in mind features two chairs that are ordinary in all respects but these: their seats are approximately five feet off the ground, and their backrests top out at about eight feet. Similarly, the exhibited table top is six feet above floor level, while the dinnerware atop the table is five times the size that adults actually use. The purpose of the physical exaggerations is as obvious as the implied message: "Adult, climb onto the chair and then pretend you are eating with the giant spoon from the moon-sized plate. Next, stare down at a floor that is now so far away that you experience vertigo. Finally, let yourself fall off the chair, knowing that there is nothing to break the fall." Such a display is a physical reminder of how different the world looks to the child. Ask the child who climbed onto the stool to describe the problems of mealtime, and, if she is of an age to articulate what is on her mind, after having offered a critique of the cuisine, she will likely speak about dimension, something that is far removed from the world of fretting adults who simply want the child to be quiet and to eat her food.

When adults expound implied solutions to the problems we have chosen to address, they inevitably begin to establish a distinctive kind of power relation to a specific child. That labeling is readily related to power is obvious in instances like these: When a nation names newcomers "immigrants," citizens already on the scene often deal in unwelcoming ways with them – even though the unwelcoming ones also had been immigrants before they came to be citizens. If prejudiced heterosexuals reduce a person they label as different by seeing him only in the status of being a homosexual, they will join other heterosexuals of their sort in regarding the gay person as nothing but a problem for society. Those who do the reducing, the pointing to what someone is "nothing but," and the naming itself have taken control of the other. Or they deal with the stranger as being strange because she brings qualities and experiences that are alien to the group that is doing the naming. The group will continue to regard that personal Other chiefly as the stranger, not as someone who can herself receive or impart hospitality. (Hereafter, whenever "the other" person or type is seen beyond the definition of one's self, we shall call it "Other," signaling the transcendence of "the self.") The child, in our picture, stands in for the immigrant, the homosexual, the stranger.

Naming and classifying, within a political society, finally often involves the impulse to call upon help from governmental powers to control the child. Political scientists on occasion have defined the modern state as the agency that uniquely possesses the monopoly on legitimate power to wield lethal weapons against humans. One could similarly define adults as the agents who have the power, gained by their physical size or societal status, to determine most of the ways to limit little children. These little ones came into a world and family and society for which they did not ask and the features of which are forbidding and alienating. The child finds few instruments or actions available for response to things or people, unless we count throwing a tantrum, falling into sullen silence, or determining to be passive. The child may early on learn to transact cunningly when someone offers little bribes, to cower in the face of threats, or to acquiesce when there is no choice but to face unjust punishment. It is hard to think of such activities as anything resembling responsible agency on the part of the child. Whoever follows and observes an impatient and abusive mother cuffing and bopping her tugging child as they walk through the supermarket aisles has seen what this form of problem solving portends. It is hard to picture the abusive one ever regarding the child positively, as a mystery, when engaging in such behavior.

Conceiving and perceiving the child as being a mystery and being surrounded by mystery does not solve all the problems that experts identify. It does provide some breathing space, leisure, and perspective to serve the adult who is to address the child and, yes, her problems. Yet the temptation remains strong for the provider of care to solve those problems by seeking, gaining, protecting, and exercising control.

3. Care as Control

When a child appears to be doing wonder-full things, it is easy for providers of care to regard her with a sense of wonder. Let a child dance and play and pray, as adults look on admiringly. Let another dazzle elders as he asks questions they would not dare to ask and would never be able to answer. Look at the shelf full of ribbons and trophies about which parents brag and in which children take measured delight, and then watch others who also provide care to the same child gaze in admiration. Often when the adult world of projects and products dampens the spirit, a visit to the world of the child, a scene evidencing imagination and creativity, will inspire. If the child represents possibility, it should be easy for the adults surrounding him to assure his freedom of movement and to encourage him to express himself.

If only it were so easy. The same child often enough sits and sulks, clams up and neither asks nor answers questions. Most children do not receive "First Place" and "Second Place" or even "Honorable Mention" badges, and they display little that an adult can spontaneously praise. Although we might posit that all children can be imaginative and creative, the free spirit of experiment will not always reveal itself. Children who have a point to make or who grow angry will sit on their hands, stand still at the starting gate, or simply refuse to respond or react, no matter what the prompting or stimulus. It is hard to be romantic about the meanings of childhood in such circumstances, which, we have to admit, appear in many cases to be as frequent as the high-flying times. And those circumstances raise the classic questions of discipline.

The Temptation to Control the Child

Faced with such a child in such a situation, adults, be they very responsible or less so, will understandably find good reasons to seek ways to master the child. Adults who zealously pursue control will defend their efforts as being "good for the child." Certainly no one, least of all the child, prospers if a pattern develops in which the child is never disciplined. It would be a romantic, utopian, and in the end simply destructive counsel to urge adults to avoid all expressions of discipline. But questions arise.

Is *control* the best term to connect with *disciplining?* If so, what kind of control is proper and effective? What assumptions about a child help to determine the nature of the relation between adult and child? When does the impulse to control take on a life of its own, in which case the goal of relating positively to the child is lost? What occurs when it dawns on the child that she has become an object to be controlled, not a subject with whom to interact? What does it teach about power relations if the larger and older but not necessarily better partner in the adult-child nexus simply wins all contests, even if he cannot back the impulse to control with any reasonable philosophy that might legitimate it? Before there can be answers, there has to be room for thought.

To put the matter in perspective, we begin at the beginning. Adults who are to provide care and who regard the child as mystery or as embodying mystery will recall the sense of awe with which they greeted her at birth and in the early seasons of life. As she grows, she will not be an isolated and solitary figure on the way to becoming a finished product. She can never become one – no one can – despite all the possibilities that she represents. From the first day, like all others that follow, she is dependent on people older than she is. To live a full human life she must find herself in company or community. In the acts of both growing up and relating to others, the child will be busy learning her place in the world, especially when her will, desire, and actions collide with the will, desire, and actions of others.

Whoever is serious at all about this reality – which should mean every person of conscience, anyone who is not blighted with absolute naiveté or is not at perfect ease with chaos – will recognize that some discipline comes into play. A commentator risks sounding obvious or even silly writing reminders of this factor in the human condition, so familiar a figure is the undisciplined and spoiled child as a character in comics, tragedies, and common experience. What is at issue are the questions about the *base* from which talk of discipline starts, by what *means* one develops discipline, and what its *ends* are.

Regard the child fundamentally as representing problems, and one approach to discipline is dominant. Many of these problems are unique to infancy and childhood, and in due course the child will simply outgrow them. Still, the legacies of these may be lifelong. From that starting base, one consistent discourse about the relations of the child to the adult world will follow. In it, the first question will not have to do with awe so much as with authority, not with creativity so much as with devices of control, not with imagination but with techniques of management. The child-care manuals would not exist and would not find a market if all children did not present problems of discipline that needed to be addressed in some manner or another.

Many patterns and acts that relate an adult to a child who is seen in the context of mystery will often be congruent with those initiated when the child is regarded essentially as a presenter of problems. Every child has to learn somehow where his ego and rights end and where they are fused, overlap with, or collide with those of another. This limiting reality means, among other things, that the child needs to follow certain patterns and regulations. He has to be taught such obvious things as the meaning of a red light and the action he should take when it flashes. He has to learn that a clock or a bell signals the beginning of school. It does not come naturally to a child to take a proper position in a line, to wait his turn in public spaces, not to insist on his own way, or not to cheat. I include these observations, though they seem obvious and banal, because the accent on the mystery of the child could easily be misread as a policy of "anything goes."

Advisers who deal with the problem of discipline come in many breeds. Some are indeed of the laissez-faire school: the child is a free tyrant, and passive adults let her reign. At the other end are tyrannous adults who restrict the child's freedom and mete out physical punishment. While researching approaches to discipline, with an eye out for those whose thinking was most congruent with the idea of regarding the child as a set of problems, I came across counselor Margaret Donaldson, professor emerita of psychology at the University of Edinburgh. In several climactic paragraphs she offered common sense, a philosophy, and a practice that commends itself because she faces the issue of control directly.

After she has celebrated the wonderful and wonder-working child to the point that the reader might expect her to let such a child go her own way and have her own way, Donaldson speaks of the need for discipline. Yet many factors come into play, factors that lead the expert to focus on the social settings in which the child acts and acts up. Donaldson asks, how does the responsible adult deal with the issue? Teachers, parents, administrators of justice, and caregivers will sympathize as Donaldson wrestles with what is for most of them a basic issue. After surveying the scene in which indiscipline prevails, she empathizes with teachers and casts her judgment philosophically:

> All of this leads to a central dilemma for those who want to teach the young. There is a compelling case for control. The young child is not capable of deciding for himself what he should learn: he is quite simply too ignorant. And he needs our help to sustain him through the actual process of learning. [Alfred North] Whitehead puts it vividly: "After all the child is the heir to long ages of civilization and it is absurd to let him wander in the intellectual maze in the Glacial Epoch."[1]

Common sense usually wins out as the adult who interacts with the child employs a mixture of firmness and subtlety. The problem comes when the adult loses patience and too readily wants to turn his own impulse to master and control into providing occasions for severe punishment over the child's lapses. Call that impulse in the teacher innate or the product of original sin, as some of the theologically inspired might do, but Donaldson reaches for that common sense and keeps the end in view, speaking of modulated approaches. Her voice of experience includes some of the best analysis and advice that I have heard on this subject, especially because she implies a difference between having influence on the child and having control over him:

> I can see only one way out of this dilemma: it is to exercise such control as is needful with a light touch and never to relish the need. It is possible after all for control to be more or less obtrusive, more or less paraded. Also a great deal will depend on what the teacher sees the aim of the control to be. *If the ultimate aim of the control is to render itself unnecessary, if the teacher obviously wants the children to become competent, self-determining, responsible beings and believes them capable of it,* then I am convinced that the risk of rejection of learning will be much diminished.[2]

In those lines Donaldson has framed an issue that remains before us constantly. Her phrase "the ultimate aim of the control is to render itself unnecessary" is a wonderful counterbarrier against the temptation to in-

1. Margaret Donaldson, *Children's Minds* (New York: W. W. Norton, 1978), 125.
2. Donaldson, *Children's Minds,* 126; italics mine.

timidate and thus harm the child. When the child discovers a better way on her own, makes new connections, receives fresh rewards, she has experienced satisfactions that should make the need for discipline ever less compelling. The one who forgets the aim Donaldson describes and who concentrates on getting and keeping control will soon fall into the habit of seeking ever more efficient and intimidating control. And the child, still enclosed with her problems, will remain the loser.

A Metaphor for the Controlled Child: A Closed Home

Just as Donaldson keeps in mind the *end point* or goal of discipline, philosopher Jerome Miller decisively addresses the *beginnings,* and we must do the same if we speak of the mystery of the child. The originating conceptions that relate to adult-child and child-child relations here are crucial. An elaborated worldview, a rewarding philosophy of life, and a fulfilling sense of vocation are ingredients in healthy interactions, as they are features in Miller's book *The Way of Suffering.*[3] His writing in this book and a later book, *In the Throe of Wonder,* has served as a primer for me in my personal attempts to reorient my own life and – here comes confession! – to reconceive my by no means fully reined-in impulse to manage and control. It is difficult to give the mystery of the child fair play unless one can control the impulse to control. Therefore I am now going to carry on a sort of extended conversation with *The Way of Suffering,* elaborating and applying some of Miller's themes to the issues of childhood. I hope that this sustained exchange will help others who are trying to reconceive their outlooks and habits in respect to children and, through them, to other aspects of adult life.

Those who associate habits and tendencies with specific ethnicities might attribute my impulse to control to my Swiss-German ancestry and

3. Jerome Miller, *The Way of Suffering: A Geography of Crisis* (Washington, DC: Georgetown University Press, 1988). Page references to this book will be given parenthetically in the text.

I have never met Professor Miller, who teaches at Salisbury State University in Maryland, and I know few biographical details about him, yet his two unsung books, written in a distinctive, profound, yet unburdened mode (footnotes are not a prominent feature), have led me to reorient my thinking on many subjects. I have also tried to refine my understanding in frequent conversations with Linda Lee Nelson, with whom I have shared many critical dialogues. Both of us were writing books on childhood, and both were wrestling with issues of control.

culture. They might credit the occasional releases from the hold of these on me to the children who have played and still play a role in my life. It happens to be true that at any moment I am carrying four timepieces, each with its own function, along with two calendars or schedules. Readers may see in these an indication of an obsessive-compulsive personality. Let me reassure them that I often goof off, can nap on a moment's notice, and have not been diagnosed as being under stress. Still, the dialogue with Miller can be a chastening opportunity for people like me to review details of our autobiographies and try to change what needs changing.

To house his argument against control, Miller employs the fitting metaphor of the home, one that can be appropriate for any provider of care who feels compelled to gain mastery over the young. His first chapter title is focused: "The Closed Home: Ordinary Existence as the Will to Control." This is relevant because most dealings with the child occur in ordinary existence, not in terminal cancer wards, during finals in national spelling bees, or at the Special Olympics. The context, this surrounding world of the ordinary, determines much that follows. Miller therefore dwells on the reality of a surrounding culture, and its current condition has a bearing on both children and those who care for, ponder, and relate to them. He sets the stage: "The individual is always inseparably bound to a world, to Others, and cannot be separated from the situation in which he lives and which, to some degree, he is" (p. ix).

The world of Others is one in which people make demands of sorts that reach different adults in diverse ways. Some of them follow the lines of gender differentiation. Miller observes quite rightly that men may find it especially difficult to open the figurative home, which he says represents "ordinary existence." More than is true for many women, men's experiences lead them to be nettled by the startling, the wondrous, and, in human settings, the strange. The child is likely to appear in the world of men as a stranger, even if she carries the DNA of her father, who can often be disappointed in her or put off by her. Just as her presence can stimulate affection or evoke responsibility, it can also appear to be interruptive, upsetting, and undermining. Those interruptions caused by the child's presence may seem ordinary and trivial, but in the context that concerns Miller and now us, such jostlings represent crises.

The crises about which Miller writes "upset and undermine precisely those attitudes toward life which, in our culture at least, are deeply associated with masculinity. In that sense, the 'will to control' . . . is profoundly phallocentric." After making that comment, he confesses as if for his half of the human race, "If I refer over and over to the person undergoing crisis as a male, it is finally because it is the maleness in all of us that is devastated by it" (p. xii). Yet the impulse to control, so manifest in many of the manuals on child care (though these are often written by women and usually show women as the main characters in the illustrations), also colors the relations of women to the child-as-problem. In such cases the child becomes the object of management more than the subject of mystery or the presence that elicits wonder.

The child can be the most consistent intruder on the time and space of ordinary existence that the adult – man or woman – would prefer to have under control. Most grown-ups find it difficult to let things be as they are. One can almost hear them in soliloquy: "Interruptions and upsets evoke my adult sense that I must subdue the totality of what *is* to the plans I have made for it. The moves I make in response would repress anything that tries to disrupt the flow of my routines" (p. 8).[4] Who more regularly than the child is an interrupter? The essence of the ordinary in the face of child-induced interruption is control, and the essence of control is the will to dominate. A person recognizes how planned most days of most people are at the moments when surprises or accidents occur. The presence or actions of children make demands or cause tumult. The beckoning or threatening presence of the child reveals how captive of ordinariness our lives can be.

Our mentor Jerome Miller speaks of adults' desire to make everything fit into preconceptions and patterns. This desire follows an impulse that in the present context includes the directing of children. They ordinarily must conform to the technical interests and disciplines of parents, whether on valid grounds or not. "As the wielder of techniques," Miller confesses for the generic adult, beginning with himself, "I wrench the world into obedience." He says, and most of us can say with him, "My success is measured by the degree to which I subordinate it to my purposes." We listen to parents as they boast or complain: they brag when the child fits in, when her will is subordinated to parental purposes. Some complain when her schedules (and thus their schedules) are not wholly controllable and their child is not responsive to all commands. Adults take refuge in their busyness, such as in parental work, which they see as justifying their adult existence. One thinks: "Work itself helps me impose a pattern, a direction in life. Work gives me a sense of being in control" (pp. 10-11).

4. This is a paraphrase of Miller's compact philosophical language, not the terms one would expect to hear in ordinary speech.

Joking about the patterns of interruption can often relieve some of the inner pressure to control. When we were fifty-eight, a colleague and I ran into each other at a conference after having been out of touch for several years. He asked if we could take a walk together during a long coffee break. We were friends, and I was glad to do this. At once, wearing a half-smile, he announced his purpose. "I wanted this talk and walk with you to set you straight." Because we had been out of contact, I did not know how he could have the perception that things were crooked. Because we are both in the same academic industry, he knew that at that stage of my career I was called to be at many professional society conclaves, often with some of his and my friends present. He assumed that I ran into contemporaries at such conferences, around watercoolers in the academy.

"I know what you guys are saying," he declared. I didn't know, but he quickly told me. He had entered his second marriage with someone twenty years younger than he. As he put it, her biological clock was ticking, and they wanted a child. One had arrived a year before, and my friend took delight in him, but now came a soliloquy. "I know what you guys say: 'It's great to have the grandchildren come to visit on Friday, but we are ready to let them go on Sunday.'" Well, yes. "And when the grandchild needs a diaper change or a fresh bottle, your son or daughter-in-law provides it, and that makes relating to the infant easier." Agreed. "And when you get together and talk about us or people in our situation, you fellows say that God must have planned for people to have children when the parents are in their twenties and thirties, because later they tend to creak when they bend over the crib to pick up the child or to play on the floor." Yes, generically that was the case, though I couldn't remember applying it to him. Being an academic, he knew he would score with this: "And you people all say that if you have a child in your late fifties, you don't get much scholarly work done anymore, because the kid cries and wakes you up and you've lost your edge for the next morning." He was right on target: that is what gossips would say and others of us would think. He paused after delivering these speculations and then said, "So I want to correct you. Whatever you are thinking – *it's a lot worse than that!*"

He was coping well, treating the child in wonder mingled with frustration, and he smiled as he said the last line. At the same time he was adding to the repository of stories adults collect about who children are and what they do. Listen to adults and almost universally you will hear teachers, parents, coaches, anyone having to do with children, reporting on the intrusions of children.

Returning from that coffee-hour stroll to Miller's book, we find

Miller detecting a spiritual void behind the compulsion to speak in such terms: "The fact that we really enjoy our routines is revealed by the boasting tone that creeps into our complaints about how much we have to do; we like to demonstrate that we have made the whole of our existence a work project." The more one sees the child as the problem in need of control, the more preoccupying she becomes and the less free both she and the provider of care are. The upset agendas and schedules of the day are so binding that Miller can speak of "the Promethean Dimension of the Ordinary." In this dimension, the will to control is out of control, and we designate it to be so in order that we can "cope with," "manage," and "deal with" every situation until "the very desire to control comes to dominate one's life completely." Finally, then, as with the adult who cannot let the child be, we realize that "I cannot *let* anything *be,* including myself" (pp. 11-13).

The philosophy of Jerome Miller is pointed and direct, for a clear and impressive reason. He showed that he was not content merely to connect the will to control and to manage with the acceptance of the lot of the ordinary or with the duties that accompany it. Instead, he says, the will to control reveals a spiritual vacuum that a person is not likely to wish to confront. The mystery of the child, in my observation, discloses this void as much as any other presence. A spiritual problem is haunting: "It is this need to control that explains the antireligious drive that is unconsciously at work in our lives." An adult who begins with witness to the mystery of God, the mysteries of creation, the mystery of the child, is more ready to face the apparently limitless and transcendent features of human life. "In making a thing 'manageable,'" Miller adds, "we confine it and thus make it limited" (p. 13). This is precisely what the control-minded adult sets out to do with the child at hand.

Since walls limit, Miller's metaphor of the closed home works well. It is easy to grow reasonably content with and then completely comfortable within the confinements and limits resulting from overplanning. Miller nails his topic and beckons the reader with the chapter subheading "The Other as a Problem to Be Solved" (p. 14). Who better and more frequently fills that role than the infant or child? Once more: begin with the child as problem, and when he interrupts or is unruly he simply becomes even more of a problem standing in the adult's way. A person of any age and situation can fill this intrusive and jarring role, but whoever has regard for the child knows that no one has more right to make demands, to interrupt, to bid for attention than does the child.

The child in such situations appears to be a stranger or alien, and when she is acting as such, she inspires resentment. She counters my customary framework for dealing with life. I face the child as alien because I have set boundaries across which the child as Other is not to come to jar and mess me up. If she does, as an adult I will ordinarily and naturally try to do my best to keep that problem minor and brief. If I treat either the child as an object or the calendar as a fetish, I think I can minimize the problem. Miller summarizes: "Only now do we begin to realize how powerful the heart can be once it is determined to be in control. There is literally nothing that is able to hold out against it; for there is nothing it cannot turn into a problem to be solved. A human being can view every rupture in his life as no more than an interruption to be repaired. Nothing that happens is then able to cut through the shroud he uses to hide existence" (pp. 15-16). Wait a minute, one is tempted to urge in an effort to gain perspective on the ground we have just tried to cover: All this spiritual turmoil and deadness reveal themselves simply because a child comes into view with her bids for attention or with his distractions? Answer: Well, yes.

The more secure a practical and problem-solving person sees himself to be in the ordinary world, the less can he identify with turmoil or find his way through it. Such a person makes every effort to domesticate dramatic phenomena, turning each into something that appears to be rote. Outwardly he conforms, but inwardly he engages in squirming, in trying not to lose control. Every gap in the pattern of control can be threatening. Anything foreign – and it is as being foreign that the creative and impetuous child appears – may lead to rupture. "I don't want to have the upsetting experience which the Otherness of this Other evokes in me." Once again, the child is that Other.

In such circumstances, the outcome of an encounter can induce withdrawal on the part of an adult. "I do not want to know myself as a self just as I do not want to know the Other as Other" (pp. 19-20). To apply Miller's theme to ours: the mystery that the child presents does not take on the character of the comforting "closed home" but opens what appears to be an abyss, something that seems boundless and is beyond the grasp of anyone who seeks control.

The Potential of the Child to Become the Welcomed Stranger

If Miller left the child and the provider of care in his figurative "closed home," the result would be disastrous. Miller, however, does not position himself figuratively with the world of playwright-philosopher Jean-Paul Sartre: he is not devising a room that needs a sign that says No Exit. He does not abandon readers within a suffocating and tormenting confinement of the self in the self or leave the closed-in person to suffer ever more closure. In ways that can help those who are to provide care, he presents a whole chapter on ways to reverse the tendency to close the home when he speaks of generosity as "the welcoming of strangers." In the next paragraphs we want to conceive of the child as the potentially interruptive and not always welcome stranger in home, school, church, social events, and society itself. Up close, for instance, when the surrounding adults, beginning with parents, learn to begin to be open and generous and to keep the child's needs in mind, they will find that the first bid of the child in response may be to enlarge their commitment to leisure. He signals a wish that the older and younger generations might do some re-creative things together. Or the child will want her friends to come over to visit, to accept hospitality. Such events mean risk, because, as Miller puts it, "hospitality is a rupture of boundaries."

Anything but a romantic and never one inclined to promote nostalgia among adults, Miller pictures saying, "Here my daring is not fretless, my generosity not spontaneous." However, the child so often frets and is not spontaneously generous. The impulse to control is characteristically and inevitably present among children, egocentric as they normally will be. In that egocentric guise especially, the child reveals herself to be a stranger. That situation represents a strain for the provider of care. Hospitality, Miller says, "involves welcoming as friend the Other whom I experience as Stranger. But I can experience the Other as stranger only if I experience him as *Other,* different, independent, approaching me across a frontier which separates us" (p. 25). The child is certainly different, independent, and beckoning across the frontier about which Miller has just spoken and which most adults experience.

Any dialogue, including this written version of one carried on with Jerome Miller, will allow for some disagreements. I disagree with Miller's concept of maturation, as when he suggests that childhood must simply be a thing of the past when "the state where we enjoyed an undifferentiated interplay between ourselves and the world" ends. I will argue that some dimensions and elements of that childhood world deserve to be and can be sustained all through life in ways appropriate to various contexts. The philosopher's description of that world of the child does illustrate why seeing the child as a problem to be solved can be limiting and destructive. Miller writes both personally and generically about childhood:

"As a child I did not have to open my self to an Other since, strictly speaking, there existed for me only the play in which both my self and the Other participated. Once this dance stops, I remember it as an extraordinary time which was strangely timeless, an extraordinary space not yet surveyed and divided by boundaries" (p. 25).

There is, of course, a negative side to the efforts to sustain, recover, or re-create one dimension of childhood, efforts that Miller sees to be futile if not destructive. He draws up short and summarizes his argument: "All of this is not meant to imply that we do not often seek to recreate our childhood world. But we can see very quickly that when we attempt such a return, we are really refusing to welcome the Other as Stranger" (p. 25). He next points to adult-on-adult disruptions of the will to control the Other. An example of this loss of control comes when one truly falls in love. Falling in love is not simply experiencing sensuality, for falling in love in its fullness also involves suffering. Still, at its best, says Miller, "it is no accident that love is represented, traditionally, as a *playful* figure who persuades the hard-hearted to join in its child-like game" (p. 32).

This observation applies obviously to the world of the child when he is seen not as representing problems but as being mystery. Thus, when an experience of love presents itself and one responds, "to let one's self be so persuaded, to let down one's defenses, is precisely to suffer, *to be wounded,* to become the hapless victim of an arrow tipped with a deadly poison. Such an act of letting-be lets the Other captivate me so that I fall under the sway of her disruptive and irresistible agency" (p. 32). Emphatically, to regard the mystery of the child is *not* to be able to remove suffering from relationships. Instead, such reflection about the inevitability of being wounded, of having to be vulnerable when children enter one's world, leads to a question never quite easily resolved, given the pain they can cause: Why want children?

Why Want Children?

Given the complexity of child rearing and the multitude of surrounding decisions that go with having care of a child, sober people might ask, why then do people want to have children? To one kind of thinker about human evolution, their desire is simply the expression of "the selfish gene," which contributes to the impulse for the human race not merely to survive but to dominate and control. Profound instincts govern humans, and they will not be denied.

Beyond the possibility that the selfish gene controls the whole process, another drive that inspires parenthood is relation to the peer group. The yearning to rear children represents having what other people – especially other couples of one's vintage, locale, and culture – have. They may not calculate how the ability of a child to interrupt can disrupt patterns of control with which they are familiar and to which they have become habituated in their years of childlessness. Where peers do not have children, as is the case in much of Western Europe today, "others" will not have them either. Thus they all control their own destiny through their generation but without contributing to the risk that comes with children being present in the next. Among other reasons to have children is one that poor single mothers-to-be often voice: they want someone to love them – and also someone to whom to relate, to shape, and, they will admit, to control. In a world where all other forces seem overwhelming, having a little child at one's side gives a chance for expression, even if that relation is full of problems.

Many will cite religious reasons: their God has commanded that generations replenish themselves, and they can fulfill the will of God by having children. Many wedding ceremonies stress that demand. Responding to a command to have children will come more naturally to those who want to see themselves in a chain of command and compulsion: God makes demands on me, and I make demands on the child God ordered me to have and with which God blessed me. Therefore, when I find the child to be a problem, the impulse to control takes over again.

Caring for Children in Circumstances That Offer Control

The talk of the problem of the Other, the closed home, and the desire to cling to the controlling aspects of childhood may strike some as philosophically abstract, though it is an appropriate introduction to the world of practical decisions and habit. For a more feet-on-the-ground approach and application, reading critiques of child-care manuals and prescriptions is bracing. Ann Hulbert's book to which we have briefly referred, *Raising America: Experts, Parents, and a Century of Advice about Children,*[5] is a brisk history of twentieth-century productions. Many of the child-care

5. Ann Hulbert, *Raising America: Experts, Parents, and a Century of Advice about Children* (New York: Knopf, 2003)

manuals about which she writes were best-sellers and were much spoken about. So reading her account for me meant revisiting familiar figures and their counsels; some of these nurtured our parents, others advised my generation, and the newer ones were designed to guide two subsequent generations, and this they did.

While doing research for this book, I read Hulbert's book twice. The first reading convinced me that the century's consistent counsel treated children as problems or as having problems. If parents did not feel a need for help, why would they buy and read books such as these? Because the problem (or problems) of the child was their constant focus, the books also come across as essays on control of the child. In our context I would be tempted to call it *Controlling America: Experts, Parents and a Century of Advice about How to Deal with the Problem of Children.* Reduce the controversies over child care to essentials, and they come to this: What control over the infant, child, and youth do adults have and need? What *should* they have? By what authority do they gain it, hold it, or lose it? What motives lead them to be so preoccupied with this question?

In my second reading I imposed a plot in response to a question: How would these books read if the authors had begun by evoking a sense of wonder and treating the child as a mystery not to be explained but to be explored? One or two of the authors Hulbert examined did now and then revel in the marvel of the child, but most of them, even those who sometimes used humor to reassure worrying parents, were in rather grim pursuit of goals that focused on explanation, management, and control. As I read Hulbert's story of the lives and teachings of some major givers of advice, it occurred to me that in almost every case the experts about whom Hulbert wrote were turning the figurative and sometimes actual home of the child into the laboratory or clinic of the adult. They were thereby closing the door to mystery, to awareness of contingency, to recognition that the child as mystery or surrounded by mysteries is fathomless.

As I embark on this page-through, I realize that I should face a critique from those who have written these problem-centered books and offered the practical advice that I am questioning. Countering them with reference to "wonder" and "mystery" can sound dismissive of material and strategies that can be helpful at one time or another to all providers of care. Is it useful to treat the child with an awareness that she is not explicable, that many of her problems are intractable, that what is most interesting about her is fathomless and surprising? I contend that it is, so long as the awareness is coupled with a sense of readiness to deal with the child in practical ways. Retaining the sense of wonder and refusing to dispel the mystery of the child is not just for happy times, good days, and the "highs" of a child's life. These strategies are full of the richest potential when, for instance, parents keep a vigil at the bedside of a very ill child, when teachers face long-lasting discipline problems, or when a child betrays the confidence parents have shown her.

In her thoughtful and creatively posed survey of advice manuals in the United States throughout the twentieth century, Hulbert focused on competing counsel through a sequence of approximately twenty-five-year periods. In each case one leader and one school could be called "hard," because it accented authority, discipline, and overt attempts to control behavior – often through harsh and stringent means – "for the child's own good." Similarly, in each period she focused on what we may call a "soft" counsel, offered by someone or some school that paid close attention to the child's internal development and growing autonomy. Her book includes stories of heroes and villains, the permissive and the rigid, the well-intended and the ideologically driven or even cruel. Overall, Hulbert is empathic and not condescending, even though the perspective of hindsight makes it possible for her to see follies in the past, and the moralist in her gets to chide posthumously some whose counsel turned out to be destructive. Both stories are instructive for any who provide care for the child.

Though Hulbert deals with the span of a whole century, what concerns us here is the near-contemporary scene, the situation at the turn of the new century. The names of those who appear in the most recent period lack the clinical and secular cachet of celebrities of old, such as Benjamin Spock and Bruno Bettelheim, who represented, in turn, a "soft" and a "hard" counsel during their domination some decades ago. Similarly, recent exemplars of scientific self-assurance, despite their best-selling books, have not received celebrity status and are not likely to leave as long a shadow as did John B. Watson or B. F. Skinner, masters of control in the mid-twentieth century. Still, books by contemporaries sell by the millions, and if no single individual towers, this may be partly because it is harder for one to break away from the pack of so many authors and advisers. Also, they represent great numbers of competing interest groups, marketed through mass media, books, seminars, videos, and tapes, which often tend to cancel each other out in a buyers' market.

Of special interest has to be the role of religion in the counsel that Hulbert recalls. Through many decades in the century past, American Catholic, Protestant, and fundamentalist-turned-evangelical advice-givers addressed their specific sheltered constituencies, almost as if by stealth, because few outside their communions were aware of what went on in them. Religion was seen to be a private affair, monitored by sectarian interests, while leaders in the larger context seemed to be reflexively secular. In recent decades, however, religious figures and groups have "gone public." More of them have used the media and the market in fresh ways, appealing to constituencies that transcend sectarian boundaries. Through clever marketing and by addressing the unsettling issues of the day, they attract attention along with millions of purchasers and followers. They are forces to be taken seriously in pluralist, religiously open-market America. What they teach has consequences beyond child nurture — for example, in debates over social issues and in legislatures and courts.

Many of the experts and writers whom Hulbert describes played on fears, rang alarm bells, or whined over cultural decline as they defined it and as they saw it affecting the child. In some cases the givers of advice displayed signs of near-panic among themselves or showed that they wanted to induce a sense of crisis in the world of parents and teachers. Hulbert found two spiritually armed camps in the 1990s flinging names at each other during the standoff between the "disciples of discipline," as the *New York Times* called them, and the more relaxed "'helping' professionals." Further divisions separated the "Judeo-Christian" and "parent-centered" experts, as she portrayed them in their critics' terms, from the "Eastern establishment, liberal, secular humanists," who propagated child-centered approaches. The former two groups included people who were mistrustful of government and who attacked the United States Supreme Court and many kinds of public school jurisdictions[6] because they considered such agencies to be alien. Meanwhile, the more self-assured and militant critics of whatever looked secular or liberal attacked those scientists who had spent the century figuratively pushing religious counselors off the stage. It was these secularists who, in popular culture and the market, were now being rendered ever more suspect as they turned defensive.

Hulbert paid special attention to the usually confident but in one case bemused and humble James Q. Wilson, author of *The Moral Sense*. Wilson confessed that he and other reductionists who employed "nothing but" scientific approaches had not found ways to ground their counsel when they dealt with the matter of character development. It was "surprising," he confessed in 1995, that "we do not know how character is formed in any rigorously scientific sense." In that statement of humility,

6. Hulbert, *Raising America,* 326, citing Susan Bolotin, "The Disciples of Discipline," *New York Times Magazine,* 14 February 1999, 32. Hulbert also provides references to the sources of other groups designated in these lines, 425.

just this side of penitent, Wilson provided fodder for the conservatively religious who had long attacked scientists for claiming too much.[7] Many of those who were strongly motivated by intense religious understandings countered him and his kind without expressing any awareness of self-doubts like his and were not ready to make any concessions to those with other counsel about child care.

Hulbert, with her fine sense of irony, observed a symbiosis between the two opposing camps, as she kept finding how much the two schools of advice-givers had in common. "The two kinds of experts, it turned out, were not cut from entirely dissimilar cloth. Their kinship emerged in the social and moral alarm they displayed, but also even in the style of advisory fare some of them dispensed." They both advanced ways to control the child and the cultural life to which the child related, by whatever means they could render legitimate.

How could this be, since they were not all able to isolate this control factor and showed little willingness to recognize their own interest in controlling? To answer this, Hulbert offered a response based on her finding that the two camps were borrowing from each other even as they condemned each other. In more ways than they could afford to affirm, they were united in counsel even as each dismissed the other. She fastened on the kind of language that Jerome Miller had treated in more abstract contexts. Having referred to the more secular-minded prescribers as "mentors" and those focused on spiritual understandings and strategies as "ministers," she saw congruences among them:

> Ministers and mentors alike revealed themselves to be management experts armed with systematic principles and tools for engineering a home culture of structured commitment, cooperation, and communication. And "parent-centered" traditionalists and "child-centered" psychologists embraced much the same mixed aim: to prepare children for, and protect them against, an overstimulating, alienating culture of competitive achievement and unbridled consumerism. (p. 328)

Familiarity with Miller's vocabulary has prepared us to anticipate Hulbert's stresses, as seen in her accent on themes such as *management, system, principles, tools, engineering, structure, competition,* and *consumerism.* All of them in some way demonstrated the understanding of the problem of the

7. Hulbert, *Raising America,* 327-28, quoting James Q. Wilson, *The Moral Sense* (New York: Free Press, 1993), xii. Subsequent page references to Hulbert's book will be given parenthetically in the text.

Other, now in the form of a child, as well as the presumed solution to the problem. This understanding comes in the form of prescriptions for minimizing the threat by an "Other" to adult serenity and security. Her summary matches our thesis: "What may be more startling is that the mentors' softer brand of empathetic home management could be just as stringent for parents, and for children, as the ministers' regimens of inculcating self-control – if not more so" (p. 329).

Hulbert brought forward for examination a leader of the parent-centered camp, James Dobson, whose *Dare to Discipline* in 1971 was but the first of his many salvos in the culture wars that did not then have a name. From a clerical family in the Church of the Nazarene, Dobson moved forward from his Colorado Springs base with his Focus on the Family, which attracted millions of clients and constituents. He was similarly at ease in Washington, D.C., with members of New Christian Right groups at his elbow. Thus his followers could hear Gary Bauer in the Family Research Council utter claims like, "Nothing short of a great Civil War of Values rages throughout North America." Bauer elaborated: "Two sides with vastly different and incompatible worldviews are locked in a bitter conflict that permeates every level of society. Bloody battles are being fought on a thousand fronts." At stake was the issue of "what philosophy of living, loving, begetting, and getting through life will prevail" in the century ahead (p. 329).[8]

Secular-based fellow travelers soon appeared at the side of the harder-line disciplining ministers. Among them was the self-described "loose cannon" John Rosemond, the advocate of "tough love," who was described as the "anti-psychologist's psychologist." Rosemond claimed he was only reproducing the "voice of Grandma, of common sense," as he salted his words with Bible passages and charged into politics over against "ultraliberals, leftists, socialists" (p. 330).[9] Led by the popular Dr. T. Berry Brazelton, he helped boost a market that grew drastically and suddenly.

Overcontrol as a Prescription

Ann Hulbert noted that in 1997 five times as many books of parenting counsel appeared as had been published in 1975. The growth itself was a

8. Quoting James Dobson and Gary Bauer, *Children at Risk* (Dallas: Word, 1990), 19.

9. Quoting John Rosemond, *A Family of Value* (Kansas City, MO: Andrews, McMeel, 1995), 101.

clear sign that child care was up for grabs and that the market and ideological stakes were high. In the end, she wrote, "out-of-control parents," who had been favored in 1980, had now been replaced by "over-controlling parents." The word *control* kept reappearing on all sides. The scientists were clearly on the defensive. The concept of "hyper-parenting" even made its way into a book title. Again, Hulbert is to the point: "What was particularly disorienting about the array of variously credentialed doctors was an underlying similarity between the two competing camps" (p. 334), neither of which, in our terms, left their readers much time and space for wonder over the mystery of the child and for subsequently dealing with it.

Some of these hard-right counselors, to their credit, did issue some cautions, even if their advice did not often reflect these. James Dobson found it important to stake out a claim that, despite charges and appearances, he was opposed to "*parental harshness.* Period!" He even risked borrowing the concept of self-esteem, one that his camp earlier had derided. Gary Ezzo, another counselor on the cultural right, preached against the "authoritarian household" that produced the "child who is bitter and full of resentment," while John Rosemond wanted the home to be a "benevolent dictatorship." He said he thought that his support for the adjective *benevolent* tempered whatever ominous theme the noun *dictatorship* connoted. Meanwhile, in the culture wars, the secular experts found themselves having to make clear that they were not for "permissiveness." Some among them went along with the need for "limit-setting" (pp. 35-36).[10]

In her reporting, as noted, an ironic tinge colored Hulbert's view of the various strategies. Seldom had the two parties been more strident, more aggressive, more dismissive of the other than at the end of the century. Yet they also converged on more points than they knew or might want to have called to anyone's attention. The managerial style and the presenting of detailed manuals for control marked both. Hulbert cites Dobson speaking in commercial terms: "Oh yes, *children are expensive, but they're worth the price*" (p. 337).[11] Across the spectrum the peddlers of counsel came up with step-by-step advice, often in the mode of issuing harsh and intimidating demands, as they peered over the edges to where the armies of the culture wars lined up behind each. Management became

10. Quoting James Dobson, *The New Dare to Discipline* (Wheaton, IL: Tyndale, 1992), 12; Gary and Anne Marie Ezzo, *Growing Kids God's Way: Biblical Ethics for Parenting* (Chatworth, CA: Micah 6:8, 1997), 180, 45, 312; John Rosemond, *John Rosemond's Six-Point Plan for Raising Happy, Healthy Children* (Kansas City, MO: Andrews, McMeel, 1989), 48.

11. Quoting James Dobson, *Temper Your Child's Tantrums* (Wheaton, IL: Tyndale, 1986), 6.

overmanagement; counsel became demand. And a buying public whose members evidently exemplified Miller's company of those who would control the child welcomed the controlling approaches.

In the end, Hulbert had to ask herself a question that may bemuse some readers. She had surveyed the work of counselors in opposing camps who, for all their vast differences, shared an interest in control of the child, through hard or soft means. Her implicit message for readers comes close to being "Don't listen too much to the advice-givers; pass up their books at the bookstores; twist the radio and television dials or turn them off." She is not dismissive of all efforts. It *is* difficult to relate to children responsibly while keeping an anarchic stance and remaining at a great distance from all the assumptions of the management-minded people. Parents and other caregivers obviously need practical help, and most of them, we may presume, can employ their intelligence to sort out the various approaches. What is at issue is the context, intention, and product of the competitive counsels of the approaches, or whatever might next replace them. Underlying both sets of assumptions is the implicit claim that the child can be understood, explained, and somehow cut to size, and thus will turn out in ways that will please adults with their various cultural preconceptions.

The futility of efforts at total control is obvious. The twentieth century had seen scientific experiment, religious revivals, drastic cultural jolts, and change in family structures, and yet Americans who were interested in the provision of care for children seemed not to have traveled far. Many culture critics even contended that they had retrogressed. Hulbert summarizes:

> The scientific parenting crusade has certainly not wrought widespread reform in America, much less brought calm to the home front. Instead it has been a repository of the tensions — psychological and social, moral and practical — confronting middle-class families raising children in a country that has become more competitive and meritocratic, and more culturally permissive and sexually egalitarian, over a fast-changing century. . . . Two poles have defined America's child-rearing advice from the very start, and even in the cacophonous market at the close of the century they still framed an underlying debate that sounded familiar. How much power and control do, and should, parents wield over a child's journey from dependence to independence? How much freedom and intimacy do children need, or want, along the way? (pp. 364-65)

Along her way while doing research, Hulbert had made a surprising discovery of what she called "the degree of ambivalence America's advisers themselves have betrayed about their own claims to scientific clarity and certainty on their end of the spectrum." Hard and soft counselors hedged their bets, because "children resist easy analysis, and mothers are hard to please." Here is an occasion for appraising approaches that deal with the mystery of the child.

> After all, it . . . begins to dawn on parents that no fine-tuned scheme for shaping futures lies in the experts' manuals, much less in their own homes — or even, most of the time, in their dreams. Experience conveys that lesson daily, as parents run up against the resistance and the resilience of children and the uncertainty of family, social, economic, and historical circumstances. America's conflicted experts have learned that lesson, too, not just from their labs, where studies have never been as definitive as they hoped, but also from their own lives. Their advice aims to hide the wisdom, but it can be found in reading between, and across, the experts' lines. (pp. 365-66, 370)

Hulbert's reference to "their own lives" recalls what she found in the personal parent-child interactions of most counselors. Mentioning it out of context might mean hanging soiled laundry or indulging in yellow journalism or gossip. At the same time, with a request for pardon from those who find it uncharitable to bring this up, mention of some of the outcomes in a general way will both illustrate the dangers of the impulse to control, to solve the problem, and point to the theme we earlier stressed: the role of contingency, or accident, in the life of the child. Thus when the tumults of the 1960s disrupted the presumed more serene contexts of child- and youth-rearing of the previous decades, the contingencies of cultural change brought surprise to experts in both soft and hard camps:

> Although you would not have known it from their belligerence on the barricades, the experts had been taken by surprise, too. They were ultimately forced to admit that they had no simple answers — no tidy causes or cures to be found in child-rearing theories. Each in his own way, Spock [in the soft camp] and Bettelheim [in the hard camp] arrived at a similar conclusion: their influence as experts had been far less than they had hoped (and, at times, feared). Or at any rate, it had not been at all what they had anticipated. . . . [T]heir fate, as it unfolded in the 1970s, continued to confound the adversaries. . . . [Thus] in the midst of the feminist revolt, both experts were on the defensive. (pp. 262-63)

One may have brought up a child with love and care, but things could still go wrong. We have been posing the interest in managing and controlling on the part of the adult world over against the mystery of the child, which deserves a celebration that few of the controlling counselors gave them. The issue before us, then, is this: What is the problem with management and control, and what can be done to address it? The alternative is not to come up with a new manual, a new step-by-step approach, but to call for informed observation of the child and participation with her in all her mystery and never fully controlled being.

4. The Child as Mystery

To address providers of care and citizens about the mystery of the child may appear distracting. Most practical situations involving children, however drastic and complex they are, relate to the world of the mundane or the ordinary, for which there are specialists in abundance, experts on the life of the child. It is all so simple. Medical scientists treat children's diseases. Teacher training institutions and the publishers of guidance manuals for parents deal with education and discipline. Entertainers provide entertainment. Dieticians prescribe diets.

In speaking of the seemingly less practical category of mystery, one risks sounding vague, perhaps befogged and uncertain. This is the case especially because many of us usually reserve the term *mystery* for the transcendent order and even for God. Therefore one undertakes a greater risk, even a qualitatively different one, when speaking of mystery than when speaking of the prosaic features of life. Some might even read any attempt to deal with the mystery of the child as an endeavor to endow the child with qualities that should be reserved for God alone. At this time, let me only issue a disclaimer by asserting that the mystery of the child is not about Godlike goodness, because the mystery of the child also includes reference to the mystery of evil, which takes root in both the individual and the community.

At this point it is appropriate to ask: why the mystery of the child? Why not the mystery of the human person? Is the child alone a mystery, a product of the divine Mystery, wrapped in and surrounded by mystery? The answer to that question is clear: the child is not alone in mystery. Whether one believes in divine creation or sees the human person reduced to biological and chemical factors, when one considers the changing circumstances with their apparently limitless contingencies, experiences, and choices, mystery is definitely an appropriate category of approach to understanding. We are simply concentrating on the child for her distinctive ways of being regarded, experiencing reality, and responding.

Efforts to explore the child as mystery can lead the searcher astray, particularly because of potential confusion over the word *mystery.* Setting out to clarify what is meant by the term can lead the inquirer to a shelf of books or videos that connect "mystery" with "child" in ways that are irrelevant to our purposes. A scan of this imagined shelf would find these examples, among others: *The Mystery of the Child Holding a Dove* and *The Mystery of the Child's Toy.*

The great majority of these "mystery" books and films belong to the detective story genre. Most of them end with the mystery solved. The mystery of the child points to what can never be solved, but only addressed. Similarly, casually using the term to refer to something hard to figure out is misleading. It takes little imagination to picture parents as they face a misbehaving child shrugging things off with "it's a mystery to me" why he acts as he does. Similarly, when providers of care are nonplussed or befuddled by a child's actions, they may also resort to the category of mystery, which they take to mean that about which they are ignorant or which they are ill equipped to master. Or one may think of adults who listen in awe to a seven-year-old pianist flawlessly playing a Chopin nocturne and then turn to say, "It's a mystery where he got his gifts; his parents are not even talented at the piano."

Few casual users of the word *mystery* are likely to employ two phrases that appear regularly in this book: "the child as mystery" and "the mystery of the child." But others may refer to the mysteries that surround a child. Catechetical literature in Catholicism and elsewhere may connect "the mystery of the child" and "the mystery of God," suggesting what the two hold in common and how the use of the term *mystery* differs in both cases. Those who are speaking about anatomy and biology may deal with parts of the body, such as the mysterious brain, or will be wholistic in intention and refer to "the mystery of the child's own body," especially when someone young discovers and explores fingers, toes, tummies, or private parts.

It is characteristic of religious people who speak of the mystery of the child, as a few of them on occasion do, also to talk about the mystery of the church, the mystery of faith, the mystery of communion, or the mystery that goes with the search for meaning. During controversies over human cloning, some ethicists speak of the mystery of the child. That little person is other and more than the mere result of the seed of the father and the egg of the mother and is different from what one could have imagined after careful observation of the parents. The more delicate applications of the term *mystery* allow for at least the hint of the religious dimension, as we shall see in the chapters ahead.

The Provider of Care Confronts Religious Discourse about Mystery

Mystery as we are speaking of it here, though it relates to themes in various religions, derives in no small part from understandings in the Christian traditions. Because so much in them draws from the Bible, we will begin inquiries there. The writer of the oldest letters in the Christian New Testament, Paul the apostle, on numerous occasions used the term. "Handle with care!" is the main theme that comes from the apostle's witness about the concept. The mystery of which Paul spoke belongs to God. That mystery was only partially and indirectly imparted to some who were the "stewards" of those mysteries. It is easy to see that in all such cases, where normal rational and historical argument gave out and where the time-bound and earth-bound stories and explanations came to their limit, mystery entered. It represented the limitless divine activity of the sort that had some bearing on the world of mortals and sense-bound believers, including, of course, children.

An impatient reader, or even a patient one, has good reason to ask what any talk of divinity has to do with the human child. In the open market of a pluralist society, would it not be possible, someone asks, to speak profoundly about the child without risking reference to mystery? Why not get to the point of problem solving right away? We will argue that for believer and nonbeliever alike, if one wants to do justice to the depth of the child's experience and his place in emergent culture, the concept of mystery is most appropriate. While begging for still more patience, we will call on some contemporary thinkers who have revisited the concept of mystery. They can help us connect the inexhaustible concept of "mystery" with "child" more directly.

That reference to biblical language and our promise that we will deal with the mystery of human life can lead to the use of theological language, a form of discourse foreign to most of us most of the time. In a world where the majority of people believe in God or the gods, in the Sacred or a transcendent order; in a nation where 90 percent of the people tell pollsters that they believe in God, however they define God; in a society where politics, economics, entertainment, and commerce are influenced by individuals and groups who claim to measure their decisions in the light of God, it is urgent to acquire some sense of what they mean by the word *God.*

To come closer to the theme of our argument: more than 80 percent of the people in North American society take their belief in God into the precincts of Jewish and Christian traditions. Along with Muslims, they are sometimes spoken of as "People of the Book," drawing on scriptures that point to the divine mystery. Because so many providers of care for children reflect on this mystery and its shaping of the human world, there are strong reasons for nonbelievers also to take the spiritual probing seriously. Attempts to make sense of debates among citizens over the child will improve if the transcendent note, the reference to the divine, enters the reckoning.

Readers who are distanced from religious communities may not always recognize that the talk of believers, language that often to them sounds exclusive or trivial, does have a bearing on their world. Citizens today are relearning to assess the power of religion in many zones of life. For starters, notice that in this new millennium religion inspires more conflict, even more wars and terrorism, than any other force. It may also foster healing and acts of generosity more than any other form of energy around the globe. People vote in the light of their faith. They make decisions about terrorism, about war and peace, about the culture, about what is to be seen and favored in mass communications, and about what legislators and jurists should promote on the basis of it. Religious faith inspires both child care and child abuse. How people conceive of social life, beginning with the family, and how they understand biological concerns as these relate to each infant, inspire response and reaction far beyond the boundaries of their own faith communities. How they regard the mystery of the child at least indirectly affects decisions about schooling, media, health care, and many other expressions in a civil society.

For over four decades my vocation has taken me less frequently to the pulpit and sanctuary than to the classroom, the boardroom, the platform, the airwaves, and the legal forum. Therefore much of the God-talk I heard and read, whether it was convincing or not, had to make sense among people who were distant from the circles where their fellow citizens profess faith in God the Creator. However, like so many other scholars in fields like mine, I have found among many who had long been cast or miscast as "secular" a growing readiness to explore and engage religious thought – even if in the end they reject or refute it. Curiously, resistance to the exploration of the conjoined themes of mystery and child more often comes from communities of believers who, whether out of dogmatic or exclusivist impulses, do not want to hear the words of others, especially those who operate outside the closest circles of faith communities. Many of them act as if they have figured everything out and can dispense with mysteries and the mysterious.

Long aware of the difficulties in communicating about these secular-spiritual encounters, some religiously informed scholars almost reflexively suppress or disguise the religious understandings that give life to their pursuits. This is true in discourse or policy making that deals with the provision of care as much as anywhere else. Sometimes they hear that they should never employ religious discourse and instead trade only with understandings that can apply immediately to the whole culture. However, there is no such understanding in our world of variety and competition. Speaking of the child in the language of secular rationalism or in chemical or biological terms and stopping there turns out to be in its own way as sectarian as is conservative religious thought and practice. Excluding religious history and thought limits the scope of inquiry and blights efforts to communicate with the public in all its diversity.

Inquirers who have chosen to deal with religious faith and with critical thought about it, and to be aware of the possibilities these disclose, express disappointment when they see how little of the literature on our subject deals directly and systematically with the mystery of the child. How-to books on spiritual parenting, texts prepared for the religious education of the young, instructional treatises on Sunday school and youth work, and even guides to converting or disciplining children are welcomed and plentiful. People on all sides regularly express opinions and offer counsel on these subjects, often without having made efforts to understand how awareness of the mystery of the child can enhance their work.

To take an instance: the prime American Protestant public philosopher of the century past, Reinhold Niebuhr, drew on insight from his religious tradition while gaining a hearing from those who were distanced from it. Some of these called themselves "atheists for Niebuhr." They found attractive the realism of his biblically based insights that dealt with what in his major book he called "the nature and destiny of man." Many who did not share his root belief found relevant his diagnosis of the human situation. Political philosopher Hans Morgenthau, in a conversation I heard at a faculty club, was asked how his thought on social policy related to that of Niebuhr, given that they did not share religious faith. He had his answer ready. As Morgenthau saw it, Niebuhr, drawing on biblical prophetic language, analyzed the human situation most profoundly. He concluded in words along these lines: "He and I come out to just about the same practical point – only I do not need so much metaphysics to get there." With or without traditional metaphysical scaffolding, we seek approaches to the child that bring insights different from those found in the discourse dependent on secular rationalism.

Reduction: The Mystery versus the Child Who Is "Nothing but . . ."

In Niebuhr's shadow, some religious thinkers today attempt to bring distinctive perspectives – for example, the category and experience of mystery – to bear on human affairs. Trading on their achievement, one cannot immediately make a point by merely asserting that religious thought can have secular consequences. One must first hear the religious thinkers make their own case for introducing and holding to difficult concepts before they apply them to the practical scene. Much is at stake in the determination of what a child is, what her potential and resources are, and what her dreams will be. If a person who cares for a child wants to move beyond the merely practical, he will learn to welcome the many sciences that throw light on the being and ways of the child. At the same time, he will find himself called to question those approaches that assault mystery by "reducing" the subject, the child, in a particular way.

We do not picture the school counselor, the coach, the nurse, the pastor, or the grandparent theorizing about technical issues like reductionism. Nor will most of them name reductionists as villains who complicate efforts to improve care of the child. They may not read the scientific journals or even the popular press when it takes up such issues. Yet what these scientists pursue does impinge on the ways adults regard children, so we pay attention.

Scientists recognize and may employ many kinds of reduction, most of which are helpful in scientific endeavors. Reduction is thus often used for explanatory purposes, as when a scientist reduces a physicist's problem to one that a chemist can analyze within the bounds of her discipline. (Not even all scientific materialists shun categories of mystery, though they would not locate the source and end of mystery in any way in divine creation.) Such scientific reduction can advance research and discovery in positive ways.

An inhibiting version of reduction cuts phenomena to size, insisting that something mysterious is "nothing but" this or that. In this mode, the reductionist can speak of music as being nothing but a series of vibrations in the air. Similarly, it may be said that the human is nothing but a species of animal, a survival machine programmed to preserve some molecules known as genes. In such light, the unmysterious child would turn out to be nothing but this or that package of genes, survivor of a particular kind of parents, or someone plagued by misfiring neurons in the brain that lead him to destructive behavior. The child, in this light, is nothing but this at once stubborn and malleable little human machine which will come to be sufficiently comprehended after diagnosis occurs or when specific treatments are carried out.

In such materialist outlooks, everything simply manifests the physical and chemical aspects of human life, and inquiry ends there. Biology is then destiny. One might hear a scientist of a reductionist school identifying human joys and sorrows, memories and ambitions, and the sense of personal identity and free will as the activity of nerve cells and molecules; behavior is "nothing but" the action of sets of neurons.

Along with reduction to chemical, physical, and biological realities, sociological and political reduction also affect understandings of the child, and do so at the expense of mystery. Many people who do not read formal political texts or sociological treatises still know that Karl Marx explained the human story in economic terms, seeing people as "nothing but" wage slaves or greedy accumulators of capital. That was it. In our culture one often hears of economists who so isolate and elevate the market as a domain that everyone in it consequently becomes "nothing but" the *Homo economicus,* the economic human. The child is then simply the initiate into the economic order and is largely determined by it.

For another case, Sigmund Freud and the psychoanalysts of schools that were derived from his work tended to see the human as nothing but a projector of illusions, the supreme one of which was the notion of God. In the eyes of such absolutist Freudians, each child deals instinctually with traumas connected to birth and childhood experiences. Further, Charles Darwin and many evolutionists understood the human as "nothing but" the product of mere and utter chance, something realized through the expression of selfish genes. This element of chance, the Darwinists argued, readied them to explain the child in exhaustive detail.

Employing the concept of the mystery of the child cannot be a tool for refuting the "nothing but . . ." scientific approaches. In fact, it is hard to picture what a direct refutation of these would look like. I am under no delusion that invoking the category of mystery disproves any of the reductionist approaches. It is not fair to use verbal sleight-of-hand to gloss over the challenges of scientific and political materialism. The appeal to mystery attempts to help supply what novelist E. M. Forster called "breathing holes for the human spirit"[1] and to celebrate complexities for which no single mode of discourse – in this case, the scientific – accounts for everything. Similarly, keeping reductionism from becoming the all-purpose approach to the child helps buy time and space for one to adduce other factors, many of which might otherwise be overlooked.

Analogy: The Mystery of the Child and the Mystery of God

After having stood aside during our comments on scientific reduction, the child now comes back to center stage, where we relink her with mystery. I mentioned in Chapter 1 that when I was asked what focus I would bring to a scholarly project on the child in religion, law, and society, I answered, "The mystery of the child." To some that may well have sounded mystifying. Gather around a seminar table experts on medicine, law, psychology, religion, and social work, as we were chartered to do in our three-year project at Emory University, and you can expect them to name very concrete topics. My colleagues pursued mainly practical problems associated with the care of and for the child. I learned much from this congenial company and would never have ventured to write this book had I not been informed by their inquiries, arguments, and findings. Sometimes I wondered what they thought of my "mystery" theme, though most were too courteous to question. Why introduce such an elusive, almost spooky, topic like mystery? What exactly is at stake with "the mystery of the child"?

On *mystery:* The *Oxford English Dictionary* cites numerous definitions that belong in the neighborhood of our usage but do not dwell there. Out of thirteen dictionary definitions, only part of one, II.5, is helpful at all. A mystery, there, is "a matter unexplained or inexplicable." This description applies in our case because of the vast number of possibilities that one can adduce to begin to explain the mystery of the child.

The poets whom we have already met and many others provide the concept of the abyss of mystery that surrounds and pervades the child's

1. E. M. Forster, *Two Cheers for Democracy,* cited in R. D. Laing, *The Politics of Experience and the Bird of Paradise* (New York: Pantheon, 1967), 149.

existence. Whenever some scientists and other scholars give the impression that they have children all figured out, the voice of the poet, the sounds of the musician, the painted strokes of the artist are good checks against such notions. It is likely that most providers of the care of children will listen to the folksinger before they turn to the student of animal behavior, to the painter of images before the technician on humanistic subjects, and perhaps more to the pastor than to the theological professor. Still, criticizing the experts who claim too much does not mean that their analyses and prescriptions are useless.

Manifest, if selective, progress has been made on the scientific front among adults in their understanding of children, as any visit to the pages of medical and educational history books and various Websites quickly reveals. Something about the being of children tempts many experts to be overconfident when studying them, as they would not be were their subject an adult. Ann Hulbert's *Raising America* gave ample illustration of that. When a little person who is often not yet literate and is still especially vulnerable is the object of scrutiny, she can too easily be manipulated and turned into a thing. That turning is an act of profanation, a display of the mystery of evil in human interactions. This evil is magnified in the case of the child because she cannot speak distinctly for herself and cannot criticize interpretations or policies affecting her, as a free and informed adult is able to do.

My interest in writing on the mystery of the child, I realized, could be regarded with suspicion. How could a helpful contribution be made by someone who proposed that the child be seen as a subject of mystery? Enough fog surrounds inquiries into the human subject that we need not produce more of the same, losing the child among the explanations in the process. Science and humanistic studies exist to dispel fog, to push back the veil behind which ignorance hides. Bring light, not mist, is valid counsel. So why deal with the mystery of the child?

At the heart of my answer is this: treating the theme of mystery effectively can lessen the temptation of adults to seek and sustain dominance and control over the child, something that reductionism too readily makes possible. The parties tempted to exert control are the adults who are called to be providers of care. As such, they have responsibilities for discipline, nurture, understanding, and, yes, legislating in respect to the child. The biologist who studies the brain of the child needs clarity and precision and must expose to bright light the biological makeup of the little person. The teacher, to be successful, needs to find ways to teach effectively. She studies books about discipline and will not get much out of manuals counseling her to stand back in awe and wonder and enjoy chaos. In the face of those necessities, the question remains: Why do artists and poets, some religious thinkers, and this author promote the theme of mystery?

God is also at the center of the discourse. Talk about the mystery of God has to remain talk about God and not about nature or about humans within nature. This is so even though the child, made in the image of God, deserves special treatment within creation. The witness to a divine Creator who creates and interacts with humans is not utterly remote and ineffable. Whoever speaks of the child or anyone or anything else in creation as *mystery* has to detail how such usage of the term differs from that implied in God-talk. If everything is mystery, then nothing is meaningfully mysterious. Witness to the mystery of God must be protected by anyone who takes God seriously. At the heart of the mystery of the child, when it is interpreted religiously, are two claims: first, that the child is a child of God; and second, that the child is made in the image of God. Being "of God" or being "imaged" as God is far from being seen as Godlike. The most fruitful way to speak of the mystery of the child is to see such talk as *analogical,* as is all talk about God.

Here, as so often, we have introduced a term without which most people can happily live. Most providers of care for children are concerned with providing Christmas presents and summer vacations, funds for private education and visits to the doctor. They can get along indefinitely without using language last heard at college in philosophy class. Yet much of their action and thinking is analogical in ways that prepare them to understand what is at issue here.

Analogy is, among so many other things, a form of speaking or writing that stresses comparison in a particular way. The two key words associated with it in this context are *same* and *different.* When one is comparing two phenomena, the use of analogy shows awareness that on both sides there is some sameness. Otherwise, how can they be compared? At the same time, there are differences between the two. Otherwise, why should they be compared? Thus, here, God is mysterious and is a mystery, but mystery is not the same as God. For illumination, we note that God is loving and is love, but love is not God. Many things that belong to God do not belong to love, and many things that belong to love are not properly descriptions of God.

With all those precautions in mind, we will be emboldened to connect the mystery of the child with the divine mystery. Analogy became important in Christian thought because philosophers in the biblical tradition had to deal with two apparently incompatible realities, both having to do with God.

On one hand, the infinite God is so different from all finite creations that any reference to God should mean dealing with the incomparable. You cannot in any simple way compare the properties of the child to the properties of God. This means that when one relates anything said about God to anything said about the human, the two references cannot point to simple comparables. Still, since this faith is revealed to humans — and biblical witness asserts that God is participating in the creation and the world of mortals, believers must find ways to speak intelligibly about the engagement of the divine with the human. So it was that thinkers borrowed the word *analogia* from the mathematicians and put it to work. *Mystery* when related to God cannot mean the same thing as when it is related to humans and, in our case, to the human child. Yet it is appropriate to speak about both the mystery of the child and the mystery of God, so they cannot be in every way utterly different. Talk about the child "in the image of God" is obviously analogical.

When humans experience the presence of God and then speak of their encounters, or in other words, when they utter or write what comes to be regarded as a revelation of the divine, they regularly surround their witness with words about mystery. In the most familiar of such revelations, witnessed to in the biblical book of Exodus, the divine Presence comes with the voice of an angel and the sight of a bush that, though burning, is not consumed: Moses, who stands before it, is ordered to take off his shoes because the ground on which he is standing is holy ground. So goes the story in Exodus, a book that constantly demonstrates acts of dealing with God as mystery.

When Moses, bidden as he was to lead the people out of slavery, wants confirmation to give evidence that he has been called, he shows that he naturally would like to reduce the mystery. He pleads to see the face of the Lord. The Lord announces that Moses cannot see the divine glory without being annihilated. The awed man is to be hidden in the cleft of a rock and will be free to emerge after the glory of God has passed by. Then he can behold the back side, the posterior of God, who remains mysterious, but now in a different way, hidden as he is in the tracks and traces of human history (see Exodus 33:18-23).

The scientist as reductionist has little use for a concept of divine hiddenness, certainly not when dealing with the attributes of the human child. Committed to the notion that what is important has been said in a phrase such as "we are nothing but grown-up germs," some scientists will consider their assignment completed. They have studied and then expounded what their discipline turns up, witnessing to what they can know from the laboratory and clinic or in an empirical philosophy classroom that informs inquiry about the person who is a child.

When God and the human are both conceived as mysterious, we can find them connected fundamentally in the witness to God as Creator and to the child as created. Here the human imagination, limited though it may be because of finitude, contingency, and transience, comes into play. For a radical example, theologian Gordon Kaufman treats Christian thought in his book *In the Face of Mystery.*[2] What he says informs our inquiry about the child, as he sets the stage and describes an appropriate attitude for any view of creation:

> I attempt to express both my piety and my gratitude to the ultimate mystery which we daily confront. The sense of gratitude for the gift of our distinctive human qualities leads me to impute to this mystery a certain tension or movement toward humanization, even humaneness; but *my piety toward the mystery* qua *mystery* compels me to acknowledge that when we say such things as this we come up against the very limits of our language and our minds, [and] we really do not know what we are saying. . . . My convictions about mystery and about human diversity demand, of course, that I also allow a significant place for, and grant the integrity of, those who believe they can say much more – in more detail and with more certitude – about the religious meaning of our common human existence than can I. (p. xii; italics added)

In those words Kaufman deals with the gift of human qualities while invoking sacred mystery. Although I have serious differences with his expressions elsewhere on the limits of biblical witness and faith, I find this analogical argument promising. Those who provide care for the child have good reason to keep in mind some of the dimensions of response about which he speaks. His assertions derive from his witness to the creation. Using the first person, he defines his faith and piety as he speaks of what he calls

> (a) my deep sense of the ultimate mystery of life; (b) my feeling of profound gratitude for the gift of humanness and the great diversity

2. Gordon D. Kaufman, *In the Face of Mystery: A Constructive Theology* (Cambridge, MA: Harvard University Press, 1993), xii-xiii. Page references to Kaufman's book will be given parenthetically in the text.

> which it manifests; (c) my belief (with this diversity especially in mind) in the continuing importance of the central Christian moral demand that we love and care for not only our neighbors but even our enemies; and (d) my conviction (closely connected with this last point) that the principal Christian symbols continue to provide a significant resource for the orientation of human life. (p. xii)

Trading on that understanding, we see the child manifesting or reflecting aspects of the ultimate mystery, especially when recalled as created in the image of God. For those who do their interpreting from within the Christian sphere, the child becomes central in the focus of the moral demands for love and care. The same child inspires pursuit of other Christian themes that can help reorient people in a culture where human life is otherwise often devalued.

Immediately and appropriately one can picture a Jewish or Muslim thinker drawing on some of the principal motifs of the revelation or tradition on which Christianity also relies, just as she must reject others. In the case of these three forms of faith, a certain kind of author – I hope I am one – can further testify with Kaufman that many classic themes of faith can have positive consequences in the public sphere among people who do not acknowledge God or divine manifestation in Jesus Christ. We treat each other differently when we see each other as objects of divine creation, formed in the image of God.

The modest provider of care for the child can be drawn up short as he reads an epigraph for Kaufman's book, a quotation from the Jesuit theologian Karl Rahner. His words help frame what follows here, but they can also easily be turned into a challenge: "What is called knowledge in everyday parlance, is only a small island in a vast sea that has not been traveled. . . . Hence the existential question for the knower is this: Which does he love more, the small island of his so-called knowledge or the sea of infinite mystery?" Another helpful epigraph comes from Protestant theologian Karl Barth: "Theology means taking rational trouble over the mystery" (p. 2). In both cases, there is an attempt to avoid the pseudo-familiarity with the Other that comes when, as Rahner complained, some "talk of God as if we had already slapped him on the shoulder."[3]

In the usage of Rahner and Barth alike, both God and the image of God are mysteries and remain so; because as God is a mystery, so is the human, made in God's image. Kaufman writes that all human life "proceeds

3. Karl Rahner, *The Priesthood* (New York: Seabury, 1973), 8.

in face of profound mystery, and symbolic meaning is created by humans to give order and orientation to life in that situation" (p. 54). Watching a child play with a top or swing on a swing, reach for a butterfly or study the sun's reflection on fish scales, will bring one to the scene where this ordering and orienting combine in the child's mind and experience.

To deal explicitly with this theme, Kaufman takes off from assertions and urges that "the overall context within which theological work is carried on is one of mystery." Kaufman's reflection matches my own conception and usage so fittingly that I consider it worth quoting at some length. Note that his reference is to God, where the mystery is limitless, whereas we shall apply mystery analogically only to humans, who, being created, have limits. Kaufman writes,

> "Mystery" (as I use the word) does not refer to a direct perceptual experience of something, as do "darkness" (in a cellar room at night) or "dense fog" (when we cannot see anything), or as words like "unclear" or "obscure" do when used of some distant object which we cannot discern well enough to identify with confidence. To be sure, the word "mystery" sometimes conveys this aura of something — we know not what — being experienced; however, I want to focus attention on a different aspect of its meaning. "Mystery" has a fundamentally intellectual character, whatever its experiential overtones. It refers to bafflement of mind more than obscurity of perception. A mystery is something we find we cannot think clearly about, cannot get our minds around, cannot manage to grasp. If we say that "life confronts us as mystery," or "whether life has any meaning is a mystery," or "the fact that there is something not nothing is a mystery," we are speaking about intellectual bafflements. We are indicating that what we are dealing with here seems to be beyond what our minds can handle. (p. 60)

So how do humans, when they relate in thought or action to the child, for instance, get a handle on the concept of the image of God? The best way to answer is indeed by analogy, though saying that this is the case does not resolve everything. Thus religious thinkers consistently find themselves arguing over how Creator and created — including here, the child — relate to each other. The simple materialist dismisses the whole idea of the image of God as being contrary to the natural way of looking at things.

Those hundreds of millions of people worldwide who are responsive to the Bible, however, have something with which to wrestle. Both in Genesis and in the writings of the apostle Paul we find relevant references. Not only does the image of God appear primevally in the creation story; it soon reappears in the command to humans not to murder, because the human is made "in the image of God." Such a reassertion does not resolve a classic debate within Christian circles over whether the image of God in the human has been shattered or has merely been marred in the human condition or in consequence of human action or inheritance. However Christians understand the claim that humans bear the image of God, they agree with the witness that they were made in it. That witness describes the intention of God as grasped in the communities of faith. In the case of Paul, the believer has been "predestined to be conformed to the image of [God's] Son" (Romans 8:29).

In these biblical contexts, the references to the image of God obviously cannot mean that there are ordinary physical reflections; rather, reason, the will, and consciousness belong to both God and humanity, thanks to the generous creative and sustaining activity of God. In developing these spiritual ties, we have reason to be nervous about thinking of what is often called "the analogy of 'being,'" because doing so would lead us to assign properties to the child that can belong only to the Being of God. So we join those who have spoken of an "analogy of relation," through which the human and God somehow participate in each other's activity. The accent in the analogy is not from the human viewpoint, comparing human qualities to God's qualities, but the other way around. When believers consider that something of the nature of God has been revealed, they think about counterparts of God's nature that develop as gifts to humans.

The point here is to connect the mystery of the child, just as one would the experience of the adult in analogous relation, with the mystery of God and participation in that mystery. Here the metaphor may shift from the divine *image* to that of the divine *mirror*, which carries the image back and forth between God and the human. Just as God is love but love is not God, so God is mystery but mystery is not God. Limitlessness belongs only to God, who is an abyss of mystery. The human, including the human child, is not infinite, as God is, but still her existence cannot be reduced by science or definition.

Were it not for "the analogy of relation," the religious thinker as well as the provider of care for the child would lack a language with which to connect the being or doing of the Creator and the created child. In summary, it is to the point to think of the child, who henceforth occupies center stage, as a subject of wonder and as a wondering subject.

When the Provider Employs "Mystery"

An agenda based on credible questions develops among those who treat the child not only as problem but as mystery: What difference does it make to refer to the child thus? What am I to do if I find talk about the mystery in any way compelling? One is not likely to hear such practical questions whenever the concentration is on problems, because, as we have seen, problems have potential solutions, and responsible adults can address them.

While all questions about the problems of the child remain live, if one is ready to entertain issues connected with the mystery of the child, what then? Is the proper counsel to an inquiring person that he read a sacred book to delve deeper into mystery? More immediately, is the giver of care to follow up by leaning over the infant's bed, endlessly watching the child acquire skills? Is it proper to applaud the performing child, or brag, or fall silent? Although a child in a tantrum may give off heat, she is not like the light of the burning bush that Moses encountered. So one must ask: How long can one sustain an intense response, or for that matter, how long should one stay with the constant stimulus, enthralled by the beauty of the child or her actions? A world of need lies beyond the nursery. It is a world in which duties make demands on people or where a typical person will find lures and distractions. A mother and father have to go about the day's work and cannot linger indefinitely in fascination at the crib.

On top of these awarenesses, consider the criticism often leveled in a culture of people who already often idolize babies and where the infants near at hand monopolize attention at the expense of children elsewhere. In such cases it cannot make much sense to lavish more resources, adult energy, and beneficence on the already overprivileged. For most people, resources, including resources of time, are limited. Yes, a responsible parent can crouch next to a child for hours and observe the dazzling variety of facial expressions, listen for all the sounds of early childhood, the forming of first words, and the singing of songs. But will one or two more hours thus spent lead a parent immediately to serve the community, the world, the child, or the adult himself better?

The contemplation of mystery, including the mystery of the child, can inspire a welter of actions that relate to questions like these: Should one rush off to chapel every few hours to give thanks for the child? Step out under the starry sky and experience the *mysterium tremendum et fascinans,* the fascinating and tremendous mystery of God? Should adults simply be there to play with the children, or try to get them to be silent, so they can practice joint meditation? All those questions may answer themselves. Some of them include hints of answers, but by themselves they alert us to the tasks and possible rewards that lie ahead.

Mystery and the Enjoyment of the Child

Although mystery inspires awe and wonder, it can also call for a response of joy, and the child as mystery will be an agent of joyful reflection. Some years ago, Samuel Sandmel, a scholar friend who had mastered scientific approaches to the Hebrew Scriptures, surprised us with a book that showed him conversing with the text. He called it *The Enjoyment of Scripture.*[4] What a novel idea, some said, that a scholar should join the people devoted to faith and poetry in enjoying those texts that were full of problems but were also written to be enjoyed: "Taste and see that the Lord is good," sang a psalmist in words quoted by Sandmel. Rabbi Sandmel taught readers in his generation to do such tasting.

The call here is for the *enjoyment* of the child to counter efforts to dominate or control him. Such efforts are soon spent, and a constant and empathic observer will find herself replacing concern for care with wonder at the miracle of infant and child life, especially at playtime. Though problems with playground discipline may arise, one does not associate play primarily with problems. Play itself is a natural expression of the mystery of the child, a sign of the enjoying child who inspires enjoyment among others.

Similarly, the approach by way of the concept of mystery offers esthetic dimensions to child rearing that get obscured when issues dominate. Getting the child to sit still for the barber, the photographer, or the teacher is a problem that prompts an emphatic practical response. The adult who is attempting to solve a problem of this sort is not likely to describe the situation as in any way beautiful. Yet such activity does not exhaust the range of children's expressions.

Ballet or any staged dance is a provocative metaphor for describing the mystery of the child, because place and time figure in it so strongly. First, the figurative hall is dark and womblike before the brief drama begins. Birth occurs, which means the stage lights go on. The dancers on

4. Samuel Sandmel, *The Enjoyment of Scripture* (New York: Oxford University Press, 1974).

stage can be graceful or menacing, their plot pleasing or jarring, their exertions languorous or strenuous, their experiments timid or daring, and their results capable of inducing perspiration among the dancers and applause from the audience. The curtain falls. The stage lights go down and the house lights brighten, as the world outside the theater beckons. Subsequently no film of the dance survives. The music lives on in the mind but not in the ear. So it is also with the mystery of the child, except that no curtain hides the scene changes.

What does the dance of childhood signify? Here the mysterious aspect of dance as an art form is illuminating. It is said that the great ballerina Anna Pavlova, while perspiring and breathing wearily after a dance, was asked what that dance meant. She replied, "My God, if I could have said it, do you think I would have danced it?" So it is with the relations of adults to children, open as the young are to contingency, surprise, and interruption. So it is also with children, who are often asked to explain too much. In the presence of adults who would like to control her, one asks: Explain the mysterious child? No, let her dance. Let her evoke responses of wonder and move on refreshed for life in the practical and ordinary world.

5. The Mystery of Change

The Mystery of the Child was chartered by a project at Emory University called "The Child in *Religion,* Law, and Society." Lifting up this religious element, as this chapter does, provides particular resources for dealing with deep dimensions of mystery and illumines particular understandings of the child. Such religious discourse is often slighted for any number of reasons. Religion has no natural place in many kinds of child-care manuals, whose authors have agendas and bring expertise other than those that occupy us here. Some writers may well be informed about religion but give it no place because they aim for audiences to whom religious insights offer little promise. A few may simply be hostile to any sort of religious approaches to the child. More may have given up on attempts to address spiritual and religious themes because of the pluralistic character of our free society and the diversity that makes it impossible to speak in terms satisfactory to everyone. I believe, however, that one can focus on faith and write about a faith tradition or community without alienating readers who do not share the tradition or the community. Jewish, Muslim, Hindu, or agnostic readers can profit from a Christian exploration, just as Christians can learn from and welcome approaches from other faiths.

Failing to focus on religion or spirituality and the sacred in general where such focus is appropriate and can be helpful deprives readers of both ancient and contemporary resources that speak profoundly to the mystery of the child. Such failing could also mean that an author has not accurately assessed and addressed the commitments and sentiments of the vast majority of people. This chapter-length illustration of an address to the sacred will draw upon Christianity and the figure of Jesus, so powerful were they in their origin and so decisive do they remain in the development of the cultures this book addresses. All the while, the book will demonstrate regard for people of other commitments who, as they tell poll-takers, have "no preference" among the faiths or "no religion."

Access to the sacred themes occurs in part through delving in sacred scriptures. Citing such texts is a practice that some will think is restricted to traditionalist churches and synagogues. In our culture, however, such texts signal attention on the part of the larger public to the sacred dimensions of mystery, dimensions that are distinctive but whose wisdom and counsel will not reach or satisfy everyone. That is, one can evoke the sacred without reference to scriptures or sanctuaries, and one can also probe the mystery of the child in the world we call secular without making reference to such texts and heritages. Not all interpretation of the Hebrew Scriptures or the New Testament occurs in the realm of literalists and Bible-thumpers. Drawing on biblical references directed to the oversight of children can challenge liberal and moderate readers to reorient themselves, to turn some conventional notions about the child topsy-turvy and thus lead these readers to face in different directions.

A stark sample of these texts about the child, central for this book, is a word of Jesus of Nazareth recorded in the Gospel of Matthew as a call to adults, who have to figure centrally in any book on children: "Unless you change and become like children, you will never enter the kingdom" (Matthew 18:3). Such ancient language, preserved not by classical authors from Greece and Rome but by the community fostered by followers of Jesus, is still conventionally privileged among Christian audiences, though we keep non-Christian overhearers also in mind. Jesus was speaking to adults who evidently held and intended to keep control over children and, presumably, also over others in their society. In a book on children, adults would be expected to have walk-on roles as parents, teachers, advisers, or writers. The biblical situating of the child has implications for people of all ages, not only those who would provide care for the child. Unfortunately for the seeker of a simple "how-to" book plot but fortunately for adults who give such basic texts as this a hearing, they will be jostled and disturbed — so that they can begin to change.

The line "unless you change and become like children" could serve as an epigraph to this book. Those who are alienated from the biblical traditions and who keep them at a distance, those who are halfhearted or indifferent about them, and those who have a view of biblical writings very different from the view offered here, may become (only momentarily, I hope) impatient or dismissive when a biblical text provides support for the theme of a whole book.

"Unless you change and become like children" combines a note of the ominous in its implied command – "Become like one!" – with a promise that there *is* a positive outcome or that there can be rich rewards if one does respond. How readers will respond on the basis of words cradled in a two-thousand-year-old document will depend in part on how directly they regard themselves to be connected with the text. The phrase shows up in all kinds of places – books of quotations, snippets of a reading in a Great Books course, discussions in a forum or around the table. In some settings the words could serve as a generic maxim about change. But these words in the Gospels have a different appeal and make a different kind of demand as they bear on the mystery of the child.

A Rationale for This Radical Approach to Change and the Child

Although precedence exists for this kind of focus, with its specific approach to a general readership, I have learned much from the argument in the preface to *The Political Meaning of Christianity: An Interpretation,* by political scientist Glenn Tinder, who has influenced my work for years. Following Tinder's lead, I also regularly draw on wisdom from books by authors representing religions other than Christianity. Were I writing a book on the child for a broader public but in the context of a Buddhist or Hindu, Muslim or Jewish culture, the reader would expect that the privileged resources in each case would be Buddhist or Hindu, Muslim or Jewish. Were it to be a Marxian, Darwinian, or Freudian interpretation, the texts would be from Marx, Darwin, or Freud. No one would find such citations strange, and most would likely feel cheated were there no such explicit references. Yet, curiously, in American culture it has often become appropriate, perhaps even necessary, to provide an apologia for Christian references in a book for the public.

This is the case because within our pluralist society the weight of biblical and Christian themes in discourse on family life, gender, and children is so heavy that they merit a fresh hearing. Their weight is a legacy from century-old historical situations but also a matter of headlines and prime-time media attention in contemporary society. In a virtual world based on statistical sampling, one in which a hundred Americans might read a book like this, eighty would identify broadly, in many cases *very* broadly, with Christian texts, traditions, communities, and memories. Tinder, who writes not about the child but about the political order, has framed his analogous case with a question: What does a set of Christian assumptions or proposals mean in a pluralistic society? He contends that

> Christian ideas are properly of concern to people who are not Christians and even to people who are entirely closed to the possibility of becoming Christians. This is simply because of the wisdom — the deep and credible good sense concerning life, as distinguished from the revealed truth concerning God — that those ideas contain. This is wisdom pertinent to public as well as personal life, and one does not have to be a Christian to accept it. For example, according to Christian principles, people are deeply and persistently selfish. There is a good deal of evidence indicating that this is so. If it is, then it is essential to our public life that the evidence not be ignored or denied, unpleasant as it is, but faced. . . .
>
> I write, therefore, with the hope of finding non-Christian, as well as Christian, readers. Is this not reasonable? It is taken for granted that non-Marxists should read and learn from Marxist writings; people who reject the atheism and materialism of Freud readily consult the writings of Freud and his followers. It seems arbitrary and hazardous to be less open-minded toward Christianity.[1]

What Tinder calls "the deep and credible good sense concerning life," here "pertinent to public as well as personal life," has direct bearing on the situation of the child in contemporary society. Children suffer in this society because of neglect, abuse, cruel punishments, broken homes, the bombardment of mass communications, and value systems that tend to treat citizens only as consumers and that commodify most human interactions. It is in such a setting that a child represents little but problems that demand address, often at the expense of her presence as a mystery surrounded by mysteries. Christians have no monopoly on efforts to spell out the problems that cause suffering or that neglect suffering where it appears. The task remains for us to explore how biblically based wisdom might speak to public and personal life. Although Christians may share concern for the mystery of the child, they have special motivations for paying attention to it and offering their insights to the public, especially to people who oversee growing children.

What is going on here within a diverse culture is first an endeavor at *ressourcement,* the French term for drawing on resources of the past in or-

1. Glenn Tinder, *The Political Meaning of Christianity: An Interpretation* (Baton Rouge: Louisiana State University Press, 1989), 5.

der to bring about change in a stale and static situation. European Roman Catholics in the middle of the last century saw a need to rediscover the resources of the long Christian past in order to address the confusion, chaos, and crisis of their present. A "return to the sources" in the midst of our own confusion, chaos, and crisis can be of help as we probe the mystery of the child against a scriptural background that speaks to our day.

Similarly, we have engaged in what Karl Rahner called *retrieval,* an exercise proposed also by others who see a need for reaching selectively into those sources. It is fruitless and even futile to try to recover vast texts and ill-defined traditions. The retrievers must concentrate on certain features. Rahner and his colleagues were well aware of the hazards that went with selection, especially the danger that it can lead to antiquarian or sectarian interests or that what was retrieved was chosen arbitrarily to promote the interests of the retrievers at the expense of other words that offer potential. This choosing and dealing with what one finds is identified with hermeneutics. Here *hermeneutics* refers to interpretation that is colored by the presuppositions a reader or a community brings to a text. All interpretation is thus colored, whether everyone recognizes this tinting or not. An American who sings "God Bless America" may intend to be merely patriotic, but her words and the event in which she sings will strike some fellow citizens as chauvinistic and some foreigners as exclusivist and aggressively imperial. When a person recognizes her special involvement with a text and the bias that may come with treatment of it, we expect an explanation of the choices made in it. These are based upon some awareness of why the author holds certain presuppositions. Mine have to do with efforts to plumb something of the mystery of the child and to see what such an effort can do to improve relations of adults to children and the life of children as such.

The Terrible Words That Call for Change

French novelist Georges Bernanos, in a line from his *Journal d'un curé de campagne (The Diary of a Country Priest),* alerted me to the dreadful and at the same time promising call of a Gospel text. This fictional work appears in the form of a reflective journal written by a cancer-ridden young priest sent to minister in a forlorn French parish. Often thwarted in his efforts to understand and lead children, and sometimes even rendered a ridiculous figure by some of their cruel ploys, he takes counsel from an older priest, the curé of Torcy, who in one conversation quotes the Gospel text in which Jesus breaks barriers that adults have set up. He sets the quotation in a context of his time and place but one that is applicable to our own. Then follow the startling words about change, about becoming like children:

> You hear the hypocrites, the sensualists, the Scrooges, the rotten rich – with their thick lips and gleaming eyes – cooing over [Jesus' invitation] *Sinite parvulos,* "Let the little children come to me," without any indication that they're taking note of the words that follow – some of the most terrible ever heard by human ears, "If you are not like one of these little ones, you will not enter the Kingdom of God."[2]

The priest is quoting a verse from the Gospel of Mark (10:15), which has a parallel in Matthew 19:14, "Let the little children come to me . . . whoever does not receive the kingdom of God as a little child will never enter it." This is perfectly consistent and faithful to the source to add the more radical note that Matthew includes in another story (18:3): "unless you change and become like children, you will never enter the kingdom of heaven." The call to change is the most stringent in these episodes. The call to receive the kingdom as a little child is also set off strikingly. People were bringing little children to Jesus to have him touch them. The disciples – did they want to be in control, or did they consider Jesus too busy or too weary? – rebuked them. Then, for only one of two times in the Bible, the Gospel writer lets Jesus' anger show: "when Jesus saw this, he was indignant," and said the line that the priest quoted: *sinite parvulos,* let the little children come to me, because the kingdom belonged to "such as these."

2. Quoted in translation in John Saward, *The Way of the Lamb: The Spirit of Childhood and the End of the Age* (San Francisco: Ignatius, 1999), 101. Curiously, this paragraph (and numbers of others) are not included in the English translation of the book, and there is no explanation of, nor are there signs of, elision. Because the passage is so central to the theme of this chapter, I reproduce it here: "Tu entends l'hypocrite, le luxurieux, l'avare, le mauvais riche – avec leurs grosses lippes et leurs yeux luisants – roucouler le *Sinite parvulos* sans avoir l'air de prendre garde à la parole qui suit – une des plus terribles peut-être que l'oreille de l'homme ait entendue: 'Si vous n'êtes pas comme l'un de ces petitits, vous n'entrerez pas dans le royaume de Dieu." Georges Bernanos, *Journal d'un curé de campagne* (Édition établie à partir du manuscript et de l'édition originale; Libraire Plon, 1936 et 1974 pour la présente edition), 71-72.

Revising Images of a Kingdom

As if the implicit demand to change and "become like little children" were not a sufficient hurdle for ears of modern adults, the words that follow them make the theme even more off-putting. One is to be like the little children in order "to enter the kingdom of heaven." We can blurt out a question in response: Who wants a kingdom? The images of kingdoms begin with representations of kings. Americans got rid of them in 1776, and most remaining kings elsewhere are tyrannous or clownish survivors. Kingdoms imply fortresses and armaments, revenues and exploitation. Those who would provide care for children are trying to distance themselves from these symbols. Talk about the kingdom of heaven is also alien if it means waiting for fulfillment in a life to come and a place far away. Such talk would do little to improve the care of children now or to help the modern world escape the judgment of which Bernanos spoke. And kingdoms suggest kings, male figures of authority who sit atop hierarchies of princes and bishops and who set out to dominate, not to pay attention to insignificant subjects like little children. If *kingdom* sounds out of place, it is appropriate to be concerned about authoritarian and hierarchical patterns in society and even in intimate spheres like family life. Reference to a kingdom needs a great deal of explaining.

Nothing is as useless as an answer to an unasked question or a potential solution where there is no problem. Some of the answers and solutions to questions and problems posed by the Gospel reference to the kingdom are anticipated in the Gospels themselves, in the image and model and words of Jesus himself, as remembered by the writers. Just as by elevating the child while upsetting the adults in the biblical stories Jesus turns everything topsy-turvy, so references to his role and place should lead to a complete revision of life in the kingdom. He washes the feet of disciples as a gesture of humility. He eats with the wrong people and scorns the powerful. If he is a king, he is one who rules from below, not in any hierarchy. Becoming a part of his reign is always seen as liberating and, in the end, as offering solace and new moral direction. So with all those revisions, *kingdom* can stand and be a subject of desire.

Such a kingdom is no base for "the will to control"; it is the scene for "welcoming the stranger." Among the strangers, and perhaps the best representative of them all, are the children. With them at the center of the drama we can legitimately regard the words of Jesus as addressing those who would seize or hold on to control, especially control of the child. At the same time, in focusing attention on the child as the model and on the change to nurturing childlikeness as a goal, his words promote awareness of the mystery of the child. In this understanding there can be a side benefit: the child thus conceived can be an empathic provider of care to other children.

Lingering with the stories of children in the Gospels can breed such familiarity that a reader can eventually forget how distinctive they are. Children play such a bold role that one can speak of their presence as a kind of revelation. Scholars contrast these accounts with what we know of other ancient examples. They say that in no known case in the classic literature of Greece and Rome was a child projected as a paradigm for adult behavior and intention. Children do receive prominent attention in Judaism, and Jewish lore and stories influence other cultures. The child is of almost immeasurable importance in Jewish thought and life, and the Hebrew Scriptures include grand references to the place of children. In one vision of the future, "a little child shall lead them" (Isaiah 11). In Psalm 8 we read, "Out of the mouths of babes and infants" God has manifested strength or praise.

Scholars such as Judith M. Gundry-Volf point to a particular role of children in Judaism. She stresses that "knowledge of and obedience to the law is the essence of piety in Judaism; thus in this tradition an unlearned child can scarcely be an illustration of religious greatness."[3] It is not to say anything negative about Jews to point out that this reference to an incident in Jesus' life and teaching would not be applicable in the face of Jewish concepts of law and the maturing child. Gundry-Volf cites another biblical scholar as she sets out to render the saying even more radical. Willi Egger

> argues that Jesus takes a typical Jewish formula about what was necessary for entering the reign of God and turns it on its head by stating not *what works of the Law* are required for entrance but rather "whoever does not receive the reign of God *as a child* will never enter it." Since children were not even *required* to follow the Law, much less did they actually fulfill it, Jesus can be taken to challenge the perception that adults who are under obligation to the Law, and do fulfill it, are thereby qualified to enter the reign of God. Egger thus concludes that the phrase "as a child" means "as one who has neither obedience nor obligation to the Law."[4]

3. Judith M. Gundry-Volf, "The Least and the Greatest: Children in the New Testament," in *The Child in Christian Thought,* ed. Marcia J. Bunge (Grand Rapids: Eerdmans, 2001), 39n.41.

4. Gundry-Volf, "The Least and the Greatest," 39.

This contrast among classical, Jewish, and other religious traditions with Christian origins illustrates that no single religion has a monopoly and that all will make distinctive contributions. A good guide for this understanding is philosopher George Santayana, who wrote that "any attempt to speak without speaking any particular language is not more hopeless than the attempt to have a religion that shall be no religion in particular." At the moment we are less interested in "having" a religion than in learning from one and applying that learning to the contemporary scene. Santayana continues:

> Thus every living and healthy religion has a marked idiosyncrasy. Its power consists in its special and surprising message and in the bias which that revelation gives to life. The vistas it opens and the mysteries it propounds are another world to live in, and another world to live in — whether we expect ever to pass wholly over into it or no — is what we mean by having a religion.[5]

To the powerful who surrounded and often opposed the Jesus of the Gospel story, his making a model of the child certainly looks idiosyncratic, and it still is so to those who want to be in control. The story and the message — "terrible," Bernanos's priest called it — was and is "special and surprising." It "opens vistas and propounds mysteries," as Santayana said that such traditions do. And, if our whole argument holds up, considering the child as mystery surrounded by mystery does mean moving into "another world to live in" than the one dominated by problems and control.

The Vistas Opened in Such Texts

First Bernanos and now we are relocating in a new setting the sayings from the Gospels of Matthew, Luke, and Mark. They change character when read in isolation from the rest of the text. Thus on the walls of homes or religious schools or nurseries we can read words like these preserved in antique samplers that banner soft sayings. Safely framed and mounted, they are designed to soothe anyone's conscience or speak in the spirit of gentle greeting cards. This particular stitches-worthy Gospel story about children comes without reference to time or place. The

5. Quoted in Clifford Geertz, *The Interpretation of Cultures* (New York: Basic, 1973), 87.

writer may have had any of a number of reasons to situate the event where he did in the life of Jesus, but we do not at this point need to know what they were or to settle disputes about them. They have little bearing on what gets stitched and framed for reflection here and stamped on consciences.

One of Bernanos's modern interpreters, John Saward, connects this kind of testimony from the fictional diary entry by the novelist to his journal, which he published in 1938 after the *Diary of a Country Priest* had appeared. This time Bernanos called attention to the role of the child in his own voice, not in that of the priest-character:

> The world is going to be judged by children. The spirit of childhood is going to judge the world. . . . Become children again, rediscover the spirit of childhood. . . . It's your last chance, and ours. Are you capable of rejuvenating the world, yes or no? The Gospel is always young; it is you who are old. . . . I have always thought that the modern world has been sinning against the spirit of youth, and that this crime would kill it.[6]

Words from the Gospels dealing with children often get read for comfort and solace, not to be commented on or to induce terror. The country priest was dealing instead with what might be called an existential terror, one that can strike at the heart of any individual who is seeking meaning in life or among the members of any culture or society that has become complacent about traumas and trials, one that stands in need of judgment and must undergo rejuvenation.

The priest of his novel and Bernanos himself would counter the sentimental images of Jesus whose story and preserved utterances, remote from us in time, have been domesticated. This particular story of him in the company of children with adults who huddle in the surrounding background is a favorite, often reduced to cliché when pictured in Sunday school booklets or in stained glass windows. Whoever "hears" many of Jesus' words knows that some of them are shocking, but his invitations to children would not ordinarily be clustered among them. Through the ages millions of believers have so frequently read and heard them that they have lost much of their potential to shock. Given the great catastrophes of our time, the massive global concerns that press for attention and

6. *Les Grands Cimetières sous la lune,* published in English as *The Diary of My Times* (New York: Macmillan, 1938), quoted from the French edition (pp. 247, 262, 269, 289) by Saward, *Way of the Lamb,* 108.

demand response, enhanced as all of these are by the din of mass communications, the act of focusing this talk in a Gospel story about "little children" sounds like ineffectual and irrelevant whispering. A reader can easily dismiss reference to it as hyperbole, rhetorical showboating, or a side trip to adult Sunday school.

The priest as created by Bernanos clearly thought that both the promise and the threat of the word about the need to be as a little child ought still to impinge on the world of hypocrites and sensualists, the rotten and the rich, and then to violate their preconceptions. That cleric walks off the page into the consciousness of readers and there remains an extremist, an alarmist. The novelist uses him to alert readers to listen and to notify them that they will be judged. In case anyone might miss the point of application, Bernanos in his published diary – let us revisit it – sounds like a sermonizer when he goes on again to startle: "The world is going to be judged by children." That prophecy is unlikely to be fulfilled in a world where the powerful and the corrupt are the ones in control. Add to that his claim that the "spirit of childhood is going to judge the world." That word takes the picture of the powerless victim-child and uses it to counter the powerful judging ruler, as the Gospel words themselves do. It does so in a setting shaped by a word that implies the elevating of the child and the toppling of the powerful. That upsetting is, on the face of it, unrealistic in the company of the brutal people whom the radical Catholic novelist Bernanos so regularly attacked.

One would have expected Bernanos's priests and himself as a diarist to reserve their passion for judgments against criminals, gougers, exploiters, killers. Yet here are stories about adults who brought their children to the rabbi Jesus, stories that also judge his disciples, who had other interests in mind than being open to the meaning of the children's presence. Still, the text affords entrance to a larger world in which readers can entertain and be open to previously closed ways of measuring what is important in the world. This means that they can help address the sufferings of children, can correct misplaced interests of adults, and can change what Bernanos called "the modern world [that] has been sinning against the spirit of youth" – if they themselves are open to change.

Many words of sages and spiritual leaders address one community of faith and then are useful to those who aspire to transcend it during their reach for what is lasting. Here the diarist fashions a universal out of his particular vision. "Become children again, rediscover the spirit of childhood." Bernanos counsels that the word about being like the child, one that is addressed to the powerful adults, offers the last chance if the world – *the world!* – is to be rejuvenated. He adds that he had "always thought that the modern world has been sinning against the spirit of youth, and that this crime would kill it."[7] Those who insist on being in control – on asserting the right to punish (and misusing the power to punish), to dismiss the imaginations and the play of children – are "sinning against the spirit of youth." These are the apparently mild manifestations of such sin. The extreme ones involve abusing, victimizing, and abandoning the child or in other ways destroying the spirit of the child.

Bernanos, in another of his writings, put himself into the story of human destiny with the question, "What does my life matter?" Then he announced his resolution: "I just want it to be faithful, to the end, to the child I used to be." Those haunting words sounded as if he was upholding a program, but the novelist clarified them by saying he did not believe in the possibility of going back. Still, he admitted in his old age that "what honor I have, and my bit of courage, I inherit from the little creature, so mysterious to me now, scuttling through the September rain across streaming meadows, his heart heavy," in one instance, "at the thought of going back to school."[8] Those lines about the mysterious recall of being a child provide a framework for the drastic themes Bernanos drew from the word of Jesus. At least figuratively and in the imagination, readers have to "go back to school" themselves to make much sense of the words by the novelist-diarist. They need this sense if they are to entertain the judgments and advice implied by Bernanos and then apply them in the wildly diverse situations in which any child appears anywhere, whether she comes with heart heavy or light.

"Going back to school" in retracing memory is one thing. Becoming "like one of these little children" is a much more complicated and, on the face of it, an apparently impossible venture. This is especially the case if our interpretation is correct: that it is the seeming insignificance of the child that matters. So important is this that we will pause to examine some references in the Gospels that throw light on the question: What is it about the child that commands this kind of notice?

7. Quoted by Saward, *Way of the Lamb,* 108.
8. Quoted by Saward, *Way of the Lamb,* 99.

What Is It about the Child?

For reasons of verbal economy and to draw on the experts, I offer brief supporting citations.[9] In Matthew 18:2, where adults are told that they must become like little children, we are reminded that "children know that they can never earn free gifts." The child is important, among other reasons, because she stands in a gift relation to those older than she (Albright and Mann, 216). In one Gospel story Jesus summons children to him and they come. So a second commentator stresses that "the trustful humility of the child who readily came to Jesus when called is the attitude that marks true greatness" (Filson, 199). A different accent, supporting my interpretation, appears in another scholarly reference: adults are to become "like children, without any status or privilege" (Fenton, 290). While some interpreters have stressed the natural humility of children, these commentators have a different slant: "The *child* is for Matthew the symbol of humility, not because a child is humble (most of them are not), but because a child has no status in society" (Fenton, 291). Another similar theme stresses that "children do not humble themselves: they are already

9. In the next several paragraphs I have used a different citation method to allow for smoother reading. I shall refer to the following works in parentheses in the text by citing the author's name and the page on which the quotation appears:

W. F. Albright and C. S. Mann, *Matthew: Introduction, Translation, and Notes* (Garden City, NY: Doubleday, 1971).

C. E. B. Cranfield, *The Gospel according to Saint Mark* (Cambridge: Cambridge University Press, 1959).

J. C. Fenton, *The Gospel of St. Matthew* (Baltimore: Penguin, 1963).

Floyd V. Filson, *A Commentary on the Gospel According to St. Matthew* (New York: Harper and Brothers, 1960).

Joseph A. Fitzmyer, *The Gospel According to Luke (I-IX)* (Garden City, NY: Doubleday, 1981).

Norval Geldenhuys, *Commentary on the Gospel of Luke* (Grand Rapids: Eerdmans, 1951).

Sherman E. Johnson, *A Commentary on the Gospel according to St. Mark* (New York: Harper and Brothers, 1960).

C. S. Mann, *Mark: A New Translation with Introduction and Commentary* (Garden City, NY: Doubleday, 1986).

D. E. Nineham, *The Gospel of Mark* (Baltimore: Penguin, 1963).

E. Basil Redlich, *St. Mark's Gospel: A Modern Commentary* (London: Duckworth, 1948).

Eduard Schweizer, *The Good News according to Matthew* (Atlanta, GA: John Knox Press, 1975).

G. H. P. Thompson, *The Gospel according to Luke* (Oxford: Clarendon, 1972).

E. J. Tinsley, *The Gospel according to Luke* (Cambridge: Cambridge University Press, 1965).

little and aware of their littleness, so that out of gratitude (or fear) for security they accept what those who are larger and stronger can give them" and that "only children are flexible and open to learning new ideas" (Schweizer, 362, 363).

In a second passage a child is singled out and lifted up as great, while those who would be great are reduced (Mark 9:33-37). Over against grasping and prideful adults, children are those who are able to receive gifts. "Receiving" and being given gifts remain marks of the child. "Children know that they can never have earned the gifts they are given" (Mann, 377). Next, on Luke 9:46-48, a comment reads: "The little child . . . is the sign of Christian greatness, precisely as the least significant and weakest member of human society" (Fitzmyer, 816). Again, the child belongs among "those of little outward status" (Thompson, 156).

The next text is Matthew 19:13-15, where the disciples are scolded for trying to keep adults from bringing children, an act the disciples saw as intrusive: "The children seemed unimportant; their coming seemed an intrusion into [Jesus'] vital work of teaching and healing. [The disciples'] officious act, Jesus saw, misunderstood who and what are important. . . . [The children] came with trusting faith and simple openness, in their simplicity, trust, and humility" (Filson, 208). Once more, "the child has no status in the world . . . [but is] a 'nobody'" (Fenton, 312). This text has returned attention to receptivity as being part of the mystery of the child. With almost wearying frequency we hear of the reception of gifts as a mark of the child. First, "children appreciate a gift as an absolute, something which they are aware they cannot have worked to deserve." And "the children are rightful recipients because they are receptive" (Mann, 396). Seconding this is another scholar, who does not reject the element of humility, but surrounds it with another element: "The point is not so much the innocence and humility [or obedience] of the children, it is rather the fact that children are unselfconscious, receptive, and content to be dependent upon others' care and bounty" (Nineham, 268). Still another scholar underscores the idea of the "childlike spirit of receptivity and responsiveness" (Redlich, 132).

In this context again, those who comment agree that *humility,* "as the word is usually understood, is not a natural characteristic of childhood." A bit of credible speculation enters here. Possibly because of "the unsophistication and freshness of the child, whose world is new and filled with marvels[,] he has a great capacity to receive impressions and is not jaded or *blasé*" (Johnson, 172). In almost all cases, the commentators stress that in the text the kingdom of God does not belong to children because of their achievements. "The reason is rather to be found in their objective humbleness, the fact that they are weak and helpless and unimportant, and in the fact that God has chosen 'the weak things of the world'" (Cranfield, 324).

Finally, on trust, which so often appears in talk about the child in the Gospel stories, Luke 18:15-17 is to the point: "If a particular characteristic of children is being singled out, it is probably their dependence, and their readiness to trust others" (Thompson, 226). As for adults who have gotten the point, they bring a "kind of openness, unsophisticated insight and unselfconsciousness that one sees best in little children" (Tinsley, 169). Adult followers are to be as receptive and trustful as little children, who are described as exemplifying "natural humility and whole-hearted faith. . . . A little child who is brought up naturally receives artlessly what is given to him, without doubting the good intentions of the givers — he believes whole-heartedly that what is given to him is good for him and accepts it without thinking conceitedly that he deserves it" (Geldenhuys, 454-55).

One must use some caution when remarking on the place of children in these texts. Most scholars are at odds with many traditional interpretations. Thus, when Jesus is quoted as speaking of "little ones" who believe in him, these experts do not think the Gospel writer meant literally or in every case children. Some references to children in three of the Gospels are intended to portray the disciples as neophytes in the believing community. Perhaps the choice of words from Jesus suggests infant baptism in the earliest church community. The scholars offer varying views of how the Gospels were put together, which sayings are possibly misplaced, which narratives are broken off or inserted at inappropriate places, and the like. In other words, these scholars are typical in their ability to disagree. One does not even have to come to a conclusion, however, about what happened or about what incidents, scenes, and sayings lay behind the stories. It is these stories that shaped the disciples and the church through the ages along with the education of children in its communities, just as they have inspired artists who designed stained glass windows. The narratives and messages are part of the special canon or surprising rule by which the believing community measures what is of value. If the community produced these stories and sayings, these stories and sayings have also produced the community for two millennia.

Although the commentators have some disagreements with each other, their points of agreement and consensus contribute to our understanding of the mystery of the child in the Gospel appearances and messages. Most important, the child lacks status and privilege; he is the weakest, most helpless, and least significant member of society. Only one Gospel writer saw humility as a natural feature of the child's situation. Rather, the heavy accent was on children's ability to be offered unsolicited gifts and to accept what was given. The same words show up in many summaries: children are unself-conscious, receptive, trusting, dependent, flexible, open to learning new ideas, evidencing trust and freshness, unsophisticated, and — this word may tell the most — responsive.

On Belonging and Being the Stranger

In modern translations, words once presumably voiced in Aramaic and certainly written in Greek still can cause shuddering among those who would want to belong to the kingdom of God. We have read that, when he was indignant, Jesus said that it was "to such as" the little children that the kingdom of God belongs. That "belonging" signals something crucial about the claims in these lines. Usually the appearance of a child, at the same time welcomed in and disruptive of the quiet of the parental home and the intimate community, is seen as a newcomer playing a particular role. She comes as a stranger to the way the powerful have characteristically liked to arrange things as well as to the way that in practice the powerful usually assert themselves against the weak. In this story, however, in a line designed to jolt, it is the child who owns the place, who does the belonging, and it is the adults who are the uncomprehending intruders on the path to the kingdom.

Sociologist Georg Simmel in an essay on the sociology of the stranger pointed out that the stranger "imports qualities" to a scene, qualities that in every instance "do not and cannot stem from the group itself."[10] In the Gospels, the group of those who thought of themselves as belonging was made up of Jesus' dismissive disciples. In the novel of Bernanos, the priest, we are reminded, scorns moderns, especially the hypocrites and sensualists, the misers and the rotten rich. In the text before us, disciples and other adults, judged by children, now become the strangers. In the stories of Jesus it is the absence of status and the insignificance of the child that is to be the model for change in adult groups and cultures.

The distance between the world of the text and that of the current

10. Georg Simmel, *The Sociology of Georg Simmel,* ed. and trans. Kurt H. Wolff (New York: Free Press, 1950), 402.

reader is admittedly difficult to bridge. In the Gospel story and in pictorial representations of it through the ages, the children are presented without description. No curriculum vitae or juvenile court record describes them. They simply have been put forward as strangers. The scene seems cozy and domestic. If they have problems, these are not described. This is not a tale of neglect, abuse, or victimization of the sort that colors talk of the problems of the child today. It is taken for granted in this account that parents or other providers of care who may have represented their families cared enough to bring the children forward. They may have had the best interests of children in view. They need not be portrayed as greedy supplicants in the face of the holy. We picture their neighbors, rabbis, parents, and townspeople forming a background and an overhearing audience.

Adults, we have seen, are almost as near the center of this story as are children, since the two are linked by the little word "such." To such as the children, the kingdom of God belongs. Then for everyone, including all adults, terror comes to be associated with that terrible word: "Unless you change and become like little children, you will never enter the kingdom of heaven." The Gospel writer hears Jesus working to influence his hearers, and now, among those who read them, new generations are to be swayed so that they might better understand the child and reshape their own response to an ultimate call. If hearers and readers in this tradition take Jesus' words seriously, and, moved by the starkness and urgency of his demand, set out to review their own situations, they will participate in the called-for change. They must respond to questions about what it is that the child brings or represents. What can the little stories in the Gospels mean to anyone who, in the words of Bernanos's diary, wants to escape judgment and keep alive the spirit of the child?

The Keys: Being Receptive and Responsive

In the Gospel texts, it is the unique *gift-character* of the kingdom that makes all the difference. With this comes *receptivity,* not of a passive sort but marked simply by openness. The achievements of very young children, included among the "little ones" in the Gospel, would have been too meager to have qualified them for Jesus' attention or access to the kingdom. The point in the Gospel references to children and other "little ones" is their circumstance, their absence of status or independent security. Children need gifts, they must be blessed, and the Gospel writers tell us that at the end of this encounter Jesus did bless them. Philip Carrington, scholarly Anglican archbishop of Quebec, pointed to the gifts that came with childhood. The kingdom, he wrote, is "for the loving, the natural, the unspoiled, the gay, the imaginative, the free-hearted, the happy, the pitiful, the playful, the unworldly."[11]

Practical theologian Bonnie Miller-McLemore, who has given much attention to these texts, suggests that it is difficult to get back to the fresh and stark biblical story because it is now in the minds of many people colored by "modern romanticized perceptions of children." For her, too, the gift-relation is what matters, accompanied by the child's receptivity. When one understands what the Gospel writer has Jesus seeing in children, we can fill in some expressions that go with receptivity. Miller keeps the focus on the child and what he represents in the Gospel stories. She wants to correct what she calls the "viable error of these modern readings" by pointing to some company for the child — a child she sees as the marginalized stranger (a figure who became familiar when we were discussing Jerome Miller on the stranger):

> The imperative to receive the kingdom "like a child" must be read in light of the imperative to receive children in themselves, in their inferior and vulnerable social status in the first century world. . . . [I]n these passages children represent another instance in which a group — like women, the poor, and the unclean — is marginalized and dominated by more powerful people. They are models of discipleship precisely from this position, as the least in family and society. . . . These passages starkly invert the assumption that children's religious knowledge depends upon obedience to a divinely ordained paternal authority.[12]

Along with receptivity we have noted *responsiveness.* There is a bid, for example, by the parents who bring their children, and also the bid by Jesus, to which adults and the little children respond as the latter come forward. The child accepts life, or is taught to accept life and all that goes with it, as a graced endowment. The postures and gestures of response mean that the initiative remains with the giver, and the child responds by accepting what the Other offers.

11. Philip Carrington, *According to Mark: A Running Commentary on the Oldest Gospel* (Cambridge: Cambridge University Press, 1960), 212.

12. Bonnie J. Miller-McLemore, *Let the Children Come: Reimagining Childhood from a Christian Perspective* (San Francisco: Jossey-Bass, 2003), 96-98.

Miller-McLemore's stress on the marginal character of the child, the child's *littleness* or *helplessness,* counts for more than the marks of self-empowerment. Some commentators speak of this child as a *nobody.* However, as I read the Gospel stories, though no child is named, the integrity or the "somebodiness" of every child matters in discourse about the kingdom. More to the point are themes such as the child's *openness to a gift,* her *readiness* to receive what is given, her being related to the Other through creative *dependence.* This dependence is not of a sort that issues in psychological dependency. Similarly, the child's *trust* does not issue in gullibility. All these characteristics and responses are congruent with the conception of the child as mystery.

When the Grown Child Looks Back

The Bernanos story provides more depth. The curé of Torcy advances what readers have learned about the mystery of the child and the kingdom to a later time, indeed even to the extreme end of life. The priest elaborates on the meaning of dependence and then relates it to all of life: "Childhood and extreme old age ought to be the two great trials of man," he said. "But it is from that very sense of his own powerlessness that the child humbly draws the source of his joy." That powerlessness does not leave the child abandoned. He has a relation, beginning with the maternal tie: "Past, present, and future, his whole life, all life is contained in a glance, and that glance is a smile."[13]

In his *Dialogues of the Carmelites,* Bernanos invented another character whose words inform our inquiry. She is the prioress of a convent, whom the novelist employed in order to revisit the cherished theme in which he connected the child with old age. She says: "Once out of childhood, we have to suffer for a long time to reenter it, just as when the night is over, we find another dawn."[14] I know of few reflections in modern literature that so distinctively relate the being of the child to adulthood and the end of life – and vice versa.

Bernanos, often in letters and other nonfiction, wanted to reinforce his vision. In a celebrated instance, he sent a letter to a little girl in Brazil after she wrote to him about becoming a poet: "Keep your faith in poets, and keep your faith in the spirit of childhood! Never become a grown-up

13. Quoted in Saward, *Way of the Lamb,* 111.

14. Quoted in Saward, *Way of the Lamb,* 113.

person!" She should note upon reading the Gospels that "there is a conspiracy among the grown-ups against the spirit of childhood." Seldom one to restrain his tendency to swing harshly, Bernanos contrasted the powerful and the weak. God had said to cardinals, theologians, essayists, historians, novelists, and everyone: "Become like a little child." Instead, through the centuries, powers such as those he mentioned "went on telling the spirit of childhood which they had betrayed: 'Become like us.'"

Bernanos urged the little girl in Brazil that, in years to come, when grown, she should think of and pray for the old writer, who became ever more and more "convinced of the impotence of the Powerful, the ignorance of the Learned, the idiocy of the Machiavellians, and the incurable frivolity of the Serious." She should know that everything beautiful in world history is due to the "mysterious accord between the ardent and humble patience of men and the gentle Pity of God." That patience, the novelist thought, was best expressed by children, whom we often picture as being impatient. In our experience, the parents drive on and on, and the little girl asks, "Are we there yet?" In this setting, however, patience is closer to the response a child gives when she is not in control. And the pity, in turn, is best imparted by God.[15]

The provider of care who has a compulsion to control is anticipated later in Mark's Gospel, this time in the context of a saying that is less stark (Mark 9:33-37). In this case, the Gospel finds Jesus setting forth the child as an example, one who by her very being is to overturn adult assumptions about importance. To grasp the meaning of this we have to range around in Mark and another Gospel for a framework. Ordinary readers have no trouble picking up on a consistent but easily overlooked feature of what most believe to be the earliest Gospel, assembled three decades or more after Jesus was no longer on the scene. "Mark," the author, in selecting which materials to include in his almost journalistic and fast-paced account, pressed a case against the original disciples.

Experts speculate why the twelve, the privileged and chosen followers and thus precisely those who ought to have known better, did not catch on to the way Jesus set priorities and violated expectations. In that Gospel's sixteen chapters, not once does the evangelist cite Jesus congratulating or praising a disciple. For a split second he has Peter saying something to the point, but seconds later Jesus dismisses him as "Satan," who must "get behind" Jesus (Mark 8:27-33). That unflattering exchange aside,

15. Quoted in Robert Speaight, *Georges Bernanos: A Study of the Man and the Writer* (New York: Liveright, 1974), 42.

nothing else affirmative about a chosen disciple survives in that Gospel. One of the best guesses about why this is so focuses on the idea that the author or compiler is writing from the viewpoint of a community that has by then experienced the reality of suffering and death and then the presence of a resurrected Lord, who had risen to new life and offered a "new creation" after having suffered death on the cross. While in Mark Jesus was seen preparing the disciples for his parting from them, they were caught doing everything they could to avoid the brunt of the message and its implications for their lives. They were in denial, hoping to be oblivious to the horror ahead, eager to come up with alternative and less painful plots for their and his destiny. If they are supposed to follow Jesus in faith, in this Gospel they appear to be weak in faith. To appear so to Jesus, as observed by the Gospel writer, meant virtually to be faith-less. Remarkably, strangers, aliens, and others who are not disciples instead give evidence of having the gift of faith — from their place at the margins and from among the unacceptables. In that company we find the child.

In the Gospel of Mark an outsider who is positioned like the child was a woman who, we presume, was a Jew and therefore should have "belonged." She was in fact seen as a stranger, an outsider to Israel's "Closed Home," as Jerome Miller would have called it. This was so because she was stigmatized and abandoned after years of hemorrhaging, and this in a culture where anything related to menstruation was abhorrent. This woman approached Jesus and touched him in a desperate desire for healing. In faith she received the healing that she wanted, plus the congratulatory word that the disciples in Mark never heard: "Daughter, your faith has made you well; go in peace, and be healed of your disease" (Mark 5:25-34). In this story the receptive woman could be a stand-in for the child.

Another story does include a child. In an astonishing reach, the evangelist hears Jesus praising a rank outsider. A woman who suffered in the shadows because she was both a woman and "a Gentile, of Syrophoenician origin," pleaded with Jesus to heal her daughter. He rudely put her off — some say he did this in order to teach her a lesson, others say he wanted to test her faith, and still others confess they do not know why. The persistent woman prevailed, penetrated Jesus' world, and, again in Miller's terms, opened his spiritual Home and as an outsider, a stranger, received a welcome. She heard him respond, "For saying that, you may go — the demon has left your daughter." And so it was. That story appears here not so much because a child is a character in it, a healed one at that, but because the Gospel narrative demonstrates how capable Jesus was of upsetting convention and the people who took refuge in it — and of favoring the vulnerable and unqualified outsider, the peer of the child (Mark 7:24-30).

The Gospel of Matthew is more favorable to the disciples than that of Mark. At least sometimes in its depictions a few of them begin to catch on. To make a point and to effect healing, however, the Jesus of this Gospel still reaches beyond the circle of his fellow Jews. Thanks to Matthew, we learn of a third instance in which Jesus turned convention upside down. This occurred when a Roman centurion, an officer of a hated occupying force, came with a request that Jesus would heal the officer's slave. This military figure who represented an oppressing force amazed Jesus by his skill at representing his servant. Still, he was an outsider. In any case, or maybe because of that situation, Jesus healed the slave at a distance and then announced that "in no one in Israel have I found such faith." From the viewpoint of those who followed and surrounded Jesus, the centurion had to be seen as a marginalized person who shared vulnerable and outsider characteristics with children and who had no choice but to be receptive (Matthew 8:5-13).

A hemorrhaging woman, a helpless child, and a military representative of an occupying power appear in this chapter not as intrusive figures in a Bible study but as figures who help us make a point that appears through this whole book. When Jesus placed the child first and the adult last, he was being consistent. Receiving the child is a radical version of what it is in the Gospels to receive any outsider, anyone weak, unclean, at the margins, or under the domain of others. The Gospel picked up where the faith of Israel had left the child: exalted far beyond the status that was accorded a child in the worlds of Rome and Greece. In Judaism, the law was regarded as God's agent. In the Gospel story of Jesus, however, the law was not mentioned. The child was simply present, and present as someone who receives.

What mattered was the intrinsic role and situation of the child. And as Judith Gundry-Volf observes, the Gospel of Mark made a point of catching Jesus in a pose in which he was identified as being with women, conversing with mothers. He knew how they took children up in their arms, in acts that were part of women's work. Now Jesus elaborately followed their example.[16]

Efforts to discuss the mystery of the child draw one into realms of ultimate meanings, where religious thinkers of all faiths do their tracking. Many of the clues to our subject come from the zone where such mean-

16. Gundry-Volf in Miller-McLemore, *Let the Children Come,* 100.

ings wait to be disinterred. We are picking up on some of those clues, not in patterns of formal philosophy but as approaches to a variety of disciplines and structures of meaning. Several sentences in an essay of Karl Rahner, who takes off from biblical texts and philosophical understandings in ways that reinforce the main thesis of this book, provide a kind of summary to this point: "Childhood is not a state which only applies to the first phase of our lives in the biological sense. Rather it is a basic condition which is always appropriate to a life that is lived aright." We have been isolating some elements that can relate to all of life, asking a question about the years after childhood. When should trust, receptivity, and openness lose the valued place in life that, according to the Gospels, Jesus assigned them? Rahner, who is more ready to use the word *perfection* than I would be, helpfully deals with all stages and phases of life in a passage from which we will draw three excerpts:

> [I]n the last analysis all the stages of life have an equally immediate relationship to God and to the individual's own ultimate perfection, even though in saying this we must fully recognize the fact that man's life advances towards God precisely through a time-sequence consisting of a series of stages following one upon another. . . . But if childhood as a basic condition were not applicable to a rightly orientated life at all times the principle stated above could no longer be upheld. And there is a further point that everyone understands, namely that for our existence to be sound and redeemed at all, childhood must be an intrinsic element in it. It must be a living and effective force at the roots of our being if that being is to be able to endure even in the depths of the mystery.

When the bruises, rough experiences, disillusionments, and need to be critical occur as life advances, can these aspects of childhood remain? Yes.

> Childhood as an inherited factor in our lives must take the form of trust, of openness, of expectation, of readiness to be controlled by another, of interior harmony with the unpredictable forces with which the individual finds himself confronted. It must manifest itself as freedom in contrast to that which is merely the outcome of a predetermining design, as receptivity, as hope which is still not disillusioned.

In that long sentence, one phrase could be troubling, because a child's readiness to be controlled can play into the adult's impulse to control, an impulse that we have been criticizing at length. In the larger context of Rahner's thought, however, there is a kind of "being controlled" that is liberating. This is a standard theme in Christian thought, where being under the lordship of Jesus places one next to a Lord who serves "from below" and without dominating. Awe before this divine Other situates the person who is awed in front of that Other who, unlike the rest of the powers one confronts, is not tyrannous.

The theologian concludes with implied advice, in as good a passage as I have read on how biological childhood gets transcended by an "other" childhood that is lifelong.

> This is the childhood that must be present and active as an effective force at the very roots of our being. Everyone understands too that the childhood which belongs to the child in the biological sense is only the beginning, the prelude, the foretaste and the promise of this other childhood, which is the childhood proved and tested and at the same time assailed, which is present in the mature man. In other words we must take childhood in this *latter* sense as the true and proper childhood, the fulness of that *former* childhood, the childhood of immaturity.

These are startling words with a force that runs counter to the usual language one hears about maturing and eventually coming to be resigned.[17]

The leap from the third millennium back to the words about becoming like a child is strenuous. One cannot take this leap for granted, given the fact that the stories about Jesus, situated in cultures remote from us in time and custom, grow ever more remote. They recede into libraries, where so much else of the past is interred and then forgotten. Biblical illiteracy and the competition by many voices and forces for the eye and ear of our contemporaries combine to make it more difficult to hear and be confronted by texts from the Gospels. It may be, however, that because these shocking words come from texts that are so often passively taken for granted, they may sound fresh and promising.

17. Karl Rahner, "Ideas for a Theology of Childhood," chap. 3 in *Theological Investigations,* vol. 8: *Further Theology of the Spiritual Life,* trans. David Bourke (New York: Herder and Herder, 1971), 47.

When the Literalist Treats the Child as a Problem, not a Mystery

Not every one in the tradition of the Gospels places accents as we have done on Jesus' call to change, or at least on his warning that the unchanged will not enter the kingdom. Literalists and counselors of certain sorts move on from such accents to concerns for disciplining the child. In current political and cultural debate we rarely hear reference to the mystery of the child or reflection on that mystery. Instead, most references to understanding or rearing children deal with the problems of the child. Many discipline-minded authors who turn their attention to children regard them as innately rebellious and therefore give highest priority to discussing appropriate punishments for them. Often such commentators boast that in contrast to soft and compromising advisers, they are interpreting the whole Bible as God's inerrant Word and that they are doing so inerrantly, or at least literally.

Doing so is problematic, because many of their books set out to replace all sense of the mystery with the demand on the part of providers of care to represent God by punishing. To clear the air immediately, let us note that anyone who wants to consistently approach the Bible literally and "fundamentalistically" would have to follow through with calls for obedience to extreme commands about the problem child, as in this directive from Deuteronomy 21:18-21:

> If someone has a stubborn and rebellious son who will not obey his father and mother, who does not heed them when they discipline him, then his father and his mother shall take hold of him and bring him out to the elders of his town at the gate of that place. They shall say to the elders of his town, "This son of ours is stubborn and rebellious. He will not obey us. He is a glutton and a drunkard." Then all the men of the town shall stone him to death. So you shall purge the evil from your midst; and all Israel will hear, and be afraid.

A believer must do hermeneutical handsprings to work this kind of text into the main plot of Judaism or Christianity today and then to use it as a judgment on the biblical faith of other believers or of others who do not identify with the Bible. If one did follow this command of the Lord, the civil authorities would step in and bring the literal-minded elders, parents, and citizens of the town to justice, no doubt invoking the very death penalty that the self-described literalists are out to defend. In the face of such consistency, humane interpreters would therefore simply turn the page or get out the scissors and snip out that passage (and many more like it), hoping that no one would miss it or remember that it lies there on the biblical page. Still, it is there, regularly to be discovered and highlighted by critics who oppose the application of biblical law to family and civil life and who see inconsistency among the literalists.

Literal-minded commentators — give them credit for taking on this burden — have to deal with such texts. Samples of their doing so are evident in most interpretations and applications of such scriptural words to contemporary situations. Among them, one of the most comprehensive is Roy B. Zuck. In his widely received *Precious in His Sight: Childhood and Children in the Bible,* Zuck has the integrity to face up to the stipulation in the Hebrew text of Deuteronomy, even if the twists he provides are not satisfying. As for the case of the disobedient son who is to be stoned to death, the author wants us to forget the extreme punishment there stipulated. He does so evidently in order to get readers to provide a context for the commanded punishment by focusing on and examining the punishers. He writes of the son, who plays the role of the scapegoat in literalists' thinking:

> Such a son was ultimately rebelling against the Lord. However, this legislation "was not cruel nor did it give parents a right to abuse their children." Contrary to its apparent severity, this law was designed to protect children and it makes a significant restraint upon the father's authority over his family. . . . We see here the beginnings of a recognition of social responsibility towards children.[18]

This in my view is a hermeneutical handspring. It is hard to read the text as anything but cruel and as legitimating abuse. It is hard to see where restraint has come in. At the end of the text and the process, the son is dead. It is hard to picture the stoning of one's own child as a case of only "apparent severity," because stoning to death did not leave the son chastened and surviving. Bringing the case to elders who were also sworn to follow God's law in civil life hardly assures the protection of the child; it does not place any restraint upon the father's authority except to take away his license to simply pick up the stones on his own authority. Such

18. Roy B. Zuck, *Precious in His Sight: Childhood and Children in the Bible* (Grand Rapids: Baker, 1996), 163. He is citing R. R. Clements, "The Relation of Children to the People of God in the Old Testament," *Baptist Quarterly* 21 (January 1986): 196.

restraint also would bring small comfort to the disobedient and now doomed son.

In more moderate biblical passages dealing with discipline, Zuck counsels, the child *will* survive, but the relation among the generations will be strained. The child will likely remain a problem, even when punishment is backed by love and good intentions. The biblical book of Proverbs is the special favorite of the groups that want to please God and train the child by firm punishment of the disobedient. The diagnosis of the problem with the child, we learn from some conservative commentators, is rooted in the "folly" that is "bound up" in the heart of a child (Proverbs 22:15).

The harsh counselors pile on text after text to support their approach, with many of them being directed against the foolish child who "hates to be rebuked [because he is] stupid" (Proverbs 12:1). The problem child who goes unpunished will at best create a bad name for his mother (29:15) and at worst bring about death and destruction (15:10; 19:18). Numerous biblical passages recommend use of "the rod." Remember, we are counseled, that the child has been nominated as the chief of fools. "A whip for the horse, a bridle for the donkey, and a rod for the back of fools" (26:3). When parents discipline children, they are said to be showing love and demonstrating that they have the best interest of the child in heart, mind, and lashing arm (13:24). Good – even "delight," we are assured – will result from such discipline (29:17). For commentator Zuck, punishing images such as these all witness to the character, action, and intention of God (Deuteronomy 8:5).[19]

In fairness to interpreter Zuck, we note that before and after he speaks of the need for harsh discipline, he offers one-word bits of positive counsel for dealing with the child who presents problems. There is no point in elaborating on them; anyone with a concordance can easily track down the scores of passages he cites. According to the headings, the parents are to lead, pray, dedicate, provide, love, enjoy, worship, model, encourage, and teach.

These are all quite obvious counsels, and in my eye they present good advice for those who take the Bible seriously. I would particularly single out the directive to *enjoy*. To stress such a point, Zuck refers to the names of the children of patriarch Jacob's wife Leah: Gad, "good fortune," and Asher, "happy." In the promised future, according to Second Isaiah, God again will serve as a model, because the Lord will hold and jostle Jerusalem as a mother does the infant on her knee (Isaiah 66:12). Had Zuck

19. Zuck, *Precious in His Sight,* 121-24, for instances from Proverbs, with comments.

approached the Bible with the mystery of the child, not the problem of the child, in the forefront, there might have been more accent on enjoyment, for adults and children alike.[20]

Head- and name-counter Zuck also serves us with textual statistics about children, citing biblical cases in which they are enjoyed or not enjoyed, enjoyable or not enjoyable. It will surprise anyone who may have thought that the biblical writers have only adults on their minds that children make frequent appearances on their pages. The words *child* and *children,* he notes, appear over 570 times, while there are 2,700 references to *son* or *sons.* These texts often evoke a sense of wonder on the part of those who read them, so much so that Zuck has to make an insertion when quoting a psalm (71:5-6, 17): "You have been my hope, O Sovereign Lord, my confidence since my youth. From birth I have relied on you [. . . a hyperbole]. . . . Since my youth, O God, you have taught me."[21] Zuck inserts the bracketed reference to hyperbole on doctrinal grounds: he does not want his writing used to make a case for infant baptism, in which he does not believe. Believers in infant baptism connect the rite with faith, something Zuck is not prepared to do.

Upsetting of the World of the Child, by the Child

In all such interpretations, the adult is called to be God's agent and avenger, a judge who is not judged, someone who would change the child without being changed himself. I am not trying to portray counselors among such biblical commentators as people incapable of repentance when they do wrong. Rather, in the light of the way the Jesus of the Gospels turns things topsy-turvy and speaks with favor not of "those who brought" children, they are not noticing the posture and openness of the little children themselves. They close themselves off from enjoying the mystery of the child so that they can have control of their problems, no matter what these are.

What is remarkable about all the child-focused verses — twelve in Matthew, ten in Mark, and eight in Luke, totaling sixteen when one subtracts those that are parallel to each other — is that they seem at first to stand in shocking contrast to most other biblical references. Most striking for our thesis is that *not one of them shows Jesus regarding the child as a*

20. Zuck, *Precious in His Sight,* 113-14.
21. Zuck, *Precious in His Sight,* 13-19.

problem. He may well have seen them as such in the course of his life, but what one scholar calls the "memory-impressions" that he left did not include any such instances. These texts instead display the disciples, religious authorities, parents, and "those who brought" children to him as being conventional and often clueless. On one level, their devotion, their readiness to follow law and custom, can be seen as admirable. They did, after all, bring children to Jesus, and they did crave a blessing on them. They are, however, shown as wanting to be in control of Jerome Miller's metaphorical Closed Home that the child would disrupt and open.

As a mystery, the child exemplifies and teaches something decisive about what the Gospel traditions consistently relate about Jesus. Focusing on that aspect of their witness prepares the reader to understand the claims and promises of this child-loving Jesus. In turn, concentrating on these portraits of Jesus when he is seen dealing with children can also provide paradigms of the full portrait of Jesus as he appears throughout the synoptic Gospels. The stories about his dealing with children, we have insisted, can be seen as pointing to the intrinsic value of each child. That something much larger than providing for the care of the child is going on is also evident. The word *topsy-turvy,* along with others such as *unsettling* or *disruptive,* points to the larger theme of the stories in the Gospels, stories of Jesus' ministry.

Christian ethicist Stanley Hauerwas has spoken of the appeal of the Gospels' testimony or witness to Jesus, in words that set us up for its upsetting character:

> What we must understand is that witness is necessary because we are so storied. If the gospel were a truth that could be known in general, then there would be no necessity to witness. All that would be necessary would be to confirm people in what they already know. If the gospel were about general human experience that is unavoidable, then there would be no necessity of being confronted by anyone as odd as a Christian. But because the story we tell of God is the story of the life and death of Jesus of Nazareth, then the only way to know that story is through witness.[22]

Recognizing the child as a problem elicits responses that belong to the category of "a truth that could be known in general," an unavoidable element in "general human experience." The gospel, however, deals not

22. Stanley Hauerwas, *After Christendom: How the Church Is to Behave If Freedom, Justice, and a Christian Nation Are Bad Ideas* (Nashville: Abingdon, 1991), 149.

with the conventional but with the particular and the exceptional, with what one naturally accepts about adults and children alike. This is not to say that only believers in the gospel can conceive of the child from the viewpoint of mystery. It *is* to say that those who do claim to follow the gospel must use the category of mystery as the beginning point in what is observed and in what one deduces and proclaims. Nowhere is this clearer than in the parables of Jesus as collected in the Gospels. Most important on this theme is the work of Paul Ricoeur, who pointed to the extravagant nature of parables:

> They speak of small seeds growing unusually large, of workers being paid far beyond what they have earned, of a prodigal son being welcomed home virtually without repentance, and so on. These represent an "intensification" of the metaphorical nature of the parables and result in a "transgression," in which "these forms of discourse point beyond their immediate signification toward the Wholly Other."[23]

It is important to come to such texts prepared with a Ricoeurian rule: never think you have understood a parable of Jesus until you realize how upsetting it is, how shattering, how much it turns the world upside down. As with the parables, so with many of the sayings and actions as framed in the Gospels or with Jesus' reported talks about children.

Zuck does the service of citing six authors who answer a question he poses: "What did Jesus mean by the words, 'become like little children'?" We will have more to say about that question apart from the reference in this text, but for now here are Zuck's witnesses:

> Answers vary from children being receptive, responsive to Jesus' call (like the little one Jesus called to him), amenable and simple, teachable, modest and unspoiled, trusting, in need of instruction, or sinless.
>
> Preferable is the view that becoming like little children means two things: recognizing one's low estate and acknowledging one's helplessness and dependence. Just as children in the ancient world were viewed as insignificant, unimportant, and lacking in status, and just as young children everywhere are totally dependent on adults to meet their needs, so Jesus' followers are to acknowledge their insignificance and weakness, and their dependence on him.

23. Quoted in Dan R. Stiver, *Theology after Ricoeur: New Directions in Hermeneutical Theology* (Louisville: Westminster John Knox, 2001), 119.

> . . . [R. C. H.] Lenski wrote that being childlike spiritually is like being children who possess nothing but need everything; who are able to do nothing but receive everything.

A footnote cites German biblical scholar Joachim Jeremias, who said that "becoming like a child means learning to say *'abba'* ('father') again."[24] And the person, young or old, who does say *abba* and invests that utterance with assent and readiness is open to the change for which Jesus calls, and ready to regard the mystery of the child with wonder.

24. Zuck, *Precious in His Sight,* 206, 207n.16.

6. Wonder in the Provision of Care

To wonder is a mark of the child's life and an activity to be encouraged in the provider of care. A glance down the "Parents and Children" shelves in large bookstores gives evidence that most of the books are concerned with something other than wonder and mystery. Most child-care materials promote control and management. Many titles suggest something powerful and encyclopedic, as if one could comprehend "the child from A to Z" or master "everything you ever wanted to know about the child." Advisers in such books set out to explain children and are preoccupied with presenting solutions to problems. When transactions across the generations begin in wonder, however, the child will probably not merely be on the receiving end of adult initiatives but will become an agent who in turn stimulates a richer sense of wonder. Such transactions can be at once terrifying and exhilarating. To reduce the potential terror without dulling the exhilaration I get help from an old friend. In 1969 Sam Keen's publisher had me write a dust-jacket endorsement of his *Apology for Wonder.*[1] That book also serendipitously introduced me to Gabriel Marcel and his distinction between "problem" and "mystery," a distinction central to *The Mystery of the Child.* Keen posed a question that opens the topic now before us: What does it mean to wonder?

1. Sam Keen, *Apology for Wonder* (New York: Harper and Row, 1969). Page references to this book in the next section will be given parenthetically in the text.

What Does It Mean to Wonder?

Keen's answer at first sounds forbidding and arcane, because he introduces the difficult concept of "ontologic wonder" as a guide to the concept of mystery. That sort of wonder is triggered, Keen wrote, by awe "that something exists rather than nothing," and all the rest follows. He quotes philosopher Ludwig Wittgenstein in words that help us locate the child: "It is not *how* things are in the world that is mystical, but *that* it is." *That* the child is also inspires awe. Although ontologic wonder may be at the root of all other kinds, Keen also refers to mundane wonder, which also comes into play when one deals with the child. This is so because, he says, it "is elicited primarily by *what* a thing is rather than *that* it is." Keeping his own sense of awe, Keen declares: "There could be no adequate catalogue of the objects that produce such mundane wonder: a loved person [a child?], a gnarled tree, a beautiful stone, a 'miraculous' event, and so on." He elaborates: "In such encounters the structure and meaning of the object rather than its bare existence are the occasions for wonder."

The child fits well into this picture, because the child is not an abstraction called "being [*ontos*]," left as if in cloudland. Instead, the child is near, accessible, familiar. The familiar, Keen adds, can be a source of wonder, because "a mature sense of wonder does not need the constant titillation of the sensational to keep it alive. It is most often called forth by a confrontation with the mysterious depth of meaning at the heart of the familiar and quotidian" (pp. 21-23). That claim is particularly useful in the case of the child for two reasons. First, acts like changing diapers and helping with homework assignments, as well as transporting to doctors' appointments and junior chess tournaments, soon dampen titillations. Also, our talk about the mystery of the child might suggest to some that we are dealing with particularly gifted or "nice" children. Whoever has dealt with a particular child through thick and thin, in terror and boredom, has to find means of nurturing the sense of wonder in the face of this "familiar" and "mundane" little human. She is a person who often challenges others and makes awe difficult to sustain. Everyone can exclaim about a prodigy or, if the observer's taste follows certain lines, about a winner of a baby beauty contest or a sack race at a Sunday school picnic. Keen, however, is interested, as are we, in any and every child as an evoker of wonder and awe.

Keen next helps readers revisit contingency. His version does not quite match David Tracy's (which we considered in Chapter 2), though both versions are factors or fates that color all human life. "As used here," he writes, "contingency means that in raw experience the object we apprehend in wonder comes to us without bearing its own explanation" (p. 24). We deal with the child who is before us, who comes into the world without a tag or instruction book: "Here I am!" This notion is consistent with our rejection of the idea that scientists, humanists, and parents can *explain* the child. The talk of wonder instead connects at once with mystery, a linkage that emboldens Keen to treat them together. It is this connection that originally quickened my own interest and still sustains me in thinking about the child or about relating to one.

Keen quoted as witness for his own approach an epigram reproduced by Gabriel Marcel: "Mysteries are not truths that lie beyond us; they are truths that comprehend us" (p. 25).[2] Keen's own summary deals with this point: "When I am dealing with a genuine mystery, I cannot get the distance necessary for dealing with it as a pure object, because I cannot totally separate myself from the mystery under contemplation." That was a major point in Marcel's severing of the two concepts: one can "lay siege" to the other when dealing with problems, but one cannot separate one's self from the mystery. The child before me, the child that I was, the element of childlikeness that remains or is to remain within me do not allow me to "totally separate myself." Keen's next assertion is fundamental for all inquiries about mystery:

> Thus when we say objects of wonder are mysterious we do not mean they are only vaguely known. It is too often assumed that the mysterious is equivalent to the unknown and that, in the light of adequate knowledge, mystery will give way to clarity. Such a view equates mystery and ignorance. (pp. 24-25)

Few distinctions are more important in our context than the distinction between dealing with mystery and dealing with ignorance; few oppositions are more decisive than mystery versus ignorance. The following certainly applies to child rearing or even to the observation of the child. "So we can see that the mysteriousness of an object has little to do with how well or how poorly it is known." Keen offers an example by pointing to "the process of conception, gestation, and birth." In the physical sense this process "can be adequately explained," he argues, "but the event of birth is as productive of wonder for some modern men as it was for the primitive, who somehow vaguely assumed the whole process was caused by the powers of the moon."

2. Marcel does not identify B. J. Jouve as the original source of this statement.

Why Keen thought that only "*some* modern men" and women wondered over the birth of a child I do not know. It is hard to picture any thoughtful person not being in awe. As an infant grows and becomes ever more complex, this wonder does not dissipate. Keen speaks of the mysteriousness of an object, but then we see him nearly apologizing for using the word *object* to refer to persons, in this case, children. With both the Jewish philosopher Martin Buber and the Catholic existentialist Gabriel Marcel, he prefers to speak of the "presence" of the Other. It is no surprise that he is therefore sufficiently emboldened to speak at chapter length of "childhood and wonder." The chapter's epigraph by atomic physicist J. Robert Oppenheimer all but states Keen's thesis: "There are children playing in the street who could solve some of my top problems of physics, because they have modes of sensory perception that I lost long ago" (p. 42).

The wonder in the face of the child and the wonder of the child are the two occasions that prompt reflection. In either case, as Keen writes, "the association of wonder with childhood is so automatic it has become a cliché." He thereupon sets out to remove it from its convenient status as a cliché. Remembering that wonder is an anteroom to mystery and is neither to be equated with mystery nor to be considered to exhaust the meanings of mystery, we can refresh our memories by hearing his definition:

> Wonder, in the child, is the capacity for sustained and continued delight, marvel, amazement, and enjoyment. It is the capacity of the child to approach the world as if it were a smorgasbord of potential delights, waiting to be tasted. It is the sense of freshness, anticipation, and openness that rules the life of a healthy child. The world is a surprise party, planned just for me, and my one vocation in life is to enjoy it to the fullest — such is the implicit creed of the wondering child. Reality is a gift, a delight, a surprise — in fact, a toy; it is an excessive, superabundant cafeteria of delights, and should any experience begin to be jaded by boredom and staleness, all one has to do is move on to the next. To wonder is to live in the world of novelty rather than law, of delight rather than obligation, and of the present rather than the future. (pp. 43-44)

Keen also relishes the quality of immediacy, of spontaneous enjoyment in the child, and quotes the old Chinese proverb: "Only to a child is pure happiness possible. Later it is always tainted with the knowledge that it will not last" (p. 51)

Jean Piaget, the psychologist devoted to assessing the stages of a child's life, observed that the child does not see the world as law-governed, as a place in which everything has to fit. (The adult sees it this way because she has in mind control of the child.) There is a "complete absence of necessity" in the thought of the child. The child lives in the world of the contingent, where "anything can happen, as far is he is concerned" (p. 52). This is one of the most remarkable aspects of the inner life of the child. Christian apologist G. K. Chesterton illustrates the fact that a "lack of a sense of necessity" is what allows the child "to enjoy again and again a game, a song, a story, or merely the repetition of a word":

> A child kicks his legs rhythmically through excess, not absence of life. Because children have abounding vitality, because they are in spirit fierce and free, therefore they want things repeated and unchanged. They always say, "Do it again"; and the grown-up person does it again until he is nearly dead. For grown-up people are not strong enough to exult in monotony.[3]

All that can be true, but a child's impatience, so regularly made evident, also signals wonder, because in that impatience the child shows that she is waiting for something fresh, new, and surprising. Philosophers from Plato and Aristotle to the present have stressed adults' need to stimulate wonder in the child and then enjoy it in the adult. Jerome Miller, who offered the metaphor of the Open Home as a way of seeing the Other, followed through in a second book on the implications of this approach to "openness." In his book *In the Throe of Wonder* he cites Martin Heidegger, who claimed that wonder was the "origin of all human inquiry." When better than in early childhood should one dwell on origins? Here is Miller's focus:

> It is the experience of wonder which Heidegger, like Aristotle, places not just at the origin of philosophical wisdom but at the origin of all human inquiry. Because wonder makes "the 'Why?'" spring to our lips, it is the hinge between ignorance and knowledge, between oblivion and insight, and perhaps for that reason the hinge between every past and future. What door is opened by that hinge?[4]

3. G. K. Chesterton, *Orthodoxy* (Garden City, NY: Doubleday Image Books, 1959), 60.

4. Jerome A. Miller, *In the Throe of Wonder: Intimations of the Sacred in a Post-Modern World* (Albany: State University of New York Press, 1992), 11.

Three images then draw us ever closer to the child: home, door, and hinge. Miller follows the child to the inner sanctum with a fourth, the dangerous image of a secret room. This metaphor, he writes, is

> especially suggestive when it is associated with those childhood experiences which most of us can remember vividly: the wondrous (and yet also dreadful) experience of venturing into a secret room, or exploring an uninhabited house, or even opening the lid of a chest hidden in the attic and found unexpectedly. If, as children, we seemed to live closer to the source of ourselves than we do now, perhaps it was because we were more eager to be venturers, and less able to resist the lure of dark woods and untried paths down which we were drawn by the very fact that we did not know where they led.[5]

As with such physical locations and experiences, so also it is with the mental and spiritual adventures that carried the child through such woods and on such paths – to where? In this image the teacher, the parent, and the counselor have to be concerned to keep the figurative home and door open and the hinge oiled. Most adults can remember when as children they tiptoed to an attic or a basement where frightening creatures might be hiding or where in a trunk Grandma's wedding veil was stowed out of sight and away from moths. They also will recall responding to scary dares that led them to new levels of learning that they often followed, but never without assuming risk.

Wonder, which we here celebrate, should have the field to itself, but it does not. In fact, as the years pass, it is ever more difficult for the child to keep his wondrous hold on his universe, or for adults to retain a hold on the reality of wonder that he inhabits. Therefore we may speak of an eclipse of wonder that often occurs later in the life of the growing child while he matures through adolescence into adulthood. For some contributions to this eclipse, Sam Keen faults adults, beginning with parents and teachers, who themselves "often have ceased to wonder." Subsequently, adults then "create in the child a sense of impotence to cope with novelty because of their own timidity and sense of failure," or else force children "too rapidly out of the world of play into the world of work." Over-organized adult interventions into the world of play (for example, when parents and teachers and coaches goad children into formally organized contests and athletic events) qualify here as the world of work, not the world of play.

5. Miller, *In the Throe of Wonder,* 11.

Keen signs off: "Wonder may appear pointless and impractical." Yet there is danger in stifling it, for "the underlying reason for the eclipse of wonder must be sought in the basic attitudes toward life and the fundamental models of man adopted by those who educate the wonder out of children" (pp. 57-59). It is the provider of care, the adult who educates, the parent, pastor, or coach, who bears most responsibility for the task of showing restraint when tempted to stifle wonder in the child.

Enriching the Provision of Care: Fifteen Resources of Wonder

We can mourn the eclipse of wonder in technological societies and in modernity in general, but rich resources exist for those who wish to move beyond celebration to encouragement. This theme of this book has been inspired in no small part by the work of Karl Rahner, an apparently surprising source for thinking about the child, because most of us came to know him as an aged priest who seemed far removed from the world of the child. Because his writings are heavy going for those of us who are not specialists in his field or at home with his language, I will intersperse his writings with comments that make what follows sound sometimes like a conversation and at other times like an elaboration. It is so very rare to come across a serious religious thinker dealing in depth with childhood that we shall make the most of his proposals. All of them support our focus on the mystery of the child and the response of wonder.

Rahner invited conversation on principle, and the reader is invited to respond in elaboration, because his comments are so terse that some will sound abrupt and uninviting. Yet to invite is precisely his goal. Very modestly Rahner mentioned that his was but "a modest and fragmentary approach to a theology of childhood."[6] However, fragments from the priest's scholarly table can often serve better than whole meals from lesser thinkers. These appear in his chapter "Ideas for a Theology of Childhood." Because this staged literary conversation is the centerpiece of this book, I will break the fragment into numbered statements and comment tersely. Then, in each case, in italics, I will draw out one possible practical

6. Karl Rahner, "Ideas for a Theology of Childhood," chap. 3 in *Theological Investigations,* vol. 8: *Further Theology of the Spiritual Life,* trans. David Bourke (New York: Herder and Herder, 1971), 37. Page references to Rahner's work in this section will be given parenthetically in the text.

implication of the witness, almost in mechanical form, using the phrase, *"If this is true, then the provider of care will recognize that . . ."*[7]

1. The child's existence is interpreted in a biblical matrix.

The author, again modestly, writes that he did not intend to provide guidance to parents, teachers, and the like, because in his view this was not part of his vocation. Nor did he invade the field of pedagogy, though teachers and parents could learn much from his work. His interest was in what I would call *metapedagogy*, meaning that which is "beyond" some basic advice about teaching and guiding (meta = "beyond" or "behind"). Rahner's concern also began with the Bible, which meant for him "what the divine revealed word has to say about childhood." Not first of all a biblical scholar, he announced that he would not comment on specific texts, but instead would imply scriptural themes (pp. 33, 37). Rahner's modesty can offer inspiration to providers of care for children, readers who in most cases will not be pedagogues or, for that matter, formal biblical scholars. The "divine revealed word" on this subject is accessible to all serious readers.

If this is true, the provider of care, already aware of humanistic interpretations of the mystery of the child, will find reason also to probe profound sacred literature, basically the Hebrew Scriptures and New Testament, whether or not these texts represent his own faith. Such probing will advance the reader's alertness to decisive features of the surrounding culture and the commitments of the majority in the citizenry.

2. This beginning represents mystery unveiled.

Rahner, of course, is attractive in the present context because of his immediate and regular focus on mystery. Emphatically, he wrote, "childhood is, in the last analysis, a *mystery*" (his italics). As mystery, the Jesuit wrote, the beginning of a person's life "is unveiled." Here it is important to say that in ancient times the metaphor of veiling and unveiling had special import for defining mystery. Removal of a veil did not mean that one came to a core, an essence, a concluding point. Instead, under each veil would lie another. "Unveiling" was revelatory but not conclusive (p. 42). Thinking of an infant's entry into the world as being an unveiling therefore opens the

7. I will ask the reader to keep this italicized phrase in mind in the next fifteen items.

imagination to ideas that would not come spontaneously in merely clinical connotations. A mother giving birth and those around her will be able to focus more on the development of the child while being aware of the limits of their knowledge if they keep in mind the picture of birth as an unveiling of a mystery.

If this is true, the provider of care will relish each act of unveiling and find meaning in what is revealed — especially as the child begins to relate to others.

3. The child is open to God, who is the utter mystery.

Are we ready for this next leap? This unveiling at birth connects the child with the final source of all that follows, because coming into the world and coming to life are acts that, according to Rahner, can be approached only in the light of one's being "open to the absolute beginning of God who is utter mystery, the ineffable and eternal, nameless and precisely as such accepted with love in his divine nature as he who presides over all things. Such a beginning as this cannot be otherwise than mysterious" (p. 42). Once again, the word *open* characterizes the child protected by mystery and grounded in it. In Rahner — as with other thinkers whom we are summoning — the enemy of the mystery of childhood is the adult impulse to control, to close off possibilities.

If this is true, the provider of care, without idolizing or apotheosizing the child, will learn to celebrate the mysterious aspects of her development as she increasingly assumes spiritual responsibility on her own.

4. The child is "effable" but finds her origin in God's ineffability.

My choice of the word *effable* needs explaining. It is missing in many dictionaries and marginal in others, but here it suggests some dimensions of a child's life that can be measured and explained. These include weight, temperature, appearance, health, and other visible and palpable aspects of her being. Its opposite, *ineffable,* the word applied to God, is at first hearing anything but helpful. Being ineffable — not capable of being expressed in words — seems to be irrelevant in the presence of this gasping, screaming, fluid-covered being who has been connected "effably" with a visible, tangible mother. Back up from this physical child, Rahner suggests, and contemplate the mystery of her source, and you will reach to God who is beyond words and is never reducible by explanations. In awareness of the origin and source of the child, thoughtful adults may very well gasp or fall into wonder-full silence. Doing so is excellent preparation for what lies ahead for everyone who will have care for or who will care about this child (p. 42).

If this is true, the provider of care will recognize in humility that she lacks words and ideas to penetrate the depth of the mystery of the child, who originates "in God."

5. The child is to resist efforts by adults to control.

Every attempt to contain the infant, to box her into a precast set of meanings, Rahner argues, will lead to frustration. Or the attempt can mean something worse: it may signal the impulse of a caregiver to seek control and thus lead to an eventual eclipse of the imagination of the child. Then the one in control will rely only on counsels and prescriptions designed to produce the "normal" child (p. 38).

If this is true, the provider of care will work to free himself from the impulse to manage and control all aspects of the child's life and, by such resisting, will thus contribute to the freedom of the child.

6. The child exists always at the threshold of the eternal.

"The eternal" can refer to life eternal, to the eternality of God, or to everything beyond the immediate horizon of time and place, the inexhaustible. The child is not eternal or "in the eternal" but "at the threshold" of the eternal. Rahner concentrates on "the child whom we know, since she arrives at a particular moment in a particular room," at the "relative beginning" of life. Pondering this absolute beginning sets the caregiver up to realize that the temporal, the few moments – lasting eight days or eighty years – that are given this person, have a significance that is not bounded by the calendar, precisely because it has a source in the "eternal" (p. 35).

If this is true, the provider of care will not let short-term planning be the only measure of values imparted to and discovered by the child and will try to assume the child's perspective on the passing of time.

7. The naming of the child is significant.

Upon the infant's arrival, the parents do one of the most important and dangerous things that will happen to the child: in wonder and with risk they name him. Naming always involves the imagination of parents or other adult name-givers. Through this act they can pay respect to tradition by honoring ancestors who have disappeared in the mists of memory. They can show how captive of fads and fashions they may be. Naming can be an expression of parents' egotism. In all decisions about what to call the child, adults inevitably will be participating in something that can mean exercising control. The name they choose will indicate the child throughout his life — unless upon maturity he goes to great legal lengths to change it, or unless he gets blessed or cursed with a nickname. This act of naming, as Rahner sees it, occurs in the context and presence of the nameless One, who is not bounded or described by names, even by words of address like Yahweh or Father. The child through the passage of the years gives shape to the fuller and personalized meaning of the name, and its very sound may help determine who he is. One thinks of the difference in personality among boys with "the same name," one that may come across differentiated, for instance, as Richard, Rich, Richie, Dick, or Dickie or as William, Will, Willy, Bill, or Billy. Then to be named a child of God helps shape the bearer of that name, even as that child carries the concept into the world of risk. One hears: "You don't look and *act* like a child of God!" (implied, p. 49).

If this is true, the provider of care will respect the mystery of names and the inventive ways the child who bears one lives into its meaning.

8. The child is accepted into divine love.

The beginning of this child, this mystery being unveiled, is also "open" — this is Rahner's key term throughout — to her being accepted with love, because God in God's divine nature always reaches out to accept creatures in love. The child may often deny, ignore, or even repudiate the love of God, also when it is reflected in the faces, arms, and acts of parents and others. Recovery of love, however, always can begin when that little child is allowed and encouraged to remain open to the eternal and thus is able to receive signs of divine love. Though the child is born into a world of accident, chance, contingency, and random happenings, she will finally address it in openness to the One "who presides over all things." Rahner expresses it tersely: "Childhood is openness. Human childhood is infinite openness" (p. 48).

If this is true, the provider of care will nurture love of God and help the child see it refracted in the lives of those who surround her.

9. The child is an independent and a dependent being.

From the first day of infancy, the young person is developing relationships. Rahner was a Roman Catholic "Father" who did not get to father a child, perhaps never witnessed a birth, and may or may not have been close to children through the years in which he was to forget many details of his own childhood — as all humans do. He did, however, provide a case for observing and nurturing what the child will become (p. 42). Just as the acorn bears the oak, so it is with the infant in its beginning, "because it is a mystery, and because as a beginning it bears all one's future life within itself, therefore life itself is mysterious." The child is both dependent on parents and other providers of care and all the while also an independent being, individual, distinctive, and unique. In the future of a life unfolding, he manifests the complexity of his origins at birth. The priest emphasized that the child that we all were and, in some senses, always remain — if we are "open" — will be "delivered over to mystery."

If this is true, the provider of care will give due attention to the relational demands made by the dependent child while also seeing ways to encourage independence, including independence of that provider.

10. Original childhood is preserved forever.

Then comes a shocking sentence from Rahner in a statement that the young Sam Keen could also have voiced. All this occurs and is discerned so that "life becomes for us a state in which our original childhood is preserved for ever; a state in which we are open to expect the unexpected, to commit ourselves to the incalculable, a state which endows us with the power still to be able to play, to recognize that the powers presiding over existence are greater than our own designs, and to submit to their control as our deepest good" (p. 42).

As with so much in the rest of his essay, these lines merit our contemplation. Rahner writes that one who is delivered over into mystery can say, *"life becomes for us a state in which our original childhood is preserved for ever"* (italics mine). This statement ought to startle us. In other contexts we would not speak of any part of the passages and sequences of life as a "state." Yet Rahner seems to want to stress continuity through it all. For all that flows over the river bed, its base is not mud but rock: in this metaphor, the mystery of the child remains. It is "preserved for ever," presumably in this case as a "state" that belongs to eternity and also to life after death. We need concern ourselves in this context only with life this side of death, seeing that it acts functionally "for ever." Thus when the aging Catholic professor wrote, he had in mind this mystery of childhood "preserved" still as a potential for himself. Rahner, of course, was not speaking of childishness or of what the contemporary New Age prophets sometimes call "your inner child." Instead, he referred to the whole being as viewed from the perspective of the original mystery.

If this is true, the provider of care will share with the child some experiences, terms, and ideas that connect both of them to lifelong pursuits of the mystery seen first in the child, even while finding the child a useful example for the way she relates to others.

11. The child is open to expecting the unexpected.

The decisive word *open* comes along again later in the essay. If we are "delivered over to mystery," Rahner wrote, we are "open to expect the unexpected." Whoever closely observes a life, any life, knows that "openness" of this sort is the mark of an ample and free personality. Disappointments in the career of such a life often occur in ways that are as unanticipated as are its fulfillments. Defensively, many who experience disappointment grow introverted and close the door to new and unexpected experiences. The next line in Rahner's paragraph, one that is reminiscent of the main themes of Marcel and Keen, strikes me as having most to do with childhood and what it can bear through life. He spells it out: the child and the adult have "the power still to be able to play" (p. 42).

If this is true, the provider of care will be as ready for surprise as are children, being, with them, tantalized by the mystery of human existence, so that together they will find age-appropriate ways to express this readiness.

12. Significantly, play, thus understood, has a special quality.

The child especially has the power to play. For many, growing up represents leaving behind all aspects of childhood. Such an observation as this, coming from a serious German priest, seems a hardly necessary counsel in a society where children play too many computer games, where children's vacations are many and long and entertainments are beckoning and varied. Rahner, however, was not talking about the *quantity* of opportunities to play but about another *quality* or approach to play. Such play will not always be programmed and under the control of adults; it elicits the imagination of the children on their own (p. 42).

If this is true, the provider of care will appreciate play, encourage play by the child, and play with the child.

13. The child remains in an ambiguous relation to the concept and practice of control and controlling.

The concept and experience of control and controlling present consistent problems for the provider of care, especially because so often these deprive the child of spontaneity and the freedom to develop. There is a dark side to what Rahner offers to anyone who seeks to preserve "original childhood." I am somewhat uneasy about the possible import of his phrase in the next line, where he bids us to "recognize that the powers presiding over our existence are greater than our own designs, and to submit to their control is our deepest good" (p. 42). Is this the most important and attractive portrait of the eternal and the divine to impose on the consciousness of children? I am also not sure that the healthy child regards such recognition and readiness to submit to controlling humans as positive. Adults, after all, may abuse the child whom they would control. They may also project images of God as controller-in-chief, leaving out of the picture other ways of relating to God. The child would more likely wish to remain always the president of her existence, to set forth in her earliest years her own designs, and submit to anyone only reluctantly and after having shown resistance. It is in retrospect, then, that some adults learn what to make of their childhood experience and of the powers to which they had "to submit." For now, I would leave all such reference to this most complex of Rahner's observations and here post a "Handle with Care" sign.

If this is true, the provider of care will help ensure the presence of mystery by uttering a "hands off!" to efforts, including some by himself, to control the child.

14. The child's ending is revealed in the beginning.

Rahner's next comment addresses my puzzlement over the relation of some of these metaphysical themes to the realistic childhood of the child. His whole original purpose, he writes, had been to stress "openness" as the main feature of the mystery of the child. He argues that throughout life most people will naturally be on courses in which closing, narrowing, and excluding go along with maturing and weathering. *If* there is openness and *if* repentance is present, there will be a 180-degree turning from what he observes is "naturally" occurring, and adults can manifest the durably valuable features of a child's life (p. 43). Rahner adds that through "this attitude of openness, and not without a certain *metanoia* (repentant turning), [children] become what they are – precisely children." The child does not yet know that: "however paradoxical it may appear, . . . we do not really know what childhood means at the beginning of our lives until we know what that childhood means which comes at the end of them." This turning without end refers to lifelong and regular acts of repentance, conversion, resolve, and "reception of the kingdom," for which, at any age, the advice is, as in the counsel of the Gospels, "and so become children."

Rahner is almost incantatory in his repetition of the theme of mystery: "And in the light of this, once more, we can understand that childhood invokes a mystery, the mystery of our whole existence, the ineffable element in which is God himself" (p. 43).

If this is true, the provider of care will remain open, with the child, to change. More important, the reference to the "ending" calls to mind what the being of the child can mean in the years of "near ending," old age.

15. The child is best revealed as a child of God.

All fifteen of these lines involve a lot of what philosophers call "God-talk," right in the middle of a book on child-talk, but it is the business of people of faith to keep language about God before them, as Rahner does. Here is how he does it in our context: For him everything comes down to meaning that one speaks of the child being *a child of God* (p. 43). Celebrating this kind of naming admittedly comes more easily to the person who has not been abused by a parent or left insecure by a father or a mother, but who has known protection when young, for it amounts to "the decisive influence the *experience of a secure childhood* can have" (p. 44; italics his). In contrast to this is the experience of a "lack of protection for some" (p. 47). "Childhood as an inherent factor in our lives must take the form of trust, of openness, of expectation, . . . of interior harmony with the unpredictable forces with which the individual finds himself confronted." I have cut out the phrase "readiness to be controlled by another," for reasons already mentioned in a world where the thirst to control can too easily be carried over into understandings of how God would relate to the child.

If this is true, the believing provider of care will treat the child as the child of God and follow what such a reality means for herself.

In this fifteenth case Rahner has used a term and thus posed an issue we shall have to keep facing: welcoming "protection" could easily and dangerously phase over into showing "readiness to be controlled by another." When rooted in a Gospel story of parents placing children in Jesus' arms, as we picture these little ones willingly accepting his protection and control, all is well. Control of the child, however, is such an obsessive theme in the literature of advice that it can be seen as the effort precisely to dominate, to act on the will of the other. Nowhere in the stories of Jesus that inspire and inform Rahner is there any mention of the child as an object of control. Being the child of God is central.

In Rahner there are two childhoods, though the second one has nothing to do with the colloquial "second childhood," an unfortunate term for a form of dementia. The first is the natural biological childhood, about which the youngest child cannot in any way be reflective. The second is the "state" of enduring childhood, one aspect or mode of which calls a person to be grown up but still to retain the characteristics applauded here. This is why, for Rahner as our mentor and for me as well, the childhood that belongs to the child is "only the beginning, the prelude, the foretaste and the promise of this other childhood" (p. 47). All this happens because of a childlike "orientation to God" (pp. 47-48).

Rahner at this stage displayed a readiness to condense his whole theme into a few lines that could serve as an epigraph. I quote them here, while reminding readers of how we have consistently redefined what is at stake in matters of control and how to avoid the oppressive misuse of control. Passing over what the theologian says about submission to control by another, we hear his declaration that if childhood is characterized by openness, the child will find, in Rahner's term,

> the courage to allow fresh horizons, ever new and ever wider, to be opened up before one, a readiness to journey into the untried and the untested (and all this with that deep elemental and ultimate trust which seems inexhaustible in its endurance, the trust which the sceptics and those who have made shipwreck of their lives bitterly describe as "naïve"), then in all this that transcendence of faith, hope and love in which the ultimate essence of the basic act of religion precisely consists is already ipso facto an achieved and present fact. (p. 48)

Only after having been through the exercise of connecting the first and the second situations or perspectives of being-the-child is one ready to understand why this major thinker looks to the child as mirror, model, and analogy to the divine mystery: "We can then turn our gaze back once more to the child in a biological and social sense as well" (p. 50). This we shall set out to do in the next chapter. Again, Rahner says: "In the child a man begins who must undergo the wonderful adventure of remaining a child forever."

Rahner is here speaking specifically of what the expectation of eternity does to color mortal life, but we can also see how "remaining a child forever" can inform the life of older people (p. 33). He speaks of the "unsurpassable value of childhood" and stresses how in the biological sense one cannot repeat it or return to it. Here as elsewhere there is no folksy or disdainful "second childhood" of the sort associated with senility. Seldom does Rahner get as agitated as he does when he talks about terms that point to misunderstandings of the times and the phases of life. They are, he charges, "unphilosophical, unhuman and un-Christian" (p. 34).

Rahner, in fact, gives us reason to tread cautiously. He sees danger in viewing the lifespan as a series of phases — passages? — "each of which is exhausted and leads on to the next, the very meaning of which is to disappear into the next, to be a preparation for it, to 'exist' for the further stages beyond itself." That conception of succession, he writes, is only a partial way to look at the passage of time in the life of a person. In such a scenario, he adds, "childhood itself disappears" (p. 34). Rahner criticizes Christians especially for seeing childhood as a subordinate, not intrinsically valuable, phase and thus only a preparation for adult life, which is the only goal and measure.

Reducing a human to stages that disappear in succession can lead to a focus on the child as an object instead of what Marcel and Keen call her, a presence, and one who deals with the present in especially creative ways. Rahner reminds us once more that the human "is a subject," and the child is emphatically so. The child, even early on, retains some elements of the past (p. 35), as when the four-year-old speaks of "when I was. . . ." The child will also look forward to a future that is already partially worked out, as when he says, "when I grow up. . . ." So it is that for Rahner, "we only *become* the children whom we *were* because we gather up time — and in this our childhood too — into our eternity." And thus, in one of his most memorable and revealing lines, Rahner summarizes: "*This* morning does not derive its life simply from the afternoon which follows" (p. 36).

Wonder-full Art, Stories, Play, and Imagination

Bidden or not, afternoon comes, with its own opportunities for seeking or celebrating meaning in life. Wonder, imagination, and creativity – the prime topics that come up when one appraises the child – wait to be enhanced. There appear to be nearly limitless resources in the depth of the child's reach to the point that we can speak of an abyss, plus a similar range in the apogee of discovery at the heights of that reach. Wonder will therefore prevail so long as the child is stimulated to be expressive in what we can now call the metaphoric Open Home. This open character shows itself at once in the acts of playing. A serious author is no doubt expected to apologize for introducing at such a crucial spot something that many may regard as frivolous and trivial. For this phase of the plot and the argument, however, it is the playful imagination and with it imaginative play as elements of childhood that can be key agents in sustaining proper and healthful features of being a child all through life.

First, art. Even a casual observation of the surrounding culture will provide illustrations of the cramping of the imagination, the closing of that Open Home, the effort to control by adults through their being serious and demanding that children grow up and mimic adult behavior. For a sample: More often than not, especially in the past, a kindergarten child – call him Thomas – asked to draw a house, will turn imaginatively literal and autobiographical and portray his own. Whether it is a ranch, split-level, skyscraper condominium, or lean-to makes little difference. His house is not only his castle but his home. Is not that what the teacher asked him to depict? If his home is a split-level, he may try to draw it as a split-level. If it is a house of seven or many gables, they will appear on his drawing. In his eye, he has succeeded as well as if he had produced a photograph, so we picture him beaming when the teacher comes by to inspect. He is surprised, however, by her response, in which her unease over his product is not quite suppressed, as if she was being critical and asking him for a second try.

The house he tried to draw was *his* house, not the ones that teachers and parents everywhere recognize as a child's version. The child responds and immediately goes back to drawing, repeating his earlier effort. In his eye, if in the eyes of no other, he has drawn a house. Eventually the teacher communicates that she had something else in mind. I picture many a teacher still under pressure or by instinct setting out to see a stereotypical and standard child develop. So she holds up the exemplary work of obedient and dutiful Michael, who is working at a nearby desk. We know what his house will look like, because we can quickly spot the will-to-please character of Michael, and we know how a kindergarten house should look. Compare notes with me: it will be a one- or two-story house; we do have to allow for *some* choice. It will be a head-on shot, not angled to show perspective. In most respects it will be symmetrical. A door is at the center, flanked by two windows, each delineated with sashes. A walkway may lead to the house — here is another option, since some kindergarten homes come without walkways — and, topping it off, is a chimney with smoke coming out of it, the only note of asymmetry. Bushes, trees, and clouds are also optional.

Or, for a next assignment, Thomas colors trees not green but something else. He was using his imagination, having seen trees in autumn or reflecting a pink sunset. On a field trip a well-motivated teacher will have taken him to the Impressionist galleries at the art museum. There Monet, Bonnard, Seurat, or any of a number of Impressionists will have depicted trees tinged with pink and purple in paintings worth millions of dollars, seen by thousands who are unaware of Thomas's pink truancy. For now, Michael obligingly meets expectations, accepts the single green crayon from the teacher, and pleases her. This time the tree is green. The adult remains in control.

Using their imaginations, children as artists often are heretics because they are visually reflecting some of the mystery, the uncontrolled element of their being. One will depict the judge at Jesus' trial in an airplane, since he is Pontius Pilot. Forbidden to draw the face of God, a Jewish child may draw the feet of Yahweh as he hands the two tablets of Ten Commandments to Moses. Noah's ark may come with motors and sails, the way boats are supposed to. The impulse is to render the attempts orthodox and to teach the children how to make their art conform to an approved standard set by those in control.

Those are simply snapshots of what goes on in many institutions where children learn how to draw or, more important to the teacher who represents adult achievement, how to conform. Systematically, as she hears fantastic stories and jarring poems and sees plenty of true-to-life pictorials, she will do what is required at each stage to push the child's mind into channels where only a small measure of brain power kicks in and model drawings come out. It is easy to imagine what such stifling and dimming does to the religious imagination or the mysterious character of the child. This is so especially since scriptures, stories, and even dogmas deal with wild, hard-to-imagine claims and teachings, representations that go far beyond the images of the asymmetrical house, the purple tree, or the many other symbols and objects that get pressed into molds in the mind. As I have already implied, that portrait of the kindergarten teacher who was eager to control and teach conformity in order to limit imagination has begun to be out of date and often survives in the form of a caricature. Many teachers of the very young have been reached during their college years, in workshops, or by prompting colleagues and know much more about how to stimulate the imaginations of young children than I do.

Next we turn to stories. So far, only in passing have we cited "listening to stories" as an enhancement of wonder and an instrument for helping the child gain perspective on the other. The historian in me favors attention to stories, the enactment of stories, and the play that accompanies them because they stimulate and enhance wonder in the child. I'd like to think that the observation of some storytelling scenes will produce its own point. Donald Ratcliff gathered writings by some people with know-how to present a handbook of preschool religious education. In it the editor himself and a number of the authors discuss how wonder and awe relate to more formal education, beginning with preschool education, and how this occurs through the use of story.

Rather than overwork the by-now-familiar negative issues of management and control, Ratcliff sets out positively to discuss what it means to occupy the attention of children through congenial activities, beginning with play, especially through what he calls "the enactment of stories." These fictional means help lure the child into realistic ways of dealing with "the other," through the hinged open door that we associate with the experience of wonder.[8]

Play can be spontaneous, generated by the children themselves in their "let's pretend" hours. The studied enactment of stories is less impromptu; ordinarily in such cases adults read a story, begin to interpret it, and assign roles for children to act it out. In the enactments that follow, playing helps prepare children for this use of their imaginations. Because in such enactments children have to enter into the persona of someone else and play his or her part, the opportunities for educational growth are vast. So is the danger for the child of not knowing where the particular story ends and where realities beyond the story are posed.

Handle with care is the advice given to those who select stories to be told to children, as opposed to stories invented by them.[9] A good illustra-

8. Donald Ratcliff, ed., *Handbook of Preschool Religious Education* (Birmingham, AL: Religious Education Press, 1988), 247.

9. See Ratcliff, ed., *Handbook of Preschool Religious Education,* 252-55, for comment on the selection of stories by adults.

tion of this boundary issue is most familiar in preschools or homes that leave room for religious narrative, in this case, the most familiar one, the Christmas story about the birth of Jesus. The narrative in the Gospel makes reference to the world that the contemporary child already may know from home life, because the reference to the manger and to the baby's protecting parents translate in good fashion to the ways children experience reality, or yearn to. There is a shadow story, however, that is integral to the plot. Moving too far and too fast into the biblical narrative by concentrating on the role of murderous King Herod instead of the generous Wise Men brings children to the horrendous story of the slaughter of the innocents at Bethlehem. That story strikes fear into the child, who understandably identifies with those slaughtered infants.

Because some biblical stories are so ghastly that they offer no positive possibilities, most preschool teachers and parents of the young do not need as much help as Ratcliff gives them. Thus, in case no one had noticed, he instructs: "Clearly not all biblical content is appropriate – obvious examples are Jael's murder of Sisera (Judges 4) and the rape of Tamar (II Sam. 13)." Of course. We can think of hundreds more. Even within approved stories there have to be clear emphases. Children may love the drama of the story of Noah, especially because of the part animals play on the ark. They may listen eagerly as Noah receives instruction and when floods come. Overlooked is the fact that this is not a story to tell among the youngest, for it portrays the character of God that, in isolation from context, is devastating. In it, God comes across as tyrannical and hyperjudgmental. The child reasonably asks, Weren't *some* people in the world around Noah innocent and weren't they being treated unfairly by a God who, the teacher had been saying, was supposed to represent, even to *be,* love?

Everyone who deals with children in Christian, Jewish, and Muslim contexts of faith knows how these stories reach the imagination of the young. Though some adult Christians – I wouldn't want to overestimate their number! – may adhere first, last, and most profoundly to dogma, as Jews and Muslims do not, the thoughtful among them know that the believers relate their faith and guidance largely to story, which means to those narratives in the Bible as well as to interpretations of biblical stories. Stories are more graspable because they communicate experiences and inspire experience and do not merely impart knowledge of a sort that the child may not so readily process. Even many nonreligious educators are aware of biblical stories and can chronicle the way these go into shaping values, because "the cosmic drama" in which each life plays a part gets realized and interpreted most impressively through such stories.[10]

When the Stories Speak of the Things of God

For most humans, the experience of wonder and its expression in stories and in play find focus and reach to the ultimate in the form of a character they are taught to name God. Some psychologists and educators have asked whether adults who wish to do so can both stimulate creativity and teach about God in ways appropriate for children. Ratcliff's colleagues E. Paul Torrance and J. Pansy Torrance ask that question and answer it in ways that will stimulate the inquiries of others. The two criticize teaching that is dominated by "mechanistic concepts which assume determinism in human learning." Parents not drawn to the God of the Bible may not have to deal with this issue, but the majority of citizens, bringing spiritual concerns, do. So they have reason to listen as the Torrances stress: "Our primary objection to current learning theories is that they rarely consider the infinite God" and as such are "not in harmony with the biblical teachings concerning the nature of man as being creative, made in the image and likeness of God." In sum, they are short on mystery.

> Being born in the image and likeness of God, as we see it, makes people wonderfully complex. In fact, it gives humans a touch of the infinite in terms of the way they learn and in what they are able to learn. Most learning theories tend to oversimplify the learning process and deal with mankind in finite ways.
>
> In our opinion, the weight of present evidence suggests that individuals fundamentally prefer to learn in creative ways. Teachers at all levels of education, both religious and secular, have generally insisted that it is more economical to learn by authority.[11]

Adults may be tempted to cite authority when indoctrinating children, but they can learn better through free and imaginative means. Usually this involves telling and hearing stories more than having "biblical truths" and commands pounded into them. For a story to have positive effect there has to be some corollary between it and the experience of

10. Ratcliff, ed., *Handbook of Preschool Religious Education,* 265.

11. E. Paul Torrance and J. Pansy Torrance, "Creativity and Teaching Concepts of God," in Ratcliff, ed., *Handbook of Preschool Religious Education,* 224.

the child. Adults are often tempted to ridicule or rule out the most interesting inquiries that curious children ask, and thus they stifle the impulse of children to ask the deepest questions in an environment that ought to be protective and encouraging.

It is in the case of questioning and pondering that the mystery of the child best comes to light in the earliest years. The Torrances celebrate the fact that in such transactions, children "have not yet abandoned creative ways of learning by questioning, inquiring, searching, manipulating, experimenting, and playing; in their own way they are always trying to find out the truth." Such a sentence is another implied indictment of conventional approaches. The authors' word "yet" suggests that as the child grows, the learning environment will discourage much of what goes along with questioning and experimenting on the part of the youngest. When children "discover" something about God, they want to report on their experience, but they are often stifled by protective and nervous adults who fear that three-year-olds will develop unorthodox ways and inaugurate errant mini-churches on their own.[12]

When children are dealing with the Bible, the stories they tell will often include unfamiliar twists on the plot and many surprises, because the children improvise them. Sometimes these adaptations give adults new ways to think about the same stories or themes. The teller and the hearer will have a chance to escape the humdrum, the forms of retelling that kill creativity, limit the imagination, and hinder the understanding of the mystery of the child. W. J. Gordon has even invented a term to cover what we have just called the "unfamiliar." He calls it "synectics," "the principle of making strange things familiar, or familiar things strange" in a version of brainstorming.[13] The unfamiliar term provides a promising approach to the narration and enactment of overfamiliar stories. We hear this when commentators on the Christmas story and other familiar accounts are forced to find fresh angles of vision.

Biblical stories are well poised to elicit synectic responses and experiments, especially concerning talk about God and the experience of God. Let children give their version of Jonah and the whale or, with higher risk, the resurrection of Jesus, and new insights will emerge. Thus: if the groundhog comes back every February 2, only to go back into its refuge,

12. Torrance and Torrance, "Creativity and Teaching Concepts of God," 225-26.

13. Torrance and Torrance, "Creativity and Teaching Concepts of God," 229; they are citing W. J. Gordon, *Synectics: The Development of Creative Capacity* (New York: Harper and Row, 1961).

why does not Jesus go back into the tomb after he comes back on Easter? If Jesus "died to take away our sins" but rose on the third day following, did he bring our sins back with him? In any company I've known, to bring up one or two such interpretations is to inspire a round of "my grandchild said . . ." encores.

The rendering of strange things familiar and familiar things strange will often lead to stories and conversations that veer toward the fantastic. Although the time will come for the child to learn to separate fantasy language from God-talk, there are good reasons to encourage fantasy as a tool for learning before that time. Fantasy, which belongs to the pursuit of mystery, can also be an instrument that allows for a solution to problems. Russian child psychologist K. Chukowsky may have shocked some of the staid when he argued that fantasy is "the most valuable attribute of the human mind and should be diligently nurtured from earliest childhood," but he was onto something that adults can encourage as children set out to form concepts of God in their particular traditions. He illustrates this with reference to discovery in the sciences:

> Without imaginative fantasy, there would be complete stagnation in both physics and chemistry, because the formulation of new hypotheses, the invention of new implements, the discovery of new methods of experimental research, the conjecturing of new chemical fusion — all these are products of imagination and fantasy.[14]

I have occasion to think of this role of imagination on the way to discovery daily because my desk faces a beautifully framed example of Chinese calligraphy. The characters can be translated as "Discovery is our business." Emily Fine, daughter of Nobel Prize–winning biological scientist Charles Huggins, gave it to me in 1977 out of friendship and because I spoke at Professor Huggins's memorial service. He had received the Nobel "for his discovery that prostate cancer could be slowed by shutting off the male hormone testosterone," and he became known as a father of chemotherapy. That motto about discovery, taken from his wall, served him as he spent sixty years experimenting with the fantastic in science. I've seized on it as an inspiration in the humanities, including theology. The texts with which humanists and theologians work come from ancient times and diverse cultures, but they are always open to fresh interpretations — interpretations often advanced by children. "Discovery is their business."

14. Torrance and Torrance, "Creativity and Teaching Concepts of God," 232, citing K. Chukowsky, *From Two to Five* (Berkeley: University of California Press, 1963).

Fantasy can help a person link childhood with adult creative achievement. The Torrances offer implied counsel that matches our conception. If there is not some emerging picture of God in the minds of children, they say, there is little point in trying to teach about anything in which God is an agent, such as baptism, the Lord's Supper, and the Bible, or, in Judaism and Islam — both of which formally prohibit images — about the prophets and the law. Adults who turn children loose in the use of their imaginations usually set forth a very few rudimentary concepts in the spirit of "try these on." "Love," "infinity," and "spirit" were the most urgent themes discovered in one study.[15] Dive in too far along the way in approaching a grasp of these, and imaginations will be stifled and children bored or stunned.

The Torrances ask a question that must cross the mind of most adults in a classic case like this: "What does a preschooler think when she sings, 'We thank you for sending Christ, the Savior, to take our sins away?'" Instead of abandoning children in the chaos such a line elicits, the Torrances involved children in actions that explored the three concepts of love, infinity, and spirit. They encouraged children to look at wonders in the up-close excitement of the universe that surrounded them, while they sang songs that matched these concepts. Children learned to do loving things in play. The couple experimented with colors, sounds, and the feel of love. Children found suggestions that they might do loving things for the sick, make something for persons they love, or play games about love and friendship. They also played games that suggested infinity. They could take chances on "God" in all such experiments, a God not hemmed in and limited by teacher-set boundaries. Before long children were beginning to get the concept of the time and space that separated them from the ancient Israel about which they spoke.[16]

Along with Art and Stories: Providing for Play

Fantasy and stories double back into the great eruption of the mystery of the child at play. Watching children at play when play is not controlled and rendered routine by pushy adults is a practice that reveals the imaginative capacities of children and provides a window on the mystery that is

15. Torrance and Torrance, "Creativity and Teaching Concepts of God," 234.

16. Torrance and Torrance, "Creativity and Teaching Concepts of God," 235, 237, 244-45.

the child. The portrayer of the house or the tree can picture a number of options and then seek out alternatives. Children make up games or improvise new rules for games and – observe them closely – can often think ahead to envision many options and possibilities, just as a chess player reckons with future moves to be made by herself and the opponent. That feature of chess may help explain its appeal among those children in the ghetto who, given a chance, often excel in it. Children play "pretend like . . ." and then work out some of the possibilities that follow. More and more observers notice that children creatively carry over into "real life" their ways of dealing with alternatives and their thinking through the consequences of the one chosen. They can engage in wishing, free associating, and putting emotions to work at the expense of humdrum logic. At their best, they can keep this imagination alive even when they have to slow down physically in later years.

As with imagination, so with play itself. We are not going to dip into the enormous libraries, curricula, and kits in the how-to category in the contemporary world. We will not show how to play but will address questions that have to do with the *why* of playing. The entrée to this ensuing discussion, another virtual conversation, is *Man at Play,* by Hugo Rahner, brother of Karl, with whom we have been sustaining a dialogue. Far apart as the disciplines of the two men may have been, they complement each other, and their work informs issues that concern us. While we are roving on Jesuit literary soil, we can also profit from the work of the late Walter J. Ong, S.J., a friend and mentor of mine who wrote the introduction to the English edition of Hugo Rahner's book. His introduction and translation appeared in 1967, at the height of the time when our generation, then young, was especially engrossed with various causes of freedom. These included the civil rights movement and efforts to see our nation extricated from the war in Vietnam, which we regarded as immoral and futile. "Freedom!" was our fiercely chanted theme and radical focus in studies of liberation struggles as they were being fought, especially among African Americans, among Catholics in Latin America, and in the early stages of women's liberation movements everywhere.

In his introduction, Ong reminded readers of a theme that strongly supports an aspect of the mystery of the child: that the world of play is "the world of freedom itself – of activity for its own sake, of spontaneity, of pure realization." We see that in every child and in a few adults at play. Play helps keep the child visible, but in the causes and struggles for freedom all that changes. "The child," he stresses, "so often disappears." Today, Ong continued, "we seldom associate freedom with play. Freedom is grim – something to be fought for, something that we feel may confront us with antagonisms and even hatred instead of generating effusiveness and spontaneity and joy."[17] One wonders whether the fading, collapse, or co-opting of some of the freedom movements resulted in part from reaction to this grimness, to the uncompelling joylessness of many in the struggle. No doubt too many participants left behind themselves the redeeming features of childhood that kept a few of the enduring leaders buoyant in the face of often depressing odds.

Remaining playful in some modes of expression cannot have been easy. I am always mindful of something Albert Schweitzer, musical genius and physician among Africans, once said: that it is not natural for a person to bounce out of bed in the morning with a smile and a carefree way when faced with the need to share the burdens of those who suffer injustice, disease, misery, and lack of freedom. After I read that, it occurred to me, however, that Schweitzer's devotion to the pipe organ that he had installed in his African hospital – he was a world-famed organist and musicologist – was for him a version of compensatory, correlative, and redemptive play.

In my own early adult years as I read Ong's introduction to Rahner, I would look at Martin Luther King Jr., who did not strike the world of old people as being playful, or at Dorothy Day and the Catholic Workers, who were equally serious. They had forbidding tasks and often pursued them soberly, their somber countenances reflecting their purposefulness and resolution. What endures from their struggles are the recollections, now reinforced in some memoirs and biographies, of people who had perspective on themselves, who could laugh and play without losing *gravitas* when it was appropriate, and who outlasted many of the "Sunday soldiers" who briefly invested intense but superficial commitments to the causes.

I cannot suppress one personal reference. My late wife and four sons were with me in the summer of 1961 for my week of lecturing in colleagueship with Dr. King as the preacher at the Hampton Institute in Virginia. Four hundred African American pastors were there getting signals, especially from King, and the days were demanding. In the evening, deacons from neighboring black churches would ask him, beyond the call of duty, to preach to their congregations late at night, and he did. Still he had time to do a bit of playful roughhousing with my sons, and the older ones among them recall how he would prop the one-and-a-half-year-old on a

17. Walter Ong, preface to Hugo Rahner's *Man at Play,* trans. Brian Battershaw and Edward Quinn (New York: Herder and Herder, 1967), ix.

lower tree branch, urge him to jump, and then catch him. Dr. King might lightheartedly chase another around a tree. Such gestures — seen only by us, not staged for the press — told us all much about how such a figure could sustain himself when life was on the line.

Another who kept a playful spirit — in this case through devotion to music — when life was on the line was Lutheran pastor and theologian Dietrich Bonhoeffer, executed by the Nazis whom he had tried to subvert, near the end of World War II. He was in prison and had good reason to anticipate imminent death, as his smuggled-out or cryptic letters suggested. Yet his taste in reading and his reflections on music revealed an almost childlike faith, including a faith in the value of art. That he concentrated or relaxed by playing over in his mind the music of Johann Sebastian Bach or Georg Friedrich Handel is not so surprising. But he could juxtapose reference to them with comment on bawdy musical words he had heard on the radio:

> I heard lately on the wireless (not for the first time) some scenes from Carl Orff's operas (and also *Carmina Burana*). I liked them very much; they were so fresh, clear and bright. He has also produced an orchestral version of Monteverdi. Did you know that? I also heard a *concerto grosso* by Handel, and was again quite surprised by his ability to give such wide and immediate consolation in the slow movement, as in the *Largo,* in a way in which we wouldn't dare to any more.[18]

Were I on death row, my instinct would not be to engage in such music criticism, or in care for relatives' children, as Bonhoeffer did in his letters. That is another way of saying that my kind and I have much to learn about the role of art, music, play, and children.

Ong, in the introduction to *Man at Play,* observed that a pugnacious understanding of freedom arrived with the modern age. At that time freedom became a "cause" that, he said, "with or without explanation, . . . tend[ed] to outlaw play." Play, thus outlawed and suspect, the priest contended, strikes moderns as being "inconsequential, beneath the adult's dignity, something one descends to or 'indulges' in, something childish."

Important for our understanding here is Ong's contention that "play and work derive from the same source in man's life world." To our point is this question: "When the infant first begins to use the powers which are latent within him and by using them to develop them, is he

18. Dietrich Bonhoeffer, *Letters and Papers from Prison,* trans. Reginald Fuller, rev. Frank Clarke and others (New York: Macmillan, 1967), 194.

working or playing? When he flexes his muscles, crows and coos to himself and others all day long, takes his first steps — is this *Spass* or *Ernst,* 'fun' or 'for real'?" Ong answers that there is no way to sort all this out and separate the two; the answer is both. Where both work and play enter the child's world, the potential for learning is maximal. As for the balance of two parts of life, does work take more effort than play? Not necessarily; ask the athlete. Ong regards the literature about play to be apposite for Christian thought, "which is concerned with a God who is good and thus 'diffusive of himself,' spontaneously and freely giving first existence and then redemption to his creatures, who are thus the result of his play — only not in any sinister sense but in a positive and constructive sense." In lines that underscore the theme of *The Mystery of the Child,* Ong writes:

> God's activity toward and in all his creation is like that germinal, undifferentiated activity of the child, which is both work and play, both serious application and spontaneous activity for its own sake. Thus only those who "become as little children" can enter the kingdom of heaven. In the natural life of the child, however, the juncture of work and play is fragile and doomed: soon life will cleave in two, and work and play will drift apart, even though they never entirely lose contact with one another. With God such separation never comes. God's work is always play in the sense that it is always joyous, spontaneous, and completely free.[19]

Hugo Rahner opens *Man at Play* with a sacred text from the apocryphal Ecclesiasticus 32:15-16 [11-12], which he noted was favored by Thomas Aquinas. Rahner's rendering from the German does not quite match the English translations that I consulted. In that text is this counsel: "Run home to thy house and there withdraw thyself, play and do what thou hast a mind." The more wan translations typically read, "When it is time to leave, tarry not; be off for home! There take your ease, and there enjoy doing what you wish" (New American Bible). The New Jerusalem Bible reads, "Leave in good time, do not bring up the rear, and hurry home without loitering. There amuse yourself, and do what you have a mind to." And from the New Revised Standard Version: "Amuse yourself to your heart's content." All this appears after Sirach, the presumed author, has offered detailed lessons in etiquette to the host at a banquet, a host who is to bring the event to an end so he can hurry home.[20]

19. Walter Ong, preface to Rahner's *Man at Play,* ix, xi, xii, xiv.

20. Rahner, *Man at Play,* 1-2. Page references to this text will be given parenthetically in the text.

In ways helpful to us in our concern for the mystery of the child, classicist Rahner, who was at home with Greek wisdom, displayed his enjoyment of stories that he could associate also with the Christian tradition. Thus he cited Aquinas, who retold a story of the apostle John, as first narrated in the *Collationes* of Cassian. Therein the aged apostle, it was said, liked to play with a partridge, and when he did so, as one version had it, he elicited the charming remark: "Nay, mark how this old man plays with a bird – just like a boy!" Neither for Thomas Aquinas nor for Hugo Rahner did this mean that the apostle John had become senile in "a second childhood." Rather, it pointed to the enduring character of the true child in the aged adult who is a model (p. 3).

Moderns, Rahner complains, often lose the apostle's ability to play. He cites Elisabeth Langgässer, who argued that the modern person "has become a being without mystery and a mere part of the ordered mass of termites of which one is indistinguishable from another" (p. 5). Here we can deduce what other authors who held this viewpoint would confirm: that the ability to play, as is the case in the world of the young, is connected with the very mystery of the child. Rahner argues that Carl Jung, K. Kerényi, and other students of myth "have behind them some vague awareness vehicled by the Christian truth that only 'little children' will enter the kingdom of heaven," and he adds his gloss: "Eternity will in fact be what the Paradise we have lost was – a divine children's game, a dance of the spirit, and the soul's becoming flesh in a way that is at long last wholly and eternally perfect" (p. 8).

Rahner, though leading readers through the mazes of Greek myths that may not be familiar, keeps them on course. He notes that "all the myths tell of an infant god. Dionysus, Hermes, Apollo, Heracles were, in the first instance, all world-creating children." They are "mythical expressions of the divine nature, of the timeless being-at-work even in the child – of him who is everlastingly and irresistibly formative and creative, knowing all things and doing all things, but as a child would know and do them – in fact, of the God who brings forth everything, as it were, in play" (pp. 16-17).

Foraying into Greek mythology may seem to be like taking a walk on a bypath, because most treatments of the child do not lead us through Theban myths. Yet some of the imagery the ancients used, including reference to playthings, reinforces our stress on play and demonstrates that by no means were all the classics written by or about dour or cruel adults. Thus, to picture the divine act of creation as play elevates and illumines play in the lives of children. This link was imaged when the ancient church father Clement of Alexandria preserved a fragment from the Orphic world, in which "the infant Dionysus plays with the bright playthings of which the world is made up: 'tops of different kinds and dolls with moving limbs, apples too, the beautiful golden ones of the clear-voice daughters of Hesperus.'" In that context Rahner goes further. In the Theban myth of Cabiri, the toys of the child are features of creation, and the infant Zeus has a nurse, Adrastea, who fashions the sphere that is the beautiful ball of the earth, with which he plays on Mount Ida. Eros and Aphrodite play a "fateful" ball game in the *Argonautica.* In all these myths, the world was created not under some kind of constraint but out "of the gay spontaneity of God's mind; in a word, it came from the hand of a child." Rahner encourages us to find still more illumination in Plato's *Timaeus,* where the infant Logos holds the sphere of the world within his playing hands, in the role of the *Logos-pais,* the Logos-child. Medieval pictures of Christ holding the apple still reflect this playfulness. Reference to him leads Rahner to deal with play in the Christian orbit (pp. 17-18)

Those devoted to imagination and play when commenting on the mystery of the child do not have to be content with mythology. Rahner next quotes from canonical scripture, Proverbs 8:30, where the character Wisdom picks up a theme similar to what we have seen among the Greeks, but now it is played out in front of the Creator. Wisdom says, "I was beside the master craftsman, delighting him day after day, ever at play in his presence, at play everywhere on his earth, delighting to be with the children of men" (New Jerusalem Bible).

In the Wisdom sphere of biblical poetry, these lines from Proverbs confirm Rahner's emphasis, though his translation of Proverbs 8:27-31, including "a little child," is only one possible reading of the ancient Hebrew:

> When he established the heavens, I was there, . . .
> when he marked out the foundations of the earth,
> then I was beside him, like a little child;
> and I was daily his delight,
> rejoicing before him always,
> rejoicing in his inhabited world
> and delighting in the sons of men.

The alternative reading to "a little child" — the only time the phrase appears in Scripture — is "a master workman." Rahner would have no trouble with that built-in textual ambiguity. He even found some commentaries that bring the child as Wisdom into the divine Trinity: "The

Son is called a child because of his proceeding everlastingly from the Father, because in the dewy freshness and springtime beauty of his eternal youth he eternally enacts a game before his Father" (pp. 19, 23). As is the case with so much in *Man at Play,* this is another amazing picture, because for Rahner the divine Trinity has to be the ultimate Reality, and the Son, within it, the incarnation of God's self. Yet here that Son is "called a child." Rahner brought the chapter to a climax with a quotation from Maximus:

> We ourselves, begotten and born like the other beasts, we who then become children and move forward from youth to the wrinkles of old age, we who are like flowers which last but for a moment and who then die and are transported into that other life – truly we deserve to be looked upon as a children's game played by God. (p. 25)

That is another astonishing passage, the kind of insight or affirmation that helps a person come to a new understanding of the self. Religious people picture humans as clay or clods, dust of the earth, frail flesh, embodied souls or ensouled bodies. We could picture a true revival of the spirit if humans were seen, yes, as beasts, but also as "a children's game played by God." That picture should provide perspective to the overly serious and inspiration for the child who is seeking an identity.

We can connect Rahner's Wisdom-based picture of God, or its vision of a playful God, with our understanding of the mystery of the child in the way Plotinus did:

> [We] affirm All things strive towards *theoria* [the Greek word *beholding,* behind our word *theory*], the vision of God. Does that mean that this treatise of mine is itself nothing but a kind of game? For, after all, things that play, play only because of their urge to attain to the vision of God, whether they are the seriousness of the grown man, or the play of the child. (p. 29)

In this context, Rahner asked, what are Christian saints "after all but men who enacted for our benefit a children's game played before God, a game from which every vestige of the tragic has completely disappeared?" (p. 36). Ordinarily saints appear as scowling or doleful figures in icons and paintings. In a play-centered understanding, they would be at play – still serving others, as they did on their path to sainthood.

Maximus, whom we have just met, went so far as to say of Gregory Nazianzen, another ancient church father who spoke of God's playing:

"This children's game of which Gregory speaks is the incarnation, which so completely overrides *(huperousioos)* all the natural limits of the natural order that, foreseeing it, the prophet David could say: 'In the greatness of thy strength shall thy enemies lie to thee' (Ps. 65.3)." Clement of Alexandria also spoke of the perseverance of the faithful, a pretty grim business though it appeared to be, as being like "the mystical children's game *(mystike paidia)*" (pp. 47-49).

The Hebrew Scriptures themselves are admittedly less mystical, more realistic, though in one case tinged with what later generations might call utopianism. Zechariah (8:4-5, New Jerusalem Bible) foresees the messianic age with its promise for people of all ages.

> Aged men and women once again will sit
> in the squares of Jerusalem,
> each with a stick to lean on
> because of their great age,
> and the squares of the city will be full
> of boys and girls
> playing there.

Cyril of Alexandria, still another ancient favored by Rahner, interprets this, too: "Boys who have not yet attained man's estate, little girls — this means the multitude of those who are as little children *(nepiotate elethos)*, those who have only just received the faith. It is they who, with their spiritual leaping and dancing, make so beautiful this really holy city which is the Church" (p. 50). Not all our readers are concerned with the church, but in a society in which the majority *is* so concerned, it is delicious to picture how improved church life would be were it taken up less with bureaucracy and routine, conventions and arguments, and more with little boys and girls "spiritually leaping and dancing," at play.

Jerome, one of the most scholarly of the ancient Christians, extends the vision: "May the streets of the city be full of boys and girls playing. This can only be when a city enjoys profound peace and security. . . . [H]er children shall say with David as they dance the solemn step *(tripudiante saltatus)*: 'I will dance and play before the face of the Lord'" (p. 51).[21] The harsh freedom-seeking adult world offers many kinds of visions of a

21. Rahner on occasion cites the Septuagint, the Greek translation of the Hebrew Scriptures, and neither the locations nor the translations always match the texts in the Bible as known by most Jews or Christians today. I have simply reproduced the translations from Rahner by Brian Battershaw and Edward Quinn.

peaceful and secure future, but seldom does it envision the play and dance of children in the streets as being central. Ong and Rahner would place them there.

Those testimonies from the ancient world might suggest that only very old stories and images can inform the vision of play in the mystery of the child today. Rahner gives us evidence of the enduring theme when he moves from the Bible and these ancients to reach into his own twentieth century for this from Carl Jung:

> The child is all that is abandoned and exposed and at the same time divinely powerful; the insignificant dubious beginning, and the triumphal end. The "eternal child" in man is an indescribable experience, an incongruity, a disadvantage, and a divine prerogative; an imponderable that determines the ultimate worth or worthlessness of a personality. (p. 63)

Those lines may be heavy going, but they support the simple contention that the element of play, as it lives on through all of life, does not leave the adult "childish" or the senior in a "second childhood." Instead it points to the focus of it all: seeing the "eternal child" as helping determine the worth of the person. One will not participate in any of that by limiting the imagination of the small child or limiting the element of play among children and the adults they are to become. Rahner offers a fresh spin on texts from the Gospels that we have already cited when he associates the advice to change and become like children with one of the main things children do, namely play.

> The child in man desires to play — and the final answer to that longing, the answer of truth to all our searchings, is the word of him who being himself the Word, became a little child: "Unless you become as little children, you shall not enter into the kingdom of heaven." (Matt. 18:3) That is why the streets of the heavenly city will be full of playing children and the Ancient of Days, whose face is forever young, will never cease to say to men: *"Ite et ludite."* [Go and play.] (pp. 63-64)

7. The Child's Self – in Circumstances

After theologian Karl Rahner almost incautiously pictured the little child as a kind of mirror, model, and analogy to the divine mystery, he planted his feet on the ground again, as we will now do. He wrote that "we can then turn our gaze back once more to the child in a biological and social sense as well." Turning to and acknowledging biological and social sciences might seem to be risky for anyone who is exploring the mystery of the child. It *is* risky, chiefly because the temptation in such pursuits is to reduce the child, to see her as "nothing but" that biological product. Coming from the other direction, however, the generous attention we have given to the mystery of the child in a transcendent context, as in the phrase "kingdom of heaven," can give the impression that we have forgotten to talk about mundane children. Bringing the transcendent and the mundane together inspires a delicate balancing act, but one with much promise for anyone who is to provide care for and to enjoy a child.

It may be that using the biblical language of the kingdom is misleading, but it need not be. Even princes and princesses in any kind of kingdom live lives that are in many respects ordinary. Most decisions that children make or that are made for them will be straightforwardly practical, and they do not need to be burdened by imported references to the transcendent. Some sectarian fundamentalists may insist that their religion embodies and offers all that needs to be known about the human person. The majority of citizens, including believing people, however, do not seek or find anything technically different when they enlist help from a member of one religious body as opposed to an adherent of another. Thus one does not seek Mormon or Catholic brain surgery, Buddhist auto repair, or Sikh plumbing. The customers of mechanics or physicians ordinarily insist on the best delivery of services on a nonsectarian basis and have no reason to take religious commitments into consideration when they seek such services. To speak of such transactions as practical and secular is not to regard them as anti-sacred or anti-scriptural. The word *secular,* after all, comes from the Latin *saeculum* and can simply refer to a reality that is "of this age," this time, this place.

To turn to discuss the secular, then, is to face the excitements and problems associated with the care of the child when science and practical disciplines have their say. Their say has often been centered on two alliterative terms, *nature* and *nurture,* which by now have been worked almost to death. Those who would provide care and show concern for the child do have to reckon with what both of these offer in the way of insight and prescription. Bringing forward the concern for the mystery of the child, as we are doing, will help breathe life into the terms and that to which they point. Just as the cleric is not equipped to offer medical diagnoses, biological and social scientists do not possess and do not always claim to possess a monopoly on competence in discussing nature and nurture. When providers of care and observers of children delve deeply, they confront mystery. They will find that concerns represented by the two terms overlap and intersect. Debates among biologists, psychologists, and therapists about the contributions and blights associated with the categories of nature and nurture have their place, and attitudes toward them will color approaches to the mystery of the child. We shall partly separate them out to aid in our diagnostic work and to see what light they shed on the question "What is a child?" and others that deal with providing care.

I Am Myself — and My Circumstances

Here I introduce corollary terms to *nature* and *nurture* that can enrich emphases on the mystery of the child. They derive from a saying by Spanish philosopher José Ortega y Gasset, whose thought on such subjects has strongly influenced my work and can guide some of our present inquiry. I italicize the two key words in a short sentence that summarized his philosophy and became his life motto: "I am *myself* and my *circumstances,* and if I do not save my circumstances, I cannot save myself."[1] He described

1. This phrase appeared in his first substantial book, *Meditaciones del Quijote.* In some contexts it makes most sense to translate it literally as "I am I," but in this chapter on the differentiated child's self we will cite the alternative preferred by Karl J. Weintraub: "I am

part of the life quest of all people as the "search for the sense of that which surrounds us."[2] The word *circumstance,* he liked to point out, had roots in the Latin *(circum + stantia)* and referred to "that which stands around us." Ortega never minimized the importance of the "I" (or, sometimes, "myself") and almost took it for granted when he spoke of the circumstantial reality as forming "the other half of my person."[3]

In the biblical stories we have considered, the children were in certain circumstances when they were brought to Jesus: they were children from particular homes in a particular culture and were brought by particular adults. The fact that they were not yet adolescent or adult in those stories meant that they could be described as "marginal," "unimportant," "unable to take care of themselves," "dependent on others." As the Gospels tell it, however, Jesus regarded the "I" of each as bearing great importance: he showed how in a way they represented "the other half" of Jesus' own person. Just as Jesus was part of their circumstance, those who stood around him were part of his. So rich is the dialectic, the interplay, and even the identification that — talk about mystery! — Jesus is heard saying, "Whoever welcomes one such child in my name welcomes me" (Matthew 18:5).

The Child's Self

Although the phrase "I am myself" does not correlate exactly with the "nature" side of the nature versus nurture polarity, it does point in that direction, just as "my circumstances" leans toward the "nurture" contribution to personhood. The child viewed as mystery in every case demonstrates that the two approaches to understanding intersect and overlap. Every reflective parent, teacher, or other provider of care for a child can attest to this overlapping. Failure to see the two in dynamic interaction at all points and in all events of childhood would lead to failure in relating to them.

The child regarded as a *problem* does come into the world with a genetic makeup that includes qualities that will limit or enlarge her chance

---

myself and my circumstances." Weintraub, *Visions of Culture* (Chicago: University of Chicago Press, 1966), 252.

2. Quoted in Robert McClintock, *Man and His Circumstances: Ortega as Educator* (New York: Teachers College Press, 1971), 5.

3. Quoted in Julián Marías, *José Ortega y Gasset: Circumstance and Vocation* (Norman: University of Oklahoma Press, 1970), 360.

to have impressive achievements. She may carry into the world what in the clinic come to be named genetic defects, predispositions to specific mental or physical illnesses, or inclinations that predetermine that she may get into trouble or create woe. In another child, the promise of good fortune is strong, thanks to his endowment of intelligence and the prospect of good health. He holds great promise in the eyes of those who are to provide for him and make decisions for and with him during his development. So rich is the complexity of that package that it can be tempting for evolutionary biologists, educators, and therapists to stress the "self" and its codes and underplay "the circumstances," which have such an apparently random character.

The child regarded as a *mystery* also comes into the world with a DNA package that will cause those who observe or care for her to foresee a life in which both threat and promise, misfortune and good fortune will be entangled. Those adults who are incurably sunny and optimistic when dealing with the child who stands before them and who foresee nothing but good have to learn to be realistic. The future is simply unknowable, and neither historians, sociologists, fortune-tellers, nor prophets can anticipate it. Accidents happen in the unknowable future that unfolds into the present every day in the life of the child. There is no stable point. In every age after the sacred books were written, new circumstances demanded fresh interpretations and applications of what was in them. Books on the economy or government written epochs ago may include wisdom for all ages, but relating that wisdom to new circumstances also demands constant efforts to be familiar with what is being learned in the successive periods and cultures, including our own. Adults still approach the infant with a sense of wonder, but they have different understandings of the processes of conception, gestation, and birth than did their ancestors. The particular sacred emphases of the old texts do not match in detail the faith or the nonfaith of everyone in a new day.

Providing care for the child commits adults inescapably and positively to employing scientific knowledge and beneficial technological expertise. The child is approached in fresh and ever-changing ways, thanks to instruments developed by psychologists, sociologists, educators, counselors, and religious researchers. New understandings of body, mind, and soul sometimes challenge and often replace the old inherited ones. It does the child little good to have parents and teachers who are so defensive about guarding ancient texts, so awed in contemplating the miracle of the child, or so rapt in wonder — on a child's good days! — that they neglect to put to work anything of value learned in the last two thousand years. Anyone who might fear that turning the page from archaic sacred texts to modern scientific texts will tempt or force an adult to "reduce" the child to "nothing but" this or that, at the expense of wonder, deserves immediate reassurance. The mystery remains in the scientific era and, I would argue, is now even enhanced. The more we know, the more occasions for wonder occur.

As I researched materials about the child and framed arguments about the provision of care, I grew more concerned that any expression of reservations that the child is "nothing but" this or that might be misread as a defense against scientific understandings and strategies. I pictured someone saying, "Yes, if you begin by frank and bold assertions that the infant is a child of God, a personal Creator, it is easy to stress the mystery." It remains easy to dwell on the mysterious dimensions so long as you stress transcendence on any ground. When you isolate the physical, biological, and chemical aspects, are you not saying good-bye to talk of mystery or leaving those who stress these aspects back at the starting gate where the precincts of mystery open themselves?

When such concerns pressed themselves on me, I found occasion to think about how mystery relates to strictly biological understandings. This is the case because every waking moment of a developing child's life is open to so many always surprising possibilities that attempts to anticipate everything, to explain anything completely, will be futile. Here is a sample of the number of such possibilities, from the writing of Arnold H. Modell, clinical professor of psychiatry at Harvard Medical School, a reliable representative of biology but one who tries to provide, as a chapter title suggests, "uncertain steps toward a biology of meaning":

> It is estimated that the human brain has 100 billion neurons and each neuron may have 10,000 synapses. This literally astronomical potential for synaptic connections in a human brain cannot be duplicated by computers; the scale of a computer-generated model for the brain is similar to that of an insect- or worm-sized brain. But even a worm-sized brain, such as *C. elegans* with its 302 neurons, is extremely complex.

Those who favor computer models of the brain will see algorithms as a functional unit of the mind. Their critics, says Modell, will note that "algorithms cannot account for thinking in images, for fantasy and imaginary thoughts, for error, or for novelty. How can the logic of the algorithm be applied to dreams and fantasies?" I am still pondering the "astronomical potential for synaptic connections" of even worm-sized brains, which should fill any reflective observer with wonder – and then I am asked to account for fantasy, imagination, and dreams, which are greater occasions for wonder and signals for the presence of mystery.[4]

Genes, neurons, and the chemical makeup of the brain awaken profound curiosity, and adult caregivers will always be reckoning with what scientists and philosophers discover and debate. Some years ago a University of Notre Dame television interviewer who was producing a series on spirituality surprised me with a startling and refreshing question: "When you meet your Maker, what will be your first question?" Immediately this came to mind: "I want to ask about neuron firings in the brain," from those hundred billion neurons and all those synapses and glial cells in that three-pound mess inside the skull. I want to ask this because when things go even a little bit wrong in the brain, the course of a child's life will be directed very differently from the way it will be when it appears to be going a little bit right. I see little reason to talk less about the mystery of the child among materialists than among those who come with spiritual interpretations to the same mass of brain and the same mess inside the skull.

Every adult who spends much time with children thus learns that their lives are distinctively shaped if what goes on in the chemistry of the brain predisposes them to what adults measure as genius or as obsessive-compulsive behavior, schizophrenia, attention deficit disorders, and other disorders. The parents who bring home from the maternity ward a child with Down's syndrome know that this aspect of the child's genetic makeup commits them to special kinds of care and understanding that will need to be sustained every day for the next several decades. In an impressive number of testimonies, such a child more often than not represents and quickens acts of love and generosity and learning that could not have been anticipated. Watching a child prodigy grow, caring for a child with autism, nurturing a hyperactive son, helping a little daughter cope with depression or eating disorders will be preoccupying endeavors. The need to understand these children will inspire research, laboratory or clinical work, efforts at discovery, and an increase in scientific knowledge that can inform child care and education. Anyone pondering the mystery of the child soon learns that the mystery has not been diminished because a certain kind of disposition shows up. Instead, one moves to the question that creative people voice when they come across an anomaly or a surprise that upsets their expectations: "Even so, what then?"

4. Arnold H. Modell, *Imagination and the Meaningful Brain* (Cambridge, MA: MIT Press, 2003), 8, 10.

When scientists talked of four elements — earth, air, fire, and water — they could treat them as mysteries. Though the number of recognized elements has grown, there is no reason to leave wonder behind. Conversations with astronomers and cosmologists on one end of the scale and with microbiologists on the other reveal wonder in the face of what is known and a recognition of mystery in the presence of what may never be known. Lines like this would be refreshing in the parental world: "So the child has a very high IQ? It is interesting to me to know that some of this comes from parental genes. Bizarrely, I may think that awareness of this may license me, the parent, to have bragging rights, as if I should take pride in something that was handed over to me through grandparental genes and does not represent an achievement about which I have any credentials to boast. Instead, I should put my energy into questions that have to do with the self-image of the child, with her humility or pride, with the choices she and we must make about her education and vocation."

If the child instead tends toward an eating disorder or depression, the parents will be asking what they must know, intend, and afford: will this child get appropriate medical care, be treated with proper pharmaceuticals, and offered helpful counsel, or will I pretend away her problems with a command like "Eat your food!" or "Cheer up!"? The parents will take the genetic issue into consideration, but whatever they learn from it will not diminish the number of questions still remaining about the depths of any particular situation.

The Child in His Circumstances

Suppose a parent has read enough in the scientific literature to become convinced that, whatever the apparently innate features of a particular child's neural package may be, his environment and influences on him will matter significantly in his destiny. Such an awareness and commitment will place other responsibilities on parents and teachers. They will do all they can to protect the child from sexual and other physical abuse, from negative mental influences, and the like. They will take care to help keep the child from being overwhelmed by violent images that come his way through mass media of communication. Who the playmates will be and what kind of nursery school he will attend will become urgent issues and will evoke life-changing decisions. Included in this are the religious milieux and circumstances. The child who attends church school in an environment conditioned by images of a scowling and threatening God is likely to grow up differently from one nurtured in an environment where God is a friend who is revealed and cherished as Love and who beckons that child to a secure place. As each event occurs during the development of the child, however, each influence invites reevaluations, each discovery leads to more knowledge, and what has really happened is the deepening of mystery. Why do some children succumb to certain negative influences and others face them and transcend them? These are causes for inexhaustible wondering. Solve all the problems of environment – an absurd notion to entertain even for a moment – and you will not have exhausted all that the child will encounter.

It is deceptively easier to have a child "all figured out" in the clinic or the laboratory than among chance circumstances in the social environment. Children do not spend their lives in test tubes or in research centers. Few of them exist long in solitary confinement. Instead, the manifold and complex interactions between the child and the people who make up his world offer rich possibilities for reaction and response. Although the finitude, contingency, and transience that David Tracy taught us to see in all mortal life are forever present, it is contingency that most threatens or gives promise to the being of the child when we approach the themes of circumstance and culture. The child we are contemplating might have been born as a poor Indian outcaste Hindu, as a rich Saudi princess, as a member of an African American church community whose elders sing praises while they accept her in wonder, as someone fending off physical threats in the ghetto, as a disaffiliated French Catholic secularist, or as a foster child being moved from one foster home to another. Those who deal with her cannot explain her, but they are ready to address problems that she occasions or experiences. Here is Ortega, speaking against the notion that the human has an essence:

> Man is that which has happened to him, what he has made. Other things could have happened to him, he might have made other things, but that which actually happened to him and that which he actually made, presents an unchangeable line of experience which he carries on his back as the vagabond carries his possessions. Man is the pilgrim of his being, he is substantially a wanderer. . . . [T]here is only one fixed line which is determined and given beforehand, which can orient or direct us: the past. The experiences which man made limit his future.[5]

5. Weintraub, *Visions of Culture*, 264.

The newborn knows nothing of being a "pilgrim of his being," and while he has started in the nursery on a life path that will lead to the grave, he does not know that he is "substantially a 'wanderer.'" He has to come out of the womb unaware of any history in the sense in which Ortega speaks of it. All of his subsequent life, however, he will keep on being initiated into a world that anteceded him. Trying to make sense of his surrounding world as he grows, the child as a little individual, in Ortega's phrase, cannot get his bearing in the universe except through his awareness of his people and their history. (Ortega says his "race," but that word has acquired a set of connotations that make it unusable here. That's another illustration of what circumstance and contingency can do, in this case to fundamental concepts.) The Spanish thinker elaborates: a person gets his bearing in his circumstance "because he is immersed in it like the drop of water in the passing cloud."[6] The child would not use such terms or even begin to bring such perspective to his actions and self-definition at least until he reaches adolescence, but as he progressively relates to family, school, friends, and nation, he is doing such grappling because that external world is puzzling, promising, and mysterious. The child becomes ever more aware of the natural instability of the life that surrounds him after he is no longer enjoying sheltered existence in the womb or nursery.

Ortega's images are worth unpacking and contemplating. The provider of care observes the child as the *vagabond,* the hobo or drifter who has casually filled a mental bag with the results of experiences. These might mean memories of trips to the hospital, delight in the birth of a cat, being embarrassed by Grandpa, who wants her to perform. The onlooker who is overseer is not content with the textbook definition of the child in genetic terms. He sees her as the *pilgrim* of her being. Like any pilgrim, she is uprooted from security when Grandma turns out the bedroom light, when a five-year-old friend offers a dare, when she plunges into a pool at the command of a teacher, or when the family pet dies. She is "on the way." Or the observer forgets about the essence of the child when observing him making history as a *wanderer.* The child goes forth, as Walt Whitman saw him going forth, plucking and offering a leaf of grass and asking questions about it, or going from house to house in the neighborhood, ringing doorbells and finding no one home when he is seeking directions to his own place. In all these cases, the littlest ones also are demonstrating what Ortega noted: "There is only one fixed line which is

6. Weintraub, *Visions of Culture,* 264.

determined and given beforehand, which can orient or direct" anyone: the past. That past may teach the four-year-old to avoid a vicious dog who threatened her yesterday, not to touch a hot radiator as she did last week, and to run to her parents' arms for comfort. "The experiences which [the child] made limit his future," we read, but they also open him to new possibilities.

Circumstances Defined as Culture

We have a name for what the circumstances add up to: *culture*. That is the setting in which the experiences of nurturing occur. Of course, the child would not speak of her circumstance, that which "stands around her," as culture. Most adults can do so only with caution, because it is such an ample and ambiguous concept. The child expresses involvement with it as she deals with companions on the playground and with the worlds they conjure. In her vision and vocabulary, culture might best be represented in stories. These can be stories of her family and her school, her nation and her friends, her ballet class or piano lessons, visits to her grandmother in a senior living center or outings to the state fair. Each of these helps her potentially to connect her own mystery with anything and everything that she perceives or experiences in her labyrinthine surroundings. Ortega offers a helpful definition that pushes to the abyss of mystery: "Cultures are the organs which succeed in grasping a small piece of the absolute yonder."[7] The child might ask what is behind the sky and what is behind what's behind the sky or whether her dead kitten went to heaven. The responses she receives will to a large extent depend upon the culture of which she is a part, and her reactions in turn will engage her ever further with the culture.

The child who reaches for the Calder mobile above the crib, who later learns after many a spill to ride a bike, who continually resists church-school lessons, and who is cajoled by his parents into believing that vegetarianism offers the best diet is being initiated into a variety of cultures. A culture makes possible a potentially rich base for addressing problems, including those that the child encounters. Culture, says Weintraub, paraphrasing Ortega, "is the repertory of solutions which men [and women *and children*] advance in response to the problems of their lives."[8]

7. Weintraub, *Visions of Culture,* 266.
8. Weintraub, *Visions of Culture,* 266.

This next line in Ortega may strike some as bizarrely premature or overstated in respect to the world of the child. Yet, be it of the playground, the church, the grandparents' farm, or the ghetto, the child's culture "is the conception of the world or the universe which serves as the plan, riskily elaborated by man, for orienting himself among things, for coping with his life, and for finding a direction amid the chaos of his situations."[9] It is fascinating to see a child's brow furrow when she is puzzled about the destiny of her dog that died. Watching adults cry in the face of a terrible event forces the child to make sense of their efforts to make sense of things. A child busies himself figuring out what to do about a bully or a disappointment, or how to celebrate friendship or a victory. Some will have heard a biblical story that pushes their imagination beyond boundaries or will wonder why parents retell familiar scary stories in unfamiliar ways. Watch a child play on monkey bars, try to loft a kite, fit a doll into a dollhouse, or master a new computer game, and you will see her being a part of culture, by whatever name one calls the environment and experiences.

It is not easy to find words for all this in the world and vocabulary of children. We used to enjoy telling the story of the time the German-born professor Paul Tillich began a lecture in his heavily Teutonic accent, "What child of six has not asked himself, 'Where do I belong in the structure of being?'" After chuckling, we listened more, and the longer we stayed around to hear the professor's elaborations, the more convinced we were that he was right — and also that in his naïve expression he was himself, in a way, being the child his friends knew this formidable scholar on occasion to be.

The Cases for Self and Circumstance, Nature and Nurture

To inform the debates separating those who stress the genetic package and programming of what is innate from those who stress experience and circumstance, we will listen in on a recent debate by two of the most significant figures in their field, public intellectuals of influence who bring skill to the task of framing issues, Steven Pinker and Richard Rorty. Adult providers of care probably do not wake up to their responsibilities in the morning and run to books by these two thinkers to gain points for winning arguments. More likely than not, most of them do not welcome the extremes represented in this polarity, but all would do well to become in-

9. Weintraub, *Visions of Culture,* 262.

formed about them, influential as they are in our culture, our complex of circumstances. As we read them squaring off in a scholarly journal, we are not mere bystanders but can use their debate to inform our inquiries about the mystery of the child.

Pinker looks for assured scientific accountings of what the person — in our case the child — is, and determines something of how to view, treat, and care for him. Richard Rorty asks a different set of questions and gets an answer that leads him to deride a quest like Pinker's. He does so for one main reason: the outcome of the scientifically reductionist stance in which the child is "nothing but" a biological and sociological entity, he says, does not help answer the important question: Which accounting for the person will provide advice on how human life is to be lived? It will be clear that Pinker does well to choose Ortega as the philosopher to oppose. Rorty, on the other hand, defends Ortega's concept of self and circumstances and moves beyond defense to suggest how one can begin to get guidance for life through approaches like his.[10]

The evolutionary psychologist Steven Pinker has set up Ortega as a foil because of one line especially, in which the Spanish philosopher contended, in perhaps too dramatic a contrast, that humans have no nature, but only a history. Pinker titles his essay in an argument staged in print for the American Academy of Arts and Sciences, "Why Nature and Nurture Won't Go Away." Of course, he makes the case for the pole called nature. Over against him, stressing not the "I am myself" in genetic isolation but the "I and [its] circumstances," is philosopher Richard Rorty, who begins by accusing Pinker of misinterpreting Ortega's saying that "we humans have a history rather than a nature" (Rorty, 18). Rorty's concern in quoting Ortega was to help counter those scientists who, he feared, would someday reduce the child to "nothing but" some genetic factors. Among these factors would be those that leave a mark in the child. These could include autism, a predisposition to being homosexual, having perfect pitch, being capable of lightning calculation, or other traits and abilities that differentiate some humans from others. Any of these might be found within the genetic heritage of a particular child, but they become of interest when that self meets circumstances.

The two contenders have somewhat different issues in mind and at some points talk past each other, but both speak clearly to the topic of

10. Page numbers in parentheses in the text will refer to pages in two articles — Steven Pinker's "Why Nature and Nurture Won't Go Away" and Richard Rorty's "Philosophy Envy" — in *Daedalus,* Fall 2004, 5-17 and 18-24, respectively.

our inquiry. Pinker deals with problems of behavior in the light of our inherited genes, and Rorty with theories of human experience that will color human development. Genes, Rorty readily acknowledges, *do* account for many sorts of behavior common to all humans, no matter in which culture. The evolutionary psychologists go wrong, however, in the eyes of this philosopher, when they suggest that tracing these back to the evolutionary needs of ancestors will help provide "a theory of human nature." Here Rorty has more to offer the practical provider of care among children, who listens in on the debate not idly or to satisfy intellectual curiosity but to learn more about relating to the child.

If the evolutionary biologists' theory were useful for such purposes, says Rorty, it should do what good theories in this category strive to do: offer guidance, tell people what to do with themselves, point to what may be better and worse ways for societies. *"A theory of human nature should tell us what sort of people we ought to become"* (Rorty, 18; italics added). Pinker argues in his turn that the efflorescence of the sciences of mind, brain, genes, and evolution in the past two centuries changes the nature of the inquiry about nature and nurture, essence and history. Few of the scientists on this front, he counters, are absolutists or ideologues who would deny *all* aspects of learning and culture. However, speaking for his camp, he stresses that evolutionary psychology is right to hold that there must be "complex innate mechanisms for learning and culture to be possible in the first place" (Pinker, 6). His kind of evolutionary psychologist, in our reading, sounds as sweeping in his claims as did theologians when they spoke of how human behavior in its detail was predisposed in a certain way thanks to what they called original sin. The psychologists, says Pinker, find hundreds of universals, aspects of human life that are present in all the world's cultures because of the human genetic inheritance. Thus today's humans, he argues, have a "taste for fatty foods, social status, and risky sexual liaisons," thanks to the evolutionary demands of our ancestry more than to the actual demands of the current environment. We don't need any of these, but our remote simian ancestors did, and we inherit the leftovers.

The line between the two is rather sharply drawn. Philosophers like Rorty who want to observe or make comments on theories that "tell us what sort of people we ought to become" deal with the status of the child. Evolutionary psychologists like Pinker speak less of status and more of inborn qualities.

What developmental psychologists are all about becomes clearest when they turn to children, as Pinker sees them doing, because they can show that "infants have a precocious grasp of objects, intentions, numbers, faces, tools, and language" and that temperament "emerges early in life and remains fairly constant throughout the life span." The human genome, he notes with accuracy, contains a "rich tool kit of growth factors, axon guidance molecules, and cell adhesion molecules that help structure the brain during development, as well as mechanisms of plasticity that make learning possible" (Pinker, 6). All this is to be said before one even considers circumstances, environments, and milieux in which nurturing occurs.

While Ortega stresses the environment, history, culture, and circumstances of the human child, and while Rorty advocates theories of human nature that depict how humans should live in various circumstances, Pinker keeps insisting on the primary role of the child's nature, referring to his genetic makeup: "In short, the existence of environmental mitigations doesn't make the effects of the genes inconsequential. On the contrary, the genes specify what kinds of environmental manipulations will have what kinds of effects and with what costs" (Pinker, 11). In what follows, Pinker, though he comes down on the side of nature in the classic debate, finds himself providing a bit of support for our "both/and" approach to the subject, which means the vision of the interaction at all points of what the genes carry and the environment provides:

> Though children are not pre-wired with cultural skills, they also are not indiscriminately shaped by their environment. One aspect of human nature directs children to figure out what is valued in their peer group — the social milieu in which they will eventually compete for status and mates — rather than [for example] to surrender to their parents' attempts to shape them. (Pinker, 16)

Rorty and others who share his kind of philosophical concern for qualities more than status, stress the child-in-relation. With that accent, Rorty draws on major figures to whom Pinker would give less heed, pointing out that Plato, Aristotle, Christian thinkers, and others who offered "philosophical and religious theories of human nature" steered clear of the empirical details of biological and sociological life. They did not need laboratories or clinics to set children on their way or to assess outcomes. Rorty noted how through the ages Christians spoke in relational terms and accented qualities of life, not status, when they said "that we are all children of a loving God" (Rorty, 18), even when bad things happened that seemed to provide countertestimony. Whole ways of life, philosophies of care, and strategies that changed history issue from such a proposal. There were vital alternatives to the Christian understandings, and Rorty cites some of these when he calls attention to those of Freud or Hobbes, who were useful, he writes, "not because they were accurate accounts of what human beings, deep down, really and truly are, but because they suggested perils to avoid and ideals to serve. They marketed helpful moral and political advice in fancy, disposable packaging" (Rorty, 18).

That last phrase may sound like a sneer, but Rorty has positive interests. Evidently the experiments of evolutionary psychologists and other scientists can be positive and do not need scrutiny, unless they move to an additional category of thinking. In that category, overstepping psychologists often claim predictive power and at least implicitly tell people how to live. Rorty addresses what providers of care have to keep in mind as they respond to the needs of children. They care about what the child, partly in their company, is to *become.* Rorty argues against Pinker that if the scientific theorists are "to make good on the promise of the term 'a scientific theory of human nature' [such proponents] would have to start offering advice about how we might become, individually or collectively, better people." Then, Rorty continues, having stuck their necks out, "they would have to spell out the inferences that had led them from particular empirical discovering about our genes or our brains to these particular practical recommendations" (Rorty, 19). They can tell much about the chemistry of our makeup, but they offer little that the one who deals with the mystery of the child favors most: asking questions about how to live.

While the reductionist psychologist is often portrayed as being avant-garde because of the interests he brings, Rorty instead finds an element of cultural lag. He observes that "in the last two centuries the notion that beneath all cultural overlays there lurks something called human nature, and that knowledge of this thing will provide valuable moral or political guidance, has fallen into deserved disrepute" (Rorty, 19). Major thinkers who oppose genetic determinists, he observes, now doubt "that insights provided by biology will ever help us decide which individual and social ideals to strive for." Here Rorty turns sharply:

> The books that change our moral and political convictions include sacred scriptures, philosophical treatises, intellectual and sociopolitical histories, epic poems, novels, political manifestoes, and writing of many other sorts. But scientific treatises have become increasingly irrelevant to this process of change. This is because, ever since Galileo, natural science has won its autonomy and its richly deserved prestige by telling us how things work, rather than, as Aristotle hoped to do, telling us about their intrinsic natures. (Rorty, 21-22)

Philosopher Rorty accuses scientists like Pinker of "philosophy envy," which he says is to be found among those ideological evolutionary psychologists who pride themselves on "the hardness of their disciplines." If they would stick to their empirical work, their critics would not fault them. As Rorty reads them, however, he sees them thinking "that their superior rigor qualifies them to take over the roles previously played by philosophers and other sorts of humanists – roles such as critic of culture, moral guide, guardian of rationality, and prophet of the new utopia" (Rorty, 22). Pouring on sarcasm, he continues that their advice is "get your self-image from the people who know what human beings really, truly, objectively, enduringly, transculturally are." Over against them he quotes Ortega:

> All the naturalist studies on man's body and soul put together have not been of the slightest use in throwing light on any of our most strictly human feelings, on what each individual calls his own life, that life which, intermingling with others, forms societies, that in their turn, persisting, make up human destiny. The prodigious achievement of natural science in the direction of the knowledge of things contrasts brutally with the collapse of this same natural science when faced with the strictly human element. (Rorty, 23)

In the end, Rorty has to show that he is living in the real world where the evolutionary thinkers dominate, so he acknowledges some evident debts to Darwin, who is not a misfit in Rorty's approach. I read "mystery" in the next sentence where Rorty does see that Darwin "let us see imaginative daring as a causal force comparable to genetic mutation" and helped poets dream of utopias in which human beings will have become as wonderfully different from us as we are from the Neanderthals. "Nothing that natural science tells us should discourage us from dreaming further dreams" (Rorty, 23-24). To speak in our terms in this book, nor should it discourage us from stimulating and nurturing a sense of wonder as we deal with the mystery of the child.

The Mystery of the Mind of the Child

Today not only neuroscientists are paying fresh attention to the mind of the child, as we have seen in the implications of philosopher Rorty's argument. A few specialists in philosophy who have taken pains to inquire of children are contending that young ones are in their own ways philosophers and that they ponder the mysteries of life, including of their selves and their circumstances, in ways that professional philosophers enjoy and from which they can learn. So long as grudging or neglectful approaches to the child's mind prevailed, her ideas, because she was "immature," seemed unimportant to scholars, educators, and therapists. They would wait and take interest when the child had matured to the point that she could read books and perhaps write them. Scholars also respected the aged sages and honored the minds of seniors. The child was seen as less interesting in part because she was not viewed as someone who could effect change in culture or society beyond the most intimate circle of the immediate family. Why pay attention to the babbler or scribbler? Adults knew how to gain power because they could threaten or offer promises, but the child possessed little bargaining power and normally could only wear a smile to win approval or throw a tantrum to gain attention. Such emotional responses affected only those who were in close range of a particular child. They were lost in the immense world of vocal, energetic, and muscular adults.

Conceiving of the child as mystery rather than beginning with the child as problem provocatively connects the world of human experience and nature with the mind of the child. It does not supersede or cancel out what is learned in the laboratory or the clinic, but it does provide additional perspectives and helps safeguard some valued elements in the life of the child that are at risk. Just as we have noted that specialists on the child in religious spheres complain that the child is neglected in religious thought, so the few philosophers who pay attention to the child often begin their observations with complaints that philosophers have usually forgotten about children. What is turning out to be exciting in our time is the philosophical thought of children as it bears on what Rorty called the development of theories that "tell us what sort of people we ought to become." They connect self and circumstance in revelatory ways to adults who are patient enough to listen to them.

One philosopher who listens to the child, interprets what he hears, and imparts it to those who provide care for the child is Gareth B. Matthews, who complains:

> [P]hilosophers have been, on the whole, remarkably silent on the question of what a child is. But it would be rash to conclude from this that philosophy has nothing to contribute to the theoretical discussion of childhood. Philosophy in the past has been preoccupied with

> problematic concepts like space, time, causality, God, free will, and the like. As it turns out, the concept of a child is also problematic in ways that are philosophical.[11]

And, we add, he shows that the child is also a subject of mystery in ways that are of interest to philosophers and informative to those who read philosophical works.

The familiar theories of cognitive and moral development trouble Matthews and raise alerts as well for those who want to treat the child as mystery. Although he finds value in what these theorists do, he also issues some cautions. He begins by contending that "theories of cognitive and moral development often encourage us to distance ourselves from children — both from children around us and from our own childhood selves. Such distancing sometimes produces a new respect for children." To be content with the findings of the mind or the self as evolutionary psychologists do, the listener observes the child through the developmental stages *because* they reveal constant change in the interaction or dialectic between my self and my circumstances.

We recall that Gabriel Marcel observed or defined a problem as something from which we could stand apart, though we could never get distance and extricate ourselves from mysteries. Matthews first pays respect to the approach that implies distancing: "After all, it warns us against faulting children for shortcomings that express, according to the theories, immature cognitive and moral structures that are entirely normal for children of the given age range." After that affirmation, however, comes this caution: "Yet such distancing can also encourage condescension. If we suppose that children live in conceptual worlds that are structurally different from ours, but that will naturally evolve into ours, how can we fail to be condescending toward children as moral agents?" The condescension, though understandable, he argues, is unwarranted. The antidote to the temptation to condescend is to link philosophical puzzlement with wonder in the face of the mystery of the child.

A hurrah for that insight is in order. This is the context in which we can regularly see how the child is himself a philosopher and someone who wonders, who experiences wonder, who ponders mystery. Matthews writes: "Puzzlement and wonder are closely related. Aristotle says that philosophy begins in wonder (Metaphysics 982b12). Bertrand Russell tells

11. Gareth B. Matthews, *The Philosophy of Childhood* (Cambridge, MA: Harvard University Press, 1994), 22.

us that philosophy, 'if it cannot *answer* so many questions as we could wish, has at least the power of *asking* questions which increase the interest of the world, and show the strangeness and wonder lying just below the surface in the commonest things of daily life.'"[12] Matthews also quotes the formidable twentieth-century philosopher Ludwig Wittgenstein, who wrote: "A philosophical problem has the form: 'I don't know my way about.'"[13] The philosopher addresses this bewilderment but may not find her "way about." What the thinkers from Aristotle through Russell and Wittgenstein succeed in proposing, whether it was their intention or whether it results from accident, is regard for the thinking and wondering of the child, but they do so on secular, nontranscendental grounds.

To illustrate a typical classical philosophical problem that reveals a child's grasp and groping, in this case having to do with naming entities and realities, Matthews picks up on a story that Jean Piaget told in condescension: "A little girl of nine asked: 'Daddy, is there really God?' The father answered that it wasn't very certain, to which the child retorted: 'There must be really, because he has a name!'" Piaget scoffed at the child's reasoning because it showed that a child's "inability to dissociate names from things is very curious." Matthews does not think so; instead he sees the retort of the child to be a sign of creativity that can stimulate deeper conversation and inquiry. The child as thinker, even the littlest child who can express thoughts, reveals an imagination that has to attract the interest of any thoughtful provider of care.[14]

The Special Case of Sex in Self and Circumstance

Few aspects of the life of the child — and of the adult? — attract more interest and curiosity than the sexual dimensions and expressions. Classic if sometimes wearying debates over the meanings of self and circumstance revolve around these dimensions. To use one illustration quickly: religious bodies and cultural warriors battle over homosexuality. Is it a part of nature, a predisposition that comes from the genetic base of the child's life, in which case debate will take on one character? Or is it a part of nurture, a response to stimuli in the growing child's environment? Is an at

12. Gareth B. Matthews, *Philosophy and the Young Child* (Cambridge, MA: Harvard University Press, 1980), 2.

13. Matthews, *Philosophy and the Young Child,* 2.

14. Matthews, *Philosophy and the Young Child,* 30.

this stage still hypothetical "homosexual-tending gene" determinative, or does the company one keeps, the parental nurture one receives or does not receive, or the surrounding culture do the predisposing? Even to state that polarity, as it often appears in the controversies, is to begin to see the limits of radically posing nature against nurture. I would like to think that the dialectic of "I am myself" in constant interaction with "I am my circumstances" is more illuminating.

Controversies over what is regarded to be innate in the mind of a boy versus that of a girl rage in our culture and are a subject of curiosity and concern among all who care for a child or care about children. Many of the problems of children are related to sex and gender, just as much of the mystery of the child derives from the possibilities and limits that go with gender identity.

The literature on this subject is vast, and to keep commentary at containable length I will draw upon a pair of books by Michael Gurian, *The Wonder of Boys* and *The Wonder of Girls.* A specific reason to concentrate here, even if briefly, is that the area of sex is one to which providers of care who are prone to seek to control are most attracted. Scientists try to understand and serve children, parents, teachers, and counselors when they push back the curtains of ignorance that shroud the issues of the sexual being of children. Some of the experts, when they concentrate on the evolution of the brain in the separate cases of boys and girls, helpfully account for some of the emotions and actions of children in the light of what can be learned from biology and neurology. Others devote themselves to cultural explanations of how girls and boys are shaped, thereupon stressing the influence of their surroundings. It is hard to conceive of good reasons to ask biologists or sociologists to draw up short and be content with the curtains of ignorance that have contributed to so much grief through the ages.

While applauding their efforts, however, it is in order for observers to keep their fingers crossed and to remain suspicious as they recognize how easy it is to misuse the explanations. Adults often employ these explanations to reduce the wonder of both boys and girls and to rationalize how their elders would exert or withhold discipline. Experts can create molds or set up gender stereotypes into which children have to fit. Forcing such fits is very efficient but may be harmful. In still other instances, in the eyes of some experts, children as boys or girls become mere objects brought out on stage to provide scenery for adult cultural battles. They contend that it can be easy to account for all problems in the lives of girls because they inherit and live within patriarchal and oppressive societies. In turn, those multitudes of citizens who criticize feminist interpreters often counterattack with explanations that deal with problems in the world of boys. They can assess that the problems of boys result from too-ready accusations about male misbehavior. Among these are the claims that some feminists deprive boys of the freedom to be boys because they regard male society as preparing them for cultural roles that have been set by dominant and oppressive men. All-purpose and complete explanations of the biology or the sociology, the brain or the environment, of girls and boys easily become weapons for those who would control and dominate the lives of the young along with much of the rest of society as they vote for laws dealing with "social issues."

What were once issues zoned off in the bedroom or the nursery have now been moved to the center of the most fracturing national debates. Debates over sex education in public school curricula, the nature of the images in mass media of communication, the commercialization and commodification of sexually explicit materials for children, and the controversies over homosexuality are but a few of what teachers, school boards, churches, and parents recognize as markers in battle zones. The contenders, both by their involvement and because of the passions they bring, show their recognition that almost nothing is closer to the being and identity of a person than the cast as male or female and the assigned ways of life that are presumed to accompany it. Those who claim to understand the sexual dimension are most tempted to try to control it and will have influence in public perception that the mystified or less curious and less impassioned lack. In the end, the divisive issues relating to gender often center on power: power over children or power as exercised in adult debates over being male or female or having a mixed gender identity.

No one need call experts on stage to learn about the intensity of these issues, which are so publicly visible. In this field, ordinary laypeople have no choice but to seek to understand boys and girls in their innate nature *and* their social history. Common sense serves them along the way and empowers them. Among the first devotees of this subject are the children themselves. Rather early in childhood they already engage in differentiating, and they sometimes adopt stereotyping roles that their culture bases on assumptions about gender. The tribes to which they belong, be these represented by the intimate or extended family, the school, or the place of friends and play, usually get organized along lines of girls and boys, or girls versus boys. Color-blind at birth though they may be, in the course of the years they will become alert to what it is to be African, Asian, European, or other. Among the company they keep and within the associations of which they become a part, their being boys or girls determines many of the standards and expectations of adults and other children.

Religious rites devoted to initiating the young and introducing them to the mysteries of faith and community ordinarily follow lines of gender, though Christian infant baptism is an instance in which being a boy or being a girl is not determinative. Circumcision of males in Islam and Judaism is gender conditioned. The enactment of adolescent rites that depict the child as coming of age and forming an identity are usually gender differentiated. Similarly, those who preside over marriage have historically prescribed quite defined roles for boys as they have become men and girls as they have become women. This differentiating has helped ensure that successive generations will perpetuate understandings of life within traditional gendered roles. Even unreflective people know or quickly learn how to participate in the drama of life largely on gendered lines.

In come the experts, many of whom are devoted to the school that stresses what is innate, the concentrators on "I-am-I," no matter what the circumstance. During the past fifty years biologists have put much energy into accounting for differences in the brains of boys and girls in the light of their observable, if only partly culturally conditioned, roles and vocations. Thus, because boys had to learn how to be hunters, evolutionists deduced and proposed that males needed certain kinds of mental power to direct their motor skills and aims. We hear that their heirs, little boys of today, therefore come equipped with brains that reflect this heritage and that in part help direct the conduct of boys. Such observers note how, in most cases, boys demonstrate alertness to a different kind and use of space than do girls, and the acts of dealing with spatial relations determine much of their conduct. Pushing and shoving in the preschool room, it is said, reflects that hunter ancestry. The brains of the boys, descendants of those who had to scramble for prey and protect themselves against would-be preyers, are therefore wired differently than are girls. Girls' ancestors, it is also said, necessarily stayed at home more than their male counterparts, which meant that they had to accept defined household roles.

Bracket or abolish the question of the mystery of the child for a moment and suppress any sense of wonder, and you soon find that the impulse to reduce the child to something definable and controllable is in this case very strong. In such an accounting the child is "nothing but" this or that explainable and explained being. Everything then gets reduced to the hypotheses or tentative findings of a particular and passing generation, designed as these are to explain and thus control behavior. Historians who write on the temporal course of microbiology, neurological explanations, or prescriptions concerning behavior chronicle how readily the desire to explain away or reduce issues about sexuality has produced sequences of explanations that turn out to be ephemeral and very quickly obsolete. Thus histories of how masturbation has been regarded in different periods of time can evoke both laughter and a sense of horror over how societies looked at it.

Similarly, to explain the child as a *mere* product of the environment is to grant too much to fate and to rob the young person of any measure of autonomy. That the environment of the boys' club, the gang, or the football field is conducive to one kind of behavior while that of the kitchen or ballet school influences another leads to a realization that affects how children mature and live as adults. Although study of these relationships is beneficial, problems arise when such scientific endeavors end in dispelling any sense of wonder, any aura of mystery that might serve to give the child room to breathe or a larger repertory of options for action.

The actions of many actual children, as opposed to children who show up only as statistics, will sometimes seem to confirm the findings of the behaviorists and the evolutionary psychologists but at other times will appear to inspire a gruff "Bug off, adults" to those who try too hard to control circumstances. Some parents of my acquaintance, a twosome who are heavily committed to feminist and masculinist movements, regularly proclaimed their intention to bring up their children in roles that would transcend society's expectations about gender. Their commitment led them to some extravagant experiments to enforce certain behaviors and root out others. The determinists told them that little boys are drawn or forced by culture to favor machines and all noisemaking things with wheels, while girls prefer dolls, and that they must thwart these inclinations. So they provided their little son with a doll and their little daughter with a toy auto. Some boys do like to play with dolls, and autos are not alien to girls, but in this case, when the parents returned to the room a short while after the presents had been opened, they found the boy holding and pushing the doll, now on her back, as if her shoulders could serve as wheels, while he made the appropriate r-r-r-r-r-ring sounds. Score one for children's imaginations.

While affirming the biological and social sciences for their contribution to understanding the wonder of boys and girls, we have good reasons to be critical of those who use scientific theories and knowledge to diminish the sense of mystery associated with each young human. To illustrate what I mean by urging that we go beyond the boundaries of science without trying to refute specific hypotheses or findings, let me elaborate on an observation by Eugen Rosenstock-Huessy. He pictured a student reading in a large library. "The presence of one living soul among the three million volumes of a great library offers sufficient proof against the notion that the secret of the soul is to be found by reading those three million books."[15] Great numbers of the books therein may contribute to the student's understanding of the sexual issues at hand. Yet all, taken together, do not explain her sexual drives and definitions. She is a complicated coming-together of genes and synapses, full of potential for ideas still to be developed, of connections not yet made. The universe may have hundreds of billions of galaxies, and each of these may have hundreds of billions of stars, each of which has innumerable atoms or particles or strings. Yet all together will not match the possibilities in what her eye catches, her ear hears, or her thoughts encounter at any split second of a long life.

So with the sexual realities of the boy and the girl, each as "self" and "in circumstances." After all the typing and stereotyping, the creation of molds and Procrustean beds, and the illumination that comes from provocative experiments, the possibilities of the sexual makeup and projection of children remain elusive. In short, many will say, the boy has a boy's soul and the girl has a girl's soul, though knowing that by no means exhausts explanations of who they are and what they are about. What they are about in both cases is participating in the development of their souls. My understanding of *soul* draws on Aristotle as mediated by Leon Kass, a University of Chicago colleague, an M.D., and a professor in the humanities. In this reading, the soul is not "the ghost in the machine" or "the pilot on a ship" or any *thing.* Soul is the vital power of any organic body, so long as it is open to a future, with possibility and purpose.[16] When not vital or having power or being organic — as in the case of a corpse or a finger cut off from a body — there is no soul. When there is no openness to the future, to possibility and purpose, soul is compromised. The vitality, power, and openness can be cultivated and will be so, in a variety of circumstances.

All the descriptions, prescriptions, predispositions, inclinations, in-

15. Eugen Rosenstock-Huessy, *I Am an Impure Thinker* (Norwich, VT: Argo Books, 1970), 4.

16. Leon Kass, *Toward a More Natural Science: Biology and Human Affairs* (New York: Free Press, 1985), 272-75.

timations, associations — extend the list indefinitely — that scientific knowledge proposes as explanations of the nature of boys and of girls can contribute to understanding, development, discipline, and care. Taken together, however, they do not exhaust and cannot anticipate all that belongs to any particular child, and especially to the child's sexual being. To begin with, the boy or girl is born of a cell fusion that is itself highly contingent, apparently accidental, at the time of conception. As one senior told me, he was the product of the coming together at an arbitrary moment of "one of those billions of crawling things" in his father's semen and one of those many eggs his mother issued. The sexual differentiation that occurred at conception may be altered by use of some technical engineering that is possible in the clinic today. However, after the chromosomes are lined up in such a way that they produce what will spell "b-o-y" or "g-i-r-l," they do not suffice to define and explain the person who lives out the implications of his or her gender or mix of gender ascriptions proposed by society. I am using the term *gender* here in the modern conventional sense: it has to do not with the biology of sex but with the sociology of what a culture does in defining its role.

The interactions among parents and infants, the exposure by each child to others in the nursery school, the realization of boyhood or girlhood and what each means in the three-year-old, the forming of gangs among boys and friendship circles among girls, the choice of athletic expressions and toys, the living of life within the boundaries of rules or the transgressing of these boundaries as adolescents — all are elements in the development of a human who eludes efforts at reduction, being active in creating molds, filling out or rejecting stereotypes, or satisfying the interests of scientists and human engineers. Anything that enhances the variety of options and resists reduction and predictability enlarges the possibilities of human freedom and life in community.

"I am myself" and "my circumstances." We picture a young girl, however genetically endowed, brought up in the circumstance of positive relations with her parents. Contingency remains on the scene. She goes to a party, makes new friends, watches images on television with them, is lured into early sexual expression, picks up the argot of her peers, and suddenly finds it in fashion to be nasty. Another girl, with the same potential to be drawn into nasty behavior, is drawn to a church youth group or some other religious group for young teens. She finds there a vision of a way of life that locates sexual expression in channels that she comes to see as positive and potentially rewarding lifelong. So she is induced to change. Each could have been drawn into the ways of life I have just described. I could have changed pronouns and used "he" instead of "she" in the illustration to make the point. But the fact that it is a girl or a boy making the decisions is of importance in their human vocation.

Sex, Self, and Circumstances in Community

I have pointed to the role of community in the formation of sexual outlook and expression. One often hears that much of young people's behavior — and perhaps that of older persons too — relates to their peers. We are mimetic beings, drawing many of our meanings from the impulse to imitate. Children in large measure do what their friends prefer to do. In a circle where children in their early teens engage in extreme sexual experiments, they are likely to go along with the adventurers who take risks. In another, where such young teens have chosen paths of restraint, perhaps moved by religious mandates and promises, the child makes a different "use" of his sexuality, without leaving behind tensions over how to express or repress sexual impulses.

Most boys or girls, then, belong in some way to what we will call a tribe. The tribe plays a major role in providing the circumstance of which Ortega spoke. Rosenstock-Huessy has written about the obvious: that one does not receive all values from the immediate family. The years spent in such a small circle are too brief, and the isolated family unit is too burdened to enable the young then and there to draw upon meanings and behaviors from the larger past. So the extended family, the circle of friends, the associations one forms and experiences in each case become the tribe, the *couche,* the womb of values.[17] Adults may have a difficult time crashing a particular circle of the young and becoming accepted. Or they may simply be incapable of imagining and projecting ways of life that are congenial to children in particular circumstances. Peers do much of the work. Yet there can be and is an intergenerational influence, an institutional impact.

One summer day I was attending an annual meeting of a jurisdiction of my own tribe, in a room full of reticent people of Scandinavian and German heritage. The presiding bishop in this tribe that is a church body was on stage, fielding accusations fired by those who did not welcome the denomination's investment in a study called *Your Faith and Your Sexuality.* One of the delegates from the floor asked him, "Why, in a world

17. Rosenstock-Huessy, *I Am an Impure Thinker,* 121.

of such need, is our church body spending several million dollars on a study of *Your Faith and Your Sexuality?*"

The poised and quick-witted bishop responded that he saw the venture as worthy to be compared to remedial reading. Why? Because the topic, he surmised, had been neglected in the childhood experience of most members of this church body. The first tribal circle, the family, had failed in its mission. Remedial education, was it? Yes, said the church leader, who then asked, "How many of you in the family circle as you grew up seriously discussed your faith and your sexuality?" A few hands among six hundred were raised. The bishop shielded his brow against the beams of stage lights, peered out over the audience, discerned the few hands, and questioned, "Who let those eight Italians in here?"

Such a story illustrates something of the complexity and contexts of the sexuality of the boy and the girl who rose from that family table uninformed, to become dependent on sexual differentiation and discussion in other circles of the tribe, whether a Scout troop, a church youth group, a circle of friends, or a band of impersonal intruders who crashed onto the scene by means of mass media of communication — none of whom cared much about enhancing the mystery of childhood sexuality.

No matter how helpful the tribes as here described may be in some cases, no matter how exemplary adults and peers sometimes are, the potential for things to go wrong in the world of children in respect to their sexuality is deadly. Yet those who have reference points in a constructive tribe find more clarified options than do the floundering. Cultural fads and reports on sequences of scientific proposals and findings suggest that in many cultural expressions girls experience harder times than boys. On the "who has it worse?" front, it all depends upon which factor one is isolating. Thus, as Michael Gurian reminds readers in *The Wonder of Boys,* infant boys have a 25 percent higher mortality rate than girls. They experience autism in frequencies double that of girls, they suffer more birth defects, and more of them have schizophrenia. Retarded, emotionally disturbed, learning-disabled boys greatly outnumber similarly afflicted girls. More of them suffer abuse by adults. Boys are three times as likely as girls to be victims of violence.[18]

Similarly, the notion that boys are not "born" boys but become what they are simply through social construction does not hold up in scientific studies. They are "wired" differently. They are not "inherently flawed"; nor

18. Michael Gurian, *The Wonder of Boys* (New York: Jeremy P. Tarcher/Putnam, 1996), xvii-xviii.

are girls.[19] One does not have to gird for battle with feminist researchers to make such claims. Those who pursue the mystery of the child have to confront and penetrate the issues of their gender and sexuality, but they do this best when they are unencumbered by extravagant theories and claims for either one, because either approach can easily harden into dogma and ideology.

By now it should be clear that the study of boys can well begin with – though it does well not to end with – biology, especially because of boys' higher level of the hormone testosterone, something that is measurable. Human ancestry reaches back to eons in which competition for females was intense, so the male had to act on his higher sex drive with its demand for high testosterone. When X and Y link chromosomally at conception, a boy will eventually be born, endowed with testosterone ready to motor his aggressive impulses and acts. Boys make little declarations of independence early in life and strike out on their own more readily than girls.[20] And parents have seen nothing yet: with puberty, testosterone surges become more frequent each day, fueling the boy's assertive acts. However, even as I write about testosterone surges, I am moved to qualify this by remembering that many other kinds of surges, many other dispositions and cultural expressions affect the lives of boys and make them more interesting than when they are reduced to objects controlled by testosterone.

"The urge that parents, mentors, and educators have to 'enhance their child's creativity' is a spiritual instinct," Gurian writes, "for whether we realize it or not, every act of creation is an experiential 'knowing' of what can never be rationally 'known.' We know the Great Mystery of creation by creating, not by solving its logic in our heads."[21] And, in his eyes, there is a payoff. For one example, "the more we fill hobbies with spiritual content – using them to teach wisdom, spiritual centeredness, discipline, emotional life – the more they become spiritual friends to the boy, befriending him and helping him feel grounded throughout life."[22] The mention of hobbies recognizes still another role of circumstances and culture in opening possibilities to boys and to girls.

Gurian also gives attention to spiritual development in *The Wonder of Girls.* He sees girls as more open to being relational than are boys. Reli-

19. Gurian, *The Wonder of Boys,* xix-xx.
20. Gurian, *The Wonder of Boys,* 9.
21. Gurian, *The Wonder of Boys,* 215.
22. Gurian, *The Wonder of Boys,* 218.

gious institutions are aids in forming peer relations, serving as an extended family, and enhancing rites of passage more frequently and with more intensity for girls than for boys. Gurian, the father of two girls and no boys, the author of six books on boys and only one on girls at the time of this writing, is not modest in his intentions. The basic perspective of the book, he claims, "is quite different from the books you may have read" on girls. He says he intends to provide a new way of understanding girls, thanks to his *nature-based* approach. As in his parallel book, Gurian promises to deal with "human nature" through emphases on "human sciences, neurobiology, biochemistry — checked by experience, human history, multicultural application, and just plain common sense."[23] I have to say that, ironically, in the case of both boys and girls, Gurian has little to say about the meaning of "nature" until he relates it to the cultural contexts — as Rorty had done.

As he did in the book on boys, Gurian spells out the standard current myths about girls in the form of theories that he then debunks or at least qualifies. They are sufficiently succinct and pointed that they merit quotation:

- *Girls are who they are predominantly because of the way they are socialized in our society. Nature plays a smaller part in why girls are the way they are.*
- *To be safe and successful as human beings, women must become, for the most part, independent of men. Boys and men are not inherently trustworthy; girls and women must compete with them as needed, become more like them as it is strategic to do so, and seek a social position in which they don't need the other sex.*
- *Today's girls are, first and foremost, victims of a male-dominant society.*
- *Most of our girls' social problems, especially as adolescents, grow from the gender stereotypes females are forced into by our culture. These gender types — Barbies, images of thin women, and female gender roles in the workplace and home — are the primary causes of the low self-esteem we see in young women.*[24]

Gurian is courageous enough, or foolish enough, to confront these theories but wise enough to isolate what is valuable in the insights they intend to offer. "I am not offering an extremist response to feminist the-

23. Michael Gurian, *The Wonder of Girls* (New York: Atria Books, 2002), xix.

24. Gurian, *The Wonder of Girls,* 8, 11, 13, 17. These bulleted items are italicized in the original.

ory. Feminist theory is crucial for the lives of many girls." However, he asks, to frame his book: "What might interest us most now, in the new millennium, is *which* girls?" He and his wife, who have extensive private practices involving counseling and therapy of children and who both study summaries by the National Institute of Mental Health and other research bodies, estimate that only 10 to 20 percent of American girls are experiencing some form of crisis that interferes with normal, healthy female development. These girls need attention, and the Gurians provide some, but they do not reach deeply enough into the limiting cultural factors that get associated with the concept and reality of sexism. "For abused, disturbed, or systematically disrespected girls, feminist theory is very helpful," because it deals with crisis-response theory. Then it can act as a miracle. Yet the truth that "shakes us to the bones" is that, for the other four-fifths of girls, other theories are vital, and available.[25]

It has been impossible in this accounting of sex and gender, as my comment on Gurian suggests, to keep nurture out of sight while discussing nature, just as now in the pages ahead, on what so many scholars have called nurture, meaning the social context or the circumstance, comment on nature will keep coming up. The fact that keeping the strains pure is such a difficult task supports our thesis that these are interwebbed and that specialists who isolate and then give weight only to one or the other miss something of the mystery of the child, complex as the web turns out to be. And they will fail the providers of care, who deal with the whole child, the influences upon her and what she brings to her circumstances, all that surrounds her.

25. Gurian, *The Wonder of Girls,* 22.

8. Care for the Child in Context

Parents who happen to be near when a child suffers harm and must be taken within minutes to an emergency room could represent others in thousands of similar high-risk circumstances. In some senses, every aspect of providing care for a child or learning from a child involves some form of risk. Though Ortega was writing about "man" in the lifelong situation of danger, what he said applies as well to the child: "The essence of man is always purely and simply 'danger.' Man always travels along precipices and, whether he will or not, his truest obligation is to keep his balance."[1] That is an adult way of speaking about how the child deals with the ominous sides of mystery. She affirms life, the flight of the butterfly, the joy of playing, the warmth of her father's hand as he walks with her, but she has to balance in her mind these grace-given delights with the shadowed mystery of the animals that haunt her dreams, the puzzling mystery of what mourning means at Grandfather's death, or the benumbing mystery of what inspires evil people to do bad things to children.

If the child is always traveling along precipices of which he may not be aware, those who deal with him responsibly would go mad if they conjured up all the dangers in the range of possibility. The next bike ride during which the boy under one's charge might not wear a helmet, the next shallow pool into which a fifth-grader might dive, the sudden high fever that could rage in a young person, the possibly stupid response of a kindergartener to a dare by a classmate, or the chance that a student could come under the influence of the wrong friend are the kinds of dan-

1. Ortega, quoted by Karl J. Weintraub, *Visions of Culture* (Chicago: University of Chicago Press, 1966), 269-70.

gers that are so constantly in range that no adult could function if conscious of them at all times.

Adults could easily become paralyzed with fear when they take on responsibility in the world of accidents and other contingencies. The resources on which the grown-up draws can seem to offer nothing more at the edge of a precipice than a set of weak holds. They cannot bear the weight of any adult who would like to become sure of herself in dealings with a child to whom she relates. Or, in their complexity, the threats may appear as an obscuring fog, one that inhibits discernment of real as opposed to imagined dangers and that may lead to a loss of direction or a sense of futility.

It gets worse.

The Good Provider

Ever since the time of the ancients, especially Plato and Aristotle, thinkers have focused on a triad of virtues: truth, beauty, and goodness. The serious contemporary provider of care is still called to exemplify something of that trio. If these virtues derive from intellectual endeavors and inspire books of philosophy, libraries and archives of wisdom will not suffice for shaping the art of living. Recall the student of whom Rosenstock-Huessy spoke: even taken together, the three million library books that surround her do not explain her. The responsible adult, it is true, has absorbed enough of the content from libraries, schools, churches, or other agents of literacy to learn something about guiding the young. In crises, however, book learning has its limits. For instance, how do families of desperately ill patients make decisions in that zone of danger wherein book learning as offered in medical ethics is supposed to be focused? In the lore, many circumstances do appear in which principles are clear and far-reaching. Still, addressing life experience will be complex — even, or perhaps especially, for those whose learning has been restricted more to books read than to experiences of life.

An illustration: For decades, most university courses on medical ethics have dealt with a quadrilateral of abstract philosophical themes, *justice, autonomy, beneficence,* and *nonmaleficence.* Mark Siegler, head of the clinical ethics program at the University of Chicago, a theorist, and a practitioner who takes part in conversations on these themes, once commented on how these four may appear in different guises and contexts. The modes or the voices of participants in decision making vary, he noted, depending upon who is doing the reasoning and under what circumstances. Though Siegler saw value in the philosophers' quadrilateral when experts brought it to bear in the impersonal world, such as when hospitals and legislatures set priorities or when committees debate strategies, he also clearly perceived its limits in situations where people were in crisis or on the precipices of a decision. We can picture those who provide care for a desperately ill child about whom adults are reasoning. They may have read the philosophers and even taken college courses in medical ethics. People can never learn too much, but at this point they are faced with a decision for which no tutelage will be sufficient.

A bit harder on formal philosophical ethics than I would be, Siegler described the varied contexts in which the ethical word is demanded. To paraphrase him: for many years he had experience with families as they wrestled with life-and-death issues. Those close to the dying had to ask questions such as, "Shall we 'pull the plug' and end life supports for Grandfather, who is brain dead?" "How do we make decisions concerning a newborn with spina bifida?" Siegler said, with a smile, that he knew of not one instance in which a family asked the clinic's ethics committee for counsel from an Aristotelian, an idealist, a pragmatist, or a utilitarian. Instead, such a family more characteristically asked, "What does my good doctor say?" "What does our good priest recommend?" "What would our good uncle, Grandfather's brother, say?"

Why did they describe these advisers as *good?* They came to be seen as "good" because others had experienced them as good, but also, quite likely, after each had deliberated on the meanings of goodness in philosophy or in the language of faith. Such trusted people embodied some version of goodness that patients and their families found attractive, and they put elements of it to work. Not all of them may possess the knowledge or rational equipment that is found in textbooks, but the people who are part of the patient's circumstances would be more ready than are most experts in philosophy to deal with the mysteries of the grandfather's or the infant's life and universe. They might thus help families make it more possible to live with the choices that they have to make.

When I spoke in a seminar with Emory University colleagues of this interest in finding the good doctor, the good priest, or the good uncle, they asked the same question they did when I wanted them to account for how, in a crazy world, there could be so many good children. "What do you mean by *good?*" To answer that question is seen as more difficult in a pluralistic culture than in homogeneous ones where the same single book belonged to the community and favored one interpretation of it. It was not my task in the seminars to expound a complete philosophy of the good – my role was to prompt them to think and to help them and me learn – though I hope the chapters in this book will provide some tentative clues to definitions and descriptions.

Circumstances in the Form of Historical Crises

The reference to decisions in medical emergencies might suggest that crises facing children will be intimate and focused on small circles of individuals. Yet children in any culture also have to cope with society-wide traumas. I need not elaborate here on what is doubtless on the minds of many after September 11, 2001. That date symbolizes events that shattered many structures of personal security in the citizenry at large. After the terrorist acts of that day, children saw televised images of the devastation caused by crashing airplanes, and they had to begin to cope with what they saw. While not intending to detract for a moment from the missions of those who deal with the physical problems of security and defense against terrorists, some of us are impelled by our vocations to attempt to look also at the soul and the heart of the public, including its youngest members.

Ortega has helped me relate the outer "problematic" world to the inner "mysterious" world in my own experience and as I observe others. "Decisive historical changes," he wrote, "do not come from great wars, terrible cataclysms, or ingenious inventions; 'it is enough that the heart of man incline its sensitive crown to one side or the other of the horizon, toward optimism or toward pessimism, toward heroism or toward utility, toward combat or toward peace.'"[2] One can picture America as theologian Reinhold Niebuhr did a half-century earlier: as a kind of gadget-filled paradise suspended in a hell of international insecurity. On the morning of September 11, 2001, in the skies of New York, Washington, and Pennsylvania, that cord was cut. Having lived with a sense of security provided by two wide oceans on the east and the west and friendly neighbors to the north and south, Americans could feel that attack was remote. Now they were vulnerable, as most people have been, whether in what was called primitive or tribal or feudal society in the past or in other parts of the world today. How would we react, how do we react, how do our children reckon with the sense of insecurity they can perceive in the adult world?

No adult is properly exempt from dealing with this sense of insecu-

2. Ortega, quoted by Weintraub, *Visions of Culture,* 269.

rity in our culture, which had concentrated on scientific and technical approaches to child rearing. The time now came for perceptive leaders to take second and longer looks at the values with which they would deal with "the sensitive crown" of hearts on this new horizon. Whoever would sound credible while providing care for children has had to consider the devastations and threats and then reflect on the world of children and of child rearing. Ortega spoke eloquently on this point when he used the metaphor of shipwreck: "A historical crisis exists," he wrote, "when the modification of the world is such that the world, or the system of convictions of the preceding generation, is followed by a situation in which man is without the convictions, therefore without a 'world.' It is a modification which, at first, is negative, critical." Listening to international and national debates over security and assessing what many debaters propose reveal that many approach the charge with passionate intensity but act in ways that are costly to convictions. Many radio talk-show hosts and guests as well as cable television panelists who consider the future and especially the place of children lose their bearings and indulge themselves in thoughtless and exaggerated counsel. Convictions concerning human rights, freedom, and breadth of perspectives are jettisoned. Ortega observes: "In ages of crisis one finds frequently false and hypocritical opinions. Whole generations falsify themselves, that is, they escape into artificial styles, into doctrines, into insincere political movements, merely to fill the emptiness left behind by genuine convictions."[3]

Now for the use of the metaphor: Ortega has a word about whence one might take counsel in such a time. A number who analyze the dangers, threats, and beguilements of the present culture will identify with his word: "The sense of being shipwrecked, since it is the truth about life, already means a measure of rescue. I therefore believe only in the thoughts of the shipwrecked. One should place the classics before a tribunal of the shipwrecked and ask them certain fundamental questions about life."[4] This is what we are intending to do, both by referring, as we have done, to some sacred scriptures seen as such classical texts and then by dealing with the question of "shipwrecked" children.

3. Ortega, quoted by Weintraub, *Visions of Culture,* 281.
4. Ortega, quoted by Weintraub, *Visions of Culture,* 286.

The Shipwrecked Listener and the Shipwrecked Children

When adults, without first having listened to the young, diagnose the fears of children themselves, they can fail to hear how children define their various circumstances. This failure will lead them to miss the point among children who are experiencing and defining their own crises. Until adults pay careful attention, they will lack anything approaching an accurate representation of the world of the child, and this may lead to error. I learned something of this up close. After September 11 some filmmakers asked me to convene a dozen preteen children to discuss their nightmares and their fears after the destruction in New York City. The producers were aware that some parents had joined children in repeatedly watching on television the explosions and disasters of that dire day. Others had even thoughtlessly abandoned their unmonitored children to television, where the awful scenes were frequently replayed. The children before me who were to be on camera were all highly aware of the catastrophe and the devastation. Some had already received counsel at church and school and home about how to cope with what they had seen. Most of them then went along living their young lives aware of, but not paralyzed by, the threat.

"Do you fear?" I asked these young colleagues as they faced the camera. Yes, all of them had fears in abundance. What did they fear? With the honesty that many children display, some admitted that they were scared of the dark. Then a child who lived in a ghetto, well aware of the potential of terror from the skies, also spoke up about the more immediate terror in the streets that surrounded him. Accompany him to school every morning, he dared us, as he must walk down the sidewalk between two inviting and at the same time menacing youth gangs. Have your lunch money stolen every day, and hear the threats from a cluster of bullies – "We know where *you live!*" – who promised they would get even for his having stood up against one of them. As the interviewed boy spoke, we came to empathize. His was a real and truly credible fear, and we all recognized it. No media images induced it.

It also became clear that the boy was seeking salvation by finding security in his home and on the streets. I have attended funerals of friends who lived in the inner city and have heard survivors witness to their view of heaven: there would be no more need for huge locks on the doors, no fear of predators ready to pounce. This child was resituating what Ortega called "the sensitive crown" of his heart toward a new horizon of danger and rescue. He spoke of daily threats so naturally that some of us adult onlookers had to pass over his comments in stunned silence. Only later could we give plausible accounts of our own fears, some triggered by 9/11, fears that in some cases also have their residence among the young.

Now I cannot resist lightening this dark passage by reporting that the filmmakers, parents, and pizza-providers during a long day of filmmaking also received an education about the diversity of the sources that can be used to comfort children. A five-year-old Ecuadorian-American boy, who made his contributions whenever called on through the hours of filming and who leaned forward in silence to listen as others spoke, offered his own most urgent plea as we broke up for the day: "Now," he asked, "do we get God's presents?" He evidently had experienced some sense of hope through these hours from the promise of good things or good food to follow. All day long he was mistranslating what he heard when older children spoke about being in the church where we were filming and where some of them, they said, were recognizing "God's presence." Presence = Presents. The present the child thereupon received was a pizza feast with ice cream to follow. We all learned that there are more ways than one to meet expectations in the world of the child.

Natural Circumstances

Not all circumstances represent danger in the immediate sense of which Ortega spoke. Though the natural world is threatened by pollution, it can also represent a more benign setting for the development of the child, a setting that will be conceived as a bearer of mystery. The child relates not only to human culture but to nature itself, which to the religious believer gives witness as the object of divine creation, something that can be regarded as sacred. The natural world itself "stands around" each person and is her circumstance (*circum* + *stantia,* again). To change the atmosphere and to help us regain our footing away from the precipices for a moment, we will visit this natural circumstance. To help us grasp this wonder, we will begin by inventing a little drama in which the mystery of the child meets the mystery of nature. It can be an everyday experience, heightened occasionally by attempts on the part of the providers of care to intensify the child's awareness of natural surroundings. Anyone who is not a naturalist but who walks through the woods with a naturalist is likely to be surprised, almost benumbed and humbled, when she realizes what she has been missing on her previous lonely walks. A rather quiet but important character is the questioning little child, now a mystery surrounded by mysteries.

Picture a person of inquisitive mind who has good visual, oral, and olfactory instruments and limitless curiosity going on one of those walks with a child in hand. She may carry with her a handbook that gives the names and descriptions of the birds, trees, insects, and flowers one comes across in that kind of woods in that particular part of the country. She uses her equipment well, taking note of all discoveries, perhaps recording them for future reference so that knowledge will accumulate and her familiarity with that setting will increase. This walker has also prepared herself by reading authors like Annie Dillard and Wendell Berry, essayists who reveal their spiritual affinity with what nature presents and signifies. She has thus passed her figurative qualifying examinations and is ready to be a docent in a preserve, a guide to the uninitiated and perplexed. Such a life as hers has already been enhanced in dialogue with nature. It will now be enriched by the presence of a child. The child has read none of the books, knows none of the terms, but is receptive to what will happen. I have described a guide to nature, but she may just as well be seen as someone preparing to become an exemplary provider of care to the child.

This person enrolls in a course, goes to a sylvan retreat, enters a study program, and places herself under the tutelage of an experienced naturalist. Equipped with rain gear, binoculars, compass, and mosquito repellent, her group embarks. The guide, being tactful, talks down to no one, assumes nothing, announces "we are all beginners every day when we open the book of nature," is unobtrusive but alert. That guide, being patient and generous and perhaps especially perceptive, may have been the one to invite the guest's child to go along. Tutored to behave, the child has no difficulty doing so, so rich is her experience during this venture. The party is off and walking. The naturalist then pauses: "Do you smell that?" *Of course,* we smell the leavings of a deer, the whiff of fragrance from a wildflower, the odor that wafts from a swamp that is out of visual range. We had *not* noticed them, however, until they were called to our attention. Having put nose and brain to work on hitherto unnoticed aromas and slight stenches, our walker and her group move on – and then the child smells something that the naturalist and all the adults had missed. We pause and hear reports and sharpen our sense of smell.

We move on. No, we do not: We hear the experienced guide say: "Listen. No, I mean *really* listen. The forest is not quiet. You hear the soughing of a breeze through the leaves; oh, yes, now you notice the sound of a brook, rippling not far from the path – and, unfortunately, a distant plane, or a truck roaring down the road a mile away. That's it? No, it isn't. You are hearing the song of a meadowlark rarely heard in these parts. And did you notice the croaking of frogs in the distance? In the far distance. That is remarkable, since we don't often hear frogs any-more because few have survived hereabouts. We can talk about why that is so when we get back." The child is puzzled, impatient, full of wonder. She quietly presses us to talk now, knowing that back at the base, lunch-time preoccupations will take over, and we will never get back to the frogs croaking now beyond our hearing. Another child may ask why we so seldom hear frogs and may get a little lecture from the guide about imbalances in the ecological setting, translated into talk intelligible to the child and hence to the rest of us.

Gone, forgotten, are the smells, as sounds have now taken over. The guide by now should find the group weary and satisfied, if not sensuously sated. But no: "Look at that next tree. No, you have to come over here; you just missed it as you passed by on the trail. There, follow that fork. Way out on the limb, you can just glimpse it where the sun is breaking through on it, for the moment: that nest, built by a wood thrush, shows an instinc-tual anticipation of the danger of predators. Oh, while you are looking, listen again: that's a kind of cricket that usually is heard later in the sea-son." The sense of hearing is most immediate, and the child, quickened to wonder, takes in all the sounds and listens for more.

As if the overload is not already too weighty, here is more: touch. "Just stroke that moss, will you? I said stroke it; please don't injure it. It's protected by that clump of ferns. Notice that the leaves on these ferns are *very* different from those we passed ten minutes ago. Oh, I guess I forgot to point them out. My fault; it was a noteworthy, even remarkably rare, growth for this part of the country." The child has paid attention but, be-ing closer to the ground, also noticed how the sun broke through between the tree trunks and was refracted through a drop of dew that the rest of us would not have found memorable but now found revelatory.

We might as well conclude the tour of the woods and the tour of the senses: "We are on private land; on public land you are never to pluck a wild flower. Here we will be good stewards and won't overdo it, but we *are,* after all, taking part in a learning experience. Pull just one of these tiny lilac-like flowers from the branch and gently suck through it. Now you know why the bees are so at home here. The bees! Oh, you have noticed them buzzing; all my classes are aware of the sight and sound of those buzzing creatures. When they hear them, they duck." And the child will not pick the flower, having been told so often to let nature be. She will duck when the bee comes close. Now another sense has served the child well and helped increase her awareness of the mysteries of nature.

Mentors such as that guide often stimulate a sense of wonder among otherwise jaded but still experiment-minded seniors. Typically, they can enhance the experience that evening when they are back in their rooms by opening books and reading, for example, a page that reproduces this poem from the Hebrew Scriptures. It is such an evocation of mystery that the reader can have little impulse to reduce any part of it to a guide for solving problems in nature. Among other things, the text is a reminder that nature does not merely mean a walk in the woods or a touch with the intimate and near. Instead it throws projections of nature on as large a screen as was imaginable when the book of Job was written, and, for that matter, in the reach of the imaginative, on a canvas as large as the cosmos. The voice from the whirlwind on the page confronts the questioning and suffering Job with questions that may well lead him back to the outlook he had when he was a wondering child:

> "Where were you when I laid the foundation of the earth?
>   Tell me, if you have understanding.
> Who determined its measurements – surely you know!
>   Or who stretched the line upon it?
> On what were its bases sunk,
>   or who laid its cornerstone
> when the morning stars sang together
>   and all the heavenly beings shouted for joy? . . .
>
> "Have you entered into the springs of the sea,
>   or walked in the recesses of the deep? . . .
>
> "Where is the way to the dwelling of light,
>   and where is the place of darkness . . . ?
>
> "Have you entered the storehouses of the snow . . . ?
>
> "Who has cut a channel for the torrents of rain,
>   and a way for the thunderbolt . . . ?
>
> "Can you bind the chains of the Pleiades,
>   or loose the cords of Orion? . . .
>
>   can you guide the Bear with its children? . . .

"Can you hunt the prey for the lion,
or satisfy the appetite of the young lions . . . ?

"Do you know when the mountain goats give birth?
Do you observe the calving of the deer? . . .

"Do you give the horse its might?
Do you clothe its neck with mane?
Do you make it leap like the locust? . . .

"Is it by your wisdom that the hawk soars,
and spreads its wings toward the south?"

(from Job 38-39)

If these questions are so potent that they might assault the one who hears them, yet they evoke from Job some answers, after the Lord has advised: "Deck yourself with majesty and dignity; clothe yourself with glory and splendor" (Job 40:10). Job's words follow:

"'Who is this that hides counsel without knowledge?'
Therefore I have uttered what I did not understand,
things too wonderful for me, which I did not know."

(Job 42:3)

A child may not be as stunned as this or might recover more quickly. Trust the child on a child's terms to be open to such questioning and perhaps to be aware that no one has answers to the questions from the whirlwind. The point of this detour to (or climax in) sacred scripture is not to reduce the questioner of today to the point where Job found himself: "Therefore I despise myself," though the next line may be appropriate: "and repent in dust and ashes" (Job 42:6). Instead it signals something of what is "out there" in nature, unaccountably vast, complex, and mysterious. Today, in the era of the Hubble telescope, when astronomers speak of their awareness of billions of galaxies, each including hundreds of billions of stars, we have better words for better measurements but no better ways of expressing awe before the natural world. That naturalist in the woods greatly magnifies the tour group's imaginations, but their perceptions remain infinitesimally small against the larger screen of nature. The naturalist does best to exemplify and open the group to wonder and awe. Whoever has sat in a beach chair next to a child on a night when meteor showers and the aurora borealis can be viewed will find the child most alert to the vision of the mysterious.

Alongside the language about nature is the language of science. Were I competent to do so, I would present all the names of sights, sounds, smells, tastes, and touches in their technical form. Would we have gotten closer to the depth of mystery or satisfied the child's curiosity by doing so? Whoever cherishes the walk in the woods or the language of scripture has good reason to appreciate the efforts by scientists to measure, to bring precision to everything in nature. The point is to know which language is appropriate and when, as many of the most perceptive and receptive scientists and technologists are discerning.

On the Christmas Eve when astronauts were the first to look on the world from a distance that made it possible for them to perceive it as a blue ball, they did not communicate with "the world" by broadcasting readings from their dials and other technical instruments. Instead, one of them read Genesis 1: "In the beginning God created the heavens and the earth." Although a few atheists grumbled about this "governmentally subsidized" intrusion of religious words into a scientific and international political venture, and others might have complained that the words came from the texts of a particular faith, most believers and unbelievers alike found the reading appropriate. Yet this poetic language of wonder and awe in nature had to give way to those dials and instruments in due course: you do not land a spacecraft with only a prayer.

All of this sets the stage to invoke and address our consistent subject: the mystery of the child, now among the other mysteries of nature. By adolescence, most children have begun to learn scientific terms relevant to the pursuit of knowledge of nature; without such shorthand language humans would be ill-served. Some of the young will have become familiar with the language of poetry and scripture and will have been given access to mythic approaches. Most naturalists would prefer to take a day off with children or open-minded seniors than with hardened semiprofessionals who have acquired their relative expertise from *Nature* or *National Geographic* or *Scientific American* and may have become unteachable. The German poet and scientist Johann Wolfgang von Goethe used a special verb, *schauen,* to refer to intense, profound, and perceptive ways of seeing. The child can often see in this sense.

I am not trying to endow all children with mystical powers of penetration of myth or with scientific or poetic precocity; and certainly not all children possess true readiness and openness for the awesome spirit, the Spirit of God, or the kingdom of which Jesus spoke when he insisted that all must become like a little child. Yet, with a few background assumptions in place, much of what we are describing does belong to the world of the child. Those assumptions include the understanding that the one walking in the woods or under the starlit skies has gained the confidence of the child and sets a scene in which the child is at least momentarily free from slavery to computer games, electronic entertainment, or casual ways of "hanging out" to pass the time. We speak of an ordinary child having an extraordinary day because a parent or an older friend has granted her permission to report freely and imaginatively on what she notices. It is extraordinary also because adults are permitted to listen to what the child perceives and reports to another child.

It is time to come in from the stroll in the woods or away from the table on which scriptures rest and take a figurative stroll in the book *Children and Nature.* A reader may dip in almost anywhere and find direction. To begin at the upper end of childhood, adolescence, we listen to Cynthia Thomashow reporting on a visit to a zoo, where she observed six teenagers watching a python shed its skin.[5] It writhed and, as if in empathy, they writhed. Because what emerged was a creature wearing supple new skin, while the old case of the snake was left behind, she borrowed Peter Matthiesen's finding of a metaphor for personal transformation in the performance. Thomashow heard the students make the applications themselves: they felt vulnerable, knew how hard it was to change, and took lessons from the snake. She there saw a connection between "wild nature" and adolescent development.[6]

Testimony came from Paul Shepard: "Ecological thinking requires a kind of vision across boundaries. The epidermis of the skin is ecologically like a pond surface or a forest soil, not a shell so much as a delicate interpenetration." Ecological thinking in his view becomes a contributor to the adolescent quest for identity and a marker of change perceptible to the adult who is patient and who tries to get inside the world of the adolescent, not to dominate it.[7] Thomashow pushes this further, drawing more distinctions by citing Shepard:

> Adolescence is a preparation for ambiguity, a realm of penumbral shadows. Its language includes a widening sensitivity to pun and poetry. Appropriate to its psychology is attention to the zones between categories, zones that have their own animals. The borders from

5. Cynthia Thomashow, "Adolescents and Ecological Identity: Attending to Wild Nature," in *Children and Nature: Psychological, Sociocultural, and Evolutionary Investigations,* ed. Peter J. Kahn Jr. and Stephen R. Kellert (Cambridge, MA: MIT Press, 2002), 259-78.

6. Thomashow, "Adolescents and Ecological Identity," 259.

7. In Thomashow, "Adolescents and Ecological Identity," 260.

> which obscenity and taboo arise are figured in creatures that embody a sense of overlapping reality: the insects that crawl between two surfaces, the owl flying at dusk, the bat that seems to be both bird and mammal. The adolescent person is a marginal being between stages of life, on the shifting sands of an uncertain identity. In this respect his symbols are changeling species: the self-renewing, skin-shedding snake, the amphibious frog that loses a tail and grows legs, the caterpillar that metamorphoses into a butterfly.[8]

Thomashow draws from such signals a central thesis: "that nature can – and I think must – play a key role in the healthy development of adolescent identity."[9] Poetry written by adolescents, or reports on their encounters with the natural world, are often telltale suggestions of their own inner change. In her world, adolescents become involved in issues relating to the management of public land, protecting a wildlife sanctuary, designing zoo exhibits, and more. There are "moments of entry that every educator should look for, unanticipated moments of dissonance and possibility, offering a splendid glimpse at affiliation with nature." Rather than fear what is happening, Thomashow urges others to celebrate, as does she:

> The sparkling moments of awe and wonder, the deep shudders of reverence, the churning beat of sexuality, and the rude spurts of impulse have convinced me that young people in this age group can raise the veil and grasp their "wild" nature with vigor. As an educator, I am searching for ways to use this developmental portal to nurture a more comprehensive human identity, one of self in affiliation with nature. . . . I believe that it will also increase compassion for other species and caring for the earth.[10]

Violent Behaviors

As with this upper edge of childhood, so there is something to learn through all earlier stages. Realism demands notice of the harder, even brutal side of the encounters with nature to which David W. Orr refers when he looks at youthful violence. It is also mysterious, for it "is symp-

8. Thomashow, "Adolescents and Ecological Identity," 262.
9. Thomashow, "Adolescents and Ecological Identity," 263.
10. Thomashow, "Adolescents and Ecological Identity," 277.

tomatic of something much bigger evident in diffuse anger, despair, apathy, the erosion of ideals, and the rising level of teen suicide."

Orr cites Jack Scott's reference to the high modernist surroundings of young people in our time: that means

> a muscle-bound version of the self-confidence about scientific and technical progress, the expansion of production, the growing satisfaction of human needs, the mastery of nature (including human nature), and, above all, the rational design of social order commensurate with the scientific understanding of natural laws.

The reference to the desire for mastery of nature and self goes along with our theme. Orr's reference to political economy also points to collateral effects on children. If a society divorced from natural contexts is organized only around economic growth, it will be in constant turmoil. Joseph Schumpeter accurately described the mechanism: physical capital quickly grows obsolete, thanks to what he called "creative destruction and technological dynamism," which together increase the velocity of lived experience. What the adult world calls "development," to the child in search of place and identity represents "obliteration."[11]

Orr may betray a touch of the Luddite, the would-be machine-smasher or the romantic in himself, and yet his critiques of the child being seen as a commodity and a slave of commodification at least serve as alerts that the adult world should pay attention to ways in which one can modify or counter its worst effects. A religious critique also enters, thanks to a citation of Wendell Berry, who speaks of the "modern superstition" in which "legitimate faith in scientific methodology seems to veer off into a kind of religious faith in the power of science to know all things and solve all problems." So, notes Orr, "children grow up in a thoroughly secular culture, often without awareness that life is both gift and mystery. They are, in other words, spiritually impoverished."[12]

Orr encourages attempts by parents, educators, politicians, and society to promote what E. O. Wilson calls "biophilia," which is defined as "the affinity for life and lifelike processes," or what Rachel Carson pleaded for, a developed "sense of wonder" abetted by "the companionship of at least one adult." A philosopher devoted to ecology, Thomas Berry, adds to the discourse by asking for "an intimate presence within a

11. David W. Orr, "Political Economy and the Ecology of Childhood," in Kahn and Kellert, *Children and Nature,* 286-87.

12. Orr, "Political Economy and the Ecology of Childhood," 290.

meaningful universe."[13] Quoting G. P. Nabhan and S. Trimble, Orr returns, wanting to help "find ways to let children roam beyond the pavement, to gain access to vegetation and earth that allows them to tunnel, climb, or even fall" in "playful exploration of habitat, . . . as well as the gradual accumulation of an oral tradition about the land [all of which] have been essential to child development for over a million years."[14]

The child, born of mystery, given to it, and enshrouded in it, is ennobled by it so that when she "openly confronts nature, one expects transformation." This transformation of the child, and of those who learn from her, works its effects more through experience than through intellectual apprehension, though, as Stephen R. Kellert suggests in *Children and Nature,* when "experiencing nature," the "affective, cognitive, and evaluative development all occur, both in the apprehension of nature and rejection of some of its affects."[15]

By *experiencing,* we here mean everything from dealing with pets, walking in the woods, going on field trips, spending time on the farm or in the garden, or taking courses. The experience gets diluted and turns partial if it is secondhand, as connoted by the phrase "book learning." The Danish philosopher and theologian Søren Kierkegaard wrote that you can be suspended from a ceiling and in that pose read a book on how to swim, but you learn how to swim by swimming. You experience nature not so much through an *Encyclopedia of Birds* as by spotting a particular species, hearing its song. You learn some secrets of the animal world empathically by taking home a wounded forest animal and treating it before turning it loose. The child learns about nature not just by watching a technically accurate television weather forecast that has little to do with mystery, but by camping under the stars or playing games naming cloud formations.

This is not to disdain the secondhand or mediated experience, because it can enlarge what one has seen and heard and felt up close. From prehistory to the present, many people have drawn representations of nature in burial plots or caves. They have depicted symbols and images of animals, and these have provided a vicarious challenge to experience nature. At heart is the emotional and affective contact. Watch the eyes of a child as he visually grasps something vivid in nature — the leap of a cat,

13. Orr, "Political Economy and the Ecology of Childhood," 290.

14. Orr, "Political Economy and the Ecology of Childhood," 300.

15. Stephen R. Kellert, "Experiencing Nature: Affective, Cognitive, and Evaluative Development in Children," in Kahn and Kellert, *Children and Nature,* 117-51.

the shadow cast by a giant tree, the web of a spider — and you will get some sense of how the affective realm is prime for him. Kellert illustrates this theme with the thoroughly memorable and reinforcing lines by Walt Whitman that reflect on the mystery of the child, who is open to wonders:

> There was a child went forth every day,
> And the first object he looked upon, that object he became,
> And that object became part of him for the day or a certain
> part of the day
> Or for many years or stretching cycles of years.
> The early lilacs became part of the child,
> And grass and white and red morning glories, and white
> and red clover
> And the song of the phoebe-bird
> And the Third-month lambs and the sow's pink-faint litter,
> and the mare's foal and the cow's calf.[16]

Those lines spell out something of the mystery of the child almost to the point of the dissolution of the child in the rest of nature and the absorption of the rest of nature by the child. The child is not busy looking up his experience in an encyclopedia or a guidebook. The child is occupied with emotion, sensation, feeling. Most observers of the child's wondrous tie to nature advocate a search for ways to prolong the experience, to help make it serve for memory and hope, so that it can help the child keep the sense of the mystery lifelong.

The same observers also stress, however, that while the affective tie is an end in itself, it is not the end of everything. The child, after wondering, ponders. She builds on previous experiences, mentally cataloguing this flower, her reaction to this flower among other flowers, and other responses. Certain elements in nature are likely to grab different children differently, and they will catalogue and critique the fruits of their encounters. If they have learned from the experience, they are likely to draw lessons from it that they might apply to other situations. Here is where the classroom or the family reading circle comes in as the child follows up, gaining in knowledge. The lucky ones do not leave the experience behind. The mind plays its role, and the experience itself gets filed mentally or put to practical, problem-solving use.

Try as one might, one cannot prevent the child from leaning over into the world of judgment. Kellert stands by, watching children and read-

16. Quoted in Kellert, "Experiencing Nature," 127.

ing what others have found. Taken together, the evaluative judgments in respect to nature can – one dare not say definitively, will – make a mosaic. Speaking of mosaics and their beauty, we begin with the aesthetic, the beauty the child has seen in nature. The overwhelming signals that suggest the power of the stimulus in nature also ordinarily inspire some urge on the part of humans to co-create. This impulse follows encouragement from page one in the Bible. Some children begin to blossom into young adults as they try to "explain" nature. This explaining can move all the way from trying to detail the abyss of mystery to reducing the mysteries of nature into problems to be solved.

Adults who recall their childhood or listen to children reporting will find that often the spontaneous, serendipitous, uncalled-for phenomena leave their stamp on a child. Having nearly drowned while being swept into a fast current, surviving a lightning blow not far from the tree under which one stands, being attacked by a dog, catching a glint of the sun in a drop on a leaf of grass may for a long time startle, astonish, inform, and nurture a child, while calculated contacts between child and nature may have less effect. My personal memory of being bowled over as a small boy by a farmer's overfriendly dogs during on a Sunday afternoon visit with my family colored my experience with canines in ways that I never forgot or overcame. I have left the raising of pets to others, no doubt thus depriving myself of one of the most rewarding ways to know nature. Similarly, indirect experiences also stay with children. Nursery rhymes or fairy tales about menacing wolves or pictures of serene domesticated animals color affective, cognitive, and evaluative possibilities within the child. Children's experiences with television in the last half-century offer well-documented varieties of impacts on children's imaginations. It is ever more difficult to retain balance in the horizon of the heart.

Borrowing further from Kellert's exposition, we can listen to Rachel Carson pondering on wonder, in terms that some will find romantic and overblown, yet which ring true in the experience of many children:

> A child's world is fresh and new and beautiful, full of wonder and excitement. . . . What is the value of preserving and strengthening this sense of awe and wonder, this recognition of something beyond the boundaries of human existence? Is the exploration of the natural world just a pleasant way to pass the golden hours of childhood or is there something deeper? I am sure there is something much deeper, something lasting and significant. . . . Those who contemplate the beauty of the earth find reserves of strength that will endure as long

> as life lasts. There is symbolic as well as actual beauty in the migration of the birds, the ebb and flow of the tides, the folded bud ready for the spring. There is something infinitely healing in the repeated refrains of nature.[17]

Lovers of nature mourn the creation of distance between the child and the rest of nature and criticize the creators of concrete and steel cities, the removers of children from rural life, the devisers of computer games that tempt the child to deal with the mechanical and electronic world as a surrogate for lively interaction with nature. The assault on the natural environment and the child's imagination is not total or final.

Restimulating the Sense of Wonder in Children

I spoke of Carson's quoted words as being tinged with romanticism, as casting too positive a glow on the maturing child carrying lifelong impressions and resolves based on early experiences. Peter H. Kahn Jr., in *Children and Nature,* urges the providers of care, the teachers and guides of children, to help ensure that there be new impressions. He speaks about "environmental generational amnesia" as a reality and a problem. He and his team catalogued approaches to adult "use" of childhood environmental experiences in ways that could help move the issue from the zone of problems into that of mystery. One of these problem-centered approaches they called *anthropocentric reasoning.* This approach was used, for example, when adolescents protested pollution of water as immoral because it can harm humans and their economies. The adolescents studied offered a variety of rationales for their stand: water belongs to the public, and a private "user" of a river had no right to ruin it for others; a clean river beckons swimmers, and a polluted one bars them. The child may not have worked out such rationales, but the adolescent begins to trade on them.[18]

The other approach, *biocentric reasoning,* locates contacts with nature in the zone of mystery. Here the environment is valued no matter what its preservation or destruction means for the human. Nature has intrinsic value, the believer would say, because it was created by God, or so that generations through millennia can relate to it. Animals have rights. Hu-

17. Quoted in Kellert, "Experiencing Nature," 140.

18. Peter H. Kahn Jr., "Children's Affiliations with Nature: Structure, Development, and the Problem of Environmental Generational Amnesia," in Kahn and Kellert, *Children and Nature,* 96.

mans have no right to leave beer cans on the mountain trail. The corporation does not have rights to cloud the air, making it unbeautiful and dangerous to breathe. Kahn and his colleagues also perceived and promoted what they called *isomorphic biocentric reasoning*, in which ties between humans and animal life are correlated. Growing children, as they learn rights and show empathy, can extend them to animals and plants. They will say: you have no right to cause pain in the rabbit or destruction by plucking the wildflower; what would *you* think if you were injured by a deliberate act by an adult or cut off from the sustained life you knew when you were connected to roots?[19]

In sum:

> People take the natural environment they encounter during childhood as the norm against which they measure environmental degradation later in their life. With each ensuing generation, the amount of environmental degradation increases, but each generation takes that degraded condition as the non-degraded condition, as the normal experience. The upside of environmental generational amnesia is that each generation starts afresh, unencumbered mentally by the environmental misdeeds of previous generations. But the downside is enormous. As we lose daily, intimate positive affiliations with nature and accept negative experiences (such as pollution) as the norm, we suffer physically and psychologically and hardly know it.[20]

At the very least such observations lead responsible people to two aspirations: they should do all they can to see that children's experience of nature is immediate, profound, and enduring, *and* they should help grown children trade on that experience and work to interrupt the exponential worsening of the natural environment by adult policies and practices.

The Circumstances Provided by Community

Community in its various forms is an element in the circumstance, that which "stands around" the child, and, when present, can provide the social environment so that the "I am I" is not isolated, solipsistic. Community is hard to find, develop, and sustain. Healthy community is rare; often the circle of people who make up a child's world can be oppressive and

19. Kahn, "Children's Affiliations with Nature," 97.
20. Kahn, "Children's Affiliations with Nature," 113.

will limit his freedom and imagination in thoroughly destructive ways. Where community appears as a positive context, it still needs attention, for it is never a static reality. The privilege of oversight calls each provider of care, beginning with parents and teachers, to observe and address the changes in the development of both the child and his surrounding circumstances. The maternity ward, nursery, preschool, church, hospital, playground, and teen center are settings in which these changes reveal themselves. So are the episodes of war or peace, famine or prosperity, nurture or abuse.

If providers of care have learned to see the child not simply as presenting problems but as appearing in the complex of mystery, they will have special reasons to stress the role of communities with which the child interacts. This is the case because so much of the wonder of young ones is enhanced when adults pay attention to the company children keep, the people with whom they interact. This means concern for the encounter with "the Other." Givers of care will be especially committed to making room not only for the activities but especially for the stories through which children find that Other. Such encounters should be rich within faith communities, where the door to wonder ought to open wide.

When James Michael Lee offered advice on teaching, he concentrated on community in contemporary culture, where we so often see the individual isolated from supportive company. He was writing for adults and was evidently thinking mainly of them, and he commented on only one religion, but his concepts are translatable to children and to the context of other faith communities. Here is a version of Ortega's "I am myself and my circumstances." Lee writes:

> Christianity is a religion of solitariness and socialness. Christianity is a solitary religion in that the person often meets God most deeply and most existentially in the solitariness of one's own existence. But this solitariness takes place in the broader context of socialness or corporateness. Sometimes this corporateness is remote, at other times it is immediate – but it is always there.[21]

When using half of those inelegant words ending in "-ness," Lee was pointing to the extreme individualism favored in much of the adult

21. James Michael Lee, "How to Teach: Foundations, Processes, Procedures," in *Handbook of Preschool Religious Education,* ed. Donald Ratcliff (Birmingham, AL: Religious Education Press, 1988), 215.

world. Such individualism insists that the private zone alone is the sphere of the spiritual, even among children. Community, which many critics in our culture dismiss out of hand, is disdained as it takes form in "organized religion" or "the institutional church," at which those critics sneer. Though some adults isolate children from the company of other adults, the children often circulate among the grown-ups, taking comfort from their presence. They show curiosity and, in a way, join in the partying, ready for conversation with adults. Children are dependent, social beings, and they develop healthily in the context of others, whether their peers or their elders. This "socialness," to which Lee refers in the other half of his pairings, has to be discovered, developed, and taught, through play and work alike. Such teaching will not be profitable unless providers of care devote serious attention to it.

The Formation and Roles of Community

All promoters of community engage in critique of one form or another when they face extreme individualism, and this is true also in spiritual life. Thus Mitchell L. Stevens, in *The Kingdom of Children,* a study of homeschoolers, renders judgments. He cites what sociologist Robert N. Bellah and his colleagues, in *Habits of the Heart,* called "expressive individualism." The authors contended in that book that

> it is individualism, and not equality, as Tocqueville thought, that has marched inexorably through our history. We are concerned that this individualism may have grown cancerous — that it may be destroying those social integuments that Tocqueville saw as moderating its more destructive potentialities, that it may be threatening the survival of freedom itself.[22]

All this at the expense of "the subtle ties that bind human beings to one another, leaving them frightened and alone." Stevens also cites Peter Clecak, one of a number of analysts of this phenomenon who recognize and point to some signs of recovery:

> A quest for personal fulfillment within a small community (or several communities) of significant others: this strikes me as the dominant

22. Quoted in Mitchell L. Stevens, *The Kingdom of Children: Culture and Controversy in the Homeschooling Movement* (Princeton, NJ: Princeton University Press, 2001), 181.

> thrust of American civilization during the sixties and seventies [precisely the time of the rise of the homeschooling movement]. . . . The quest . . . is a multifaceted search conducted with varying degrees of intensity and different specific aims by elements of the population as diverse as born-again Christians and atheistic feminists, gay-rights activists and red-neck males, mainline Protestants and hard-line conservatives.[23]

Stevens muses that "perhaps it is little coincidence, then, that since the 1960s Americans have developed ever more elaborate means of nurturing little selves when they are children, and for accommodating their distinctiveness as they grow." One part of the cultural ferment born in the 1960s is the field of alternative education. The market is full of books helping parents nurture "children's inner essences and catering to their individual needs."[24]

In the paragraphs that follow I am going to convoke a virtual company of educators whose writings have appeared in a printed symposium, to see what clues they offer for probing the mystery of community and the child's social circumstances. I begin with Mary Anne Fowlkes, who devotes herself to "religion and socialization" as she takes due notice of the mystery of the child in both his singularity and his associational life. Her accent is on the value of tradition, "that which is handed down," and she stresses the role of stories as a prominent means for passing elements of tradition on to the very young. Over against rootlessness and expressive individualism, she contends that a "rootedness in one's own religious tradition – developed through the rituals, sacraments, language, and symbols of the community – forms a sound basis for religious nurture for Protestants, Catholics, and Jews," and today, of course, we would add Muslims and others.[25]

Fowlkes therefore takes sides, as do I, on the issue of whether adults should set out to keep the child in isolation until she makes her choice among religious options and communities. Whoever abandons the child to such an endeavor deprives her of rich repositories of options for her creative use. Fowlkes's concern clearly counters the view often expressed by parents that the adults who provide care should be careful not to influence the child in respect to traditions of religion, faith, spirituality, and

23. Quoted in Stevens, *The Kingdom of Children,* 181.

24. Stevens, *The Kingdom of Children,* 183.

25. Mary Anne Fowlkes, "Religion and Socialization," in Ratcliff, ed., *Handbook of Preschool Religious Education,* 125.

community, all of which are partly accessible through stories. According to this view, they would do nothing to encourage belonging to or being committed to the company of other people, including other children, at church or temple.

Educator Steven Vryhof defends the role of community, pointing to the work of one of his own teachers, James C. Coleman. That mentor, after making many studies and surveys, concluded that the presence of community helps the child because it fosters *"value consistency,"* the awareness of a "shared understanding of what the world is about, what is important, and how the group should live." It also promotes what Coleman calls *"intergenerational closure,* which seals adult-child relationships and magnifies the opportunities that activate them." Together these make up what Coleman calls *social capital.*[26]

Social capital is invested to counter what another advocate, John J. DiIulio Jr., calls "moral poverty," a deprivation that derives from the absence of vital community. His emphatic word draws on the mystery of positive relationships as they help promote sympathy and common action:

> Moral poverty is the poverty of being without loving, capable, responsible adults who teach you right from wrong. It is the poverty of being without parents and other authorities who habituate you to feel joy at others' joy, pain at others' pain, happiness when you do right, remorse when you do wrong. It is the poverty of growing up in the virtual absence of people who teach morality by their own everyday example and who insist that you follow suit.[27]

For all the praise of community, especially religious community, some analysts worry with good cause that such community can become oppressive and repressive. Anyone who is regularly close to religious communities has heard horror stories of how constricting versions of these can lead to a loss of imagination and of freedom of choice when children moving toward adulthood seek a spiritual home. Some of those who have lacked an identity take refuge in new religious movements (NRMs), formerly called cults. Various authors, among them Fowlkes, reassure — or disturb — adults with the acknowledgment that when the child becomes

26. James S. Coleman, *Public and Private High Schools: The Impact of Communities* (New York: Basic Books, 1987), 36, quoted in Steven C. Vryhof, *Between Memory and Vision: The Case for Faith-Based Schooling* (Grand Rapids: Eerdmans, 2004), 4.

27. Quoted in Vryhof, *Between Memory and Vision,* 16-17.

an adult and is therefore busy putting together a philosophy of life and making commitments, she will do most deciding on her own. Therefore the child in adulthood may or may not affiliate with a religious group or find some other kind of community as she grows. She is free to ignore parental or other adult counsel. She may be emotionally crippled if childhood influences on her have been too restrictive. More likely she will do her own choosing by reaching into a repository of options. She will remain aware that there was or is a mooring from which to sail in the course of her life and will remain at least dimly familiar with ways others have measured the appropriateness of what diverse spiritual communities offer and demand.

A nagging question deserves response: When these offspring, now nurtured in a tradition or two, find reason to reject it, as so many do, is this the sign of a confused mind? Many observers of fundamentalist families see the children growing up burdened by the outlook imposed on them and vehemently rejecting their spiritual past. On the other hand, the young person who received no coherent set of symbols, whether from home, in schooling, among peers, over mass media, or at a university, will not have much knowledge on the basis of which to make informed judgments on urgent matters.

Although many counselors concentrate only on developmental stages of knowing, Fowlkes is in the company of those who propose styles of faith that will last lifelong, just as we picture certain dimensions of childhood lasting until death. She describes four styles, within which faith is "experienced, dependent, searching, owned." All are equal in value, and none has priority. In this model, the age group to which one belongs matters less than it does in approaches that stress stages of development. The family and the church, with their mix of persons in all age groups, can be major agencies for this transmission of faith.

Some who promote the communal values of stories, enactments, experiences, and common language become explicit about the mystery of faith, which in our culture more often than not is Christian. Thus G. Bedouelle introduces a refreshing concept when he explicitly speaks of the "'catholicity of childhood' being couched in the mystery of the Christ image unfolding in each of its parts, including his infancy." Over against those who associate religious community with adults, Bedouelle elaborates on "the gifts of childhood to the church," gifts that are familiar by now to anyone reading these pages but are too seldom recognized by adults. Those who followed our earlier comments on the child in the Gospels can anticipate Bedouelle, who sees the gifts of children being "spontaneity, openness to revelation, playfulness, and hunger for learning."[28]

Friendship is an element of community and is also a contributor to developmental processes in the spiritual life of children. In fact, the more one studies friendship, whether on evolutionary, strategic, or philosophical grounds, the more appropriate it is to speak of the "mystery of friendship" itself. Fowlkes addresses the question by asking "what is a peer?" and going on to discern what roles friends and peers play in stimulating social and spiritual development. Unfortunately, some friends can do much to dull the creativity and the mystery of the child, but in more cases they can also enhance these aspects. Note that "while most of the research on friendships has been done on close-age groups . . . there are untapped possibilities in the parish community for both cross-age relationships and diversity in friendship options if structured carefully." Thus a preschool child can be linked with a single adult, and if there is ethnic diversity one can build on that in a parish as well.[29] Linking a preschool child as a friend to a handicapped member who needs assistance is another way of developing such friendships. Such linkings move in two directions: both elder and younger people in the interaction learn and contribute.

One more point from Fowlkes: some readers may consider the goal of child development amid spiritual community and resources as she describes them to be an almost Utopian idea. They are not. It is true that those who choose to go heroically or hermetically on a lonely journey of spiritual discovery experience some kinds of adventure that offer glamour. The end result of such a pilgrimage can be the isolation of the grown child in spiritual individualism. Along the way, such a journey can sometimes be described as a prophetic judgment against conformist membership in religious bodies. Many biographies that follow individuals through adult life are quite consistent, however, in finding positives accompanying the continuities that healthy communities provide and support. The particular freedom that the growing child or adolescent seeks during the time of cultural transmission can thrive through a path that Fowlkes contends ensures two kinds of freedom: freedom "*from* chaos, confusion, and fragmentation and freedom *for* creative living together in a community bound together by a coherent symbol system." She seals this comment with one more: "As members are shaped, they in turn have the freedom to reshape their community."[30]

28. Quoted in Fowlkes, "Religion and Socialization," 130.

29. Fowlkes, "Religion and Socialization," 147.

30. Fowlkes, "Religion and Socialization," 126.

The Scaffold and Intersubjectivity

Laura E. Berk, in her *Awakening Children's Minds: How Parents and Teachers Can Make a Difference,* introduced the thought of I. S. Vigotsky, who wrote in the context of Soviet-era restrictions. He was a major theorist of the way the child interacts with her natural, manufactured, and human environments, and Berk, among others, applied Vigotsky's findings to the American scene in ways that I find promising for discussing spiritual development. Berk labels Vigotsky's proposal "sociocultural theory." She describes it as a dynamic, synergistic perspective that in her view "has recently captivated the field" or in our view can be seen as a valuable contributor to it. She sets the stage for Vigotsky's theory in this way:

> The central idea of sociocultural theory is that the child and his or her social surroundings join to provide direction to development; participation in social life guides and energizes the child's mastery of new, culturally adaptive skills. Because sociocultural theory focuses on children's access to and interaction with cultural experts, it has much to say to parents and teachers about how they can help children develop into responsible, contributing members of society.[31]

Berk notes that many psychologists who questioned at least some of the Piagetan views because they did not seem to give enough scope to the variety of competencies among children gravitated to Vigotsky's alternative explanatory model. It relies on cooperative dialogues "between children and more knowledgeable members of their society." These conversations and interactions occur often and spontaneously, as children and adults play, study, read stories, go on outings, and do chores together. Even the most ordinary conversations can be illuminating (pp. 30-31).

> Sociocultural theory is unique in viewing inner mental activity as profoundly social. The thoughts and imaginings that make us distinctly human are not regarded as independently constructed by the child. Rather, the child derives them from his or her history of relations with other people. . . . A basic premise of sociocultural theory is that all uniquely human, higher forms of thinking – including controlled attention to tasks, memory strategies, reflections on experiences and

31. Laura E. Berk, *Awakening Children's Minds: How Parents and Teachers Can Make a Difference* (New York: Oxford University Press, 2001), 30-31. Subsequent page references to her book will be given parenthetically in the text.

> ideas, techniques for solving problems, and imagination – are deeply affected by children's social experiences. (pp. 32-33)

In this perspective, as Berk outlines it, adults build what she calls a scaffold, which they use to support children while the young ones go about taking on culturally valued skills and ideas. The metaphor is helpful: "In scaffolding, the child is viewed as a building – actively under construction. . . . To promote development, the adult [scaffold builder] provides a dynamic flexible scaffold – or framework – that assists the child in mastering new competencies." The adults, in this metaphor, vary their assistance first by adjusting tasks so that at each stage they are appropriately challenging, but then also by tailoring the degree of adult intervention to the child's current learning need (pp. 46-47).

On this scaffolding, the role of story and stories take on special importance. If story upholds community, conversation advances it further. Through all the phases of childhood, the child will hear and contribute to conversation in different forms and at different levels in a pattern now commonly referred to as adult-child *intersubjectivity*. As the provider of care connects with the child, she offers the figurative scaffold for supporting the child who seeks some sort of mastery of fresh tasks at each level. Whenever the teacher or parent or coach offers guidance, counsels Berk, the communication must be one of "high warmth." When the climate is right and all are secure, the adults will hear children's narratives about their experiences (p. 73).

Vigotsky advances the theme as he speaks of the way play and fantasy represent a "zone" in which children experiment with a variety of skills and values. Life in that zone is especially vivid in religious contexts. One thinks of children at Seder meals, in Purim festivals, or in Christmas pageants where they represent adults. There they reach for the transcendent Other:

> [Make-believe] play creates a zone of proximal development in the child. In play, the child always behaves beyond his average age, above his daily behavior; in play it is as though he were a head taller than himself. As in the focus of a magnifying glass, play contains all developmental tendencies in condensed form and is itself a major source of development. (p. 111)[32]

32. Quoting L. S. Vygotsky, *Mind in Society: The Development of Higher Mental Processes* (Cambridge, MA: Harvard University Press, 1978), 102.

Laura Berk herself observed children as they "made-believe" and then reported on several contributions of such play to development. Children, she saw, paid attention and grew in attentiveness. Their memory was enhanced, because from game to game, scene to scene, day to day, they had to resituate themselves. Their language scope grew in this zone, as did their impulse to pursue literacy, to enhance their stories. Interestingly, they learned much about hypothetical reasoning because much of their play was, shall we say, nothing but hypothetical. From some angles, they knew this to be true. In the course of time, as we earlier noted, make-believe play taught them to separate appearance from reality. In interactions they learned self-regulation in ways they would not have otherwise. Most of all, in this zone, imagination and creativity prospered (pp. 119-29).

Berk summarized Vigotsky in ways that underscore a theme of this book, the observation and contention that dimensions of being a child are to last lifelong. From our angle, this is good news:

> [T]he drive to fantasize and engage in role play does not fade away with childhood. Instead . . . the imagination of later years is an internalized, condensed form of early childhood make-believe that can be considered play without action. We typically experience it as an elaborate stream of consciousness made up of mental images and silent self-talk that meanders along, remarking on new experiences, reflecting on the past, and predicting the future. (p. 129)

The reference in those lines to "later years" signals what was implied in the preceding pages: that the circumstances, context, and community of the child changes even as the child changes and moves through various passages into adulthood. Context, therefore, has temporal implications, usually taken up under the theme of *development,* the theme that occupies us next.

9. Receptivity "Beyond Good and Evil"

Novelist Georges Bernanos put into the mouth of a French country priest words that condense a main theme of this book on the mystery of the child. Before we treat the growth and development of the child, it is at the same time refreshing and startling to turn back to that theme. He said that "some of the most terrible [words] ever heard by human ears" are "'if you are not like one of these little ones, you will not enter the Kingdom of God.'" More radical still, we noted, is another verse from Jesus speaking in Matthew: "unless you change and become like children, you will never enter the kingdom of heaven" (Matthew 18:3).[1]

With a shelf full of biblical commentaries at hand, we isolated which feature of being a child these texts celebrated. If adults are to "change" and "become like children," what is it about children that can make them a model? Out of an array of proposed qualities, their *receptivity* best captured the meaning. Let us take a moment for review. We observed that children know that they can never have earned the gifts they are given. Children appreciate a gift as an absolute, something that they are aware they cannot have worked to deserve. As years pass, they will learn to transact with those who can reward their efforts, but at heart being a child means being dependent and thus necessarily receptive. But their receptivity is not of a passive sort, and an adult can also be "like a child." Thus we were told of an impetuous woman who "was a Gentile of Syrophoenician origin," who prevailed upon Jesus to exorcise a demon from her daughter (Mark 7:24-30). Matthew tells of another outsider, a Roman centurion, who had no choice but to be receptive (Matthew 8:5-13). Karl Rahner, in

1. See p. 71 in Chapter 5 above.

words so applicable to our theme that they merit being quoted a second time, projected the inherited factor of childhood demonstrated by both the woman and the centurion "as receptivity, as hope which is still not disillusioned" and which takes "the form of trust, of openness, of expectation, . . . of interior harmony with the unpredictable forces with which the individual finds himself confronted. It must manifest itself as freedom."[2]

Although Rahner projected this trait through all the years of life, even to the end, it is our task at the moment only to follow out what the feature of receptivity and the act of receiving mean for the early years of life – childhood into adolescence. To do so with the concept of the mystery of the child in mind necessitates sorting out and sifting through the claims, many of them helpful, that promote development and education. Our agenda is not to provide an instruction manual on how to do this, step by step. Understanding something of the act of being receptive and open to development is the present issue.

Such understanding occurs in a cultural context. Best-seller lists in the child development sections of libraries and bookstores address these themes, sometimes in ways that overadvertise the possibilities they offer. Picture the actual situation when a book is bannered as an aid because it will tell readers everything they ought to know about the child or will describe the child and her world "from A to Z." Such books have their place, yet even experts who write them find considerable difference between describing the generic child and living with any specific one. The encyclopedias draw upon laboratory and clinical studies, educational research and medical experiments. Many of those who read them become parents and soon find a great gap between two realities. There before them is a mysterious, living, breathing, kicking, excreting, gurgling, distinctive, and, of course, unique newborn. Those who profited from the reading will quickly find how important it becomes to deal with *this* child. As they do so, they will find some of the limits of practical and scientific expertise while they concentrate on the mystery of the child that is their own or under their care, the child with indefinite – we like to say with almost infinite – possibilities.

Observing the child as a subject of wonder lessens some of the urgency that has long impelled givers of advice to overdefine problems and overprescribe solutions. Suppose the child were "nothing but" the mass

2. Karl Rahner, "Ideas for a Theology of Childhood," chap. 3 in *Theological Investigations,* vol. 8: *Further Theology of the Spiritual Life,* trans. David Bourke (New York: Herder and Herder, 1971), 47.

of cells that some scientists contend she is. Even in that case it is difficult to reduce her to something that one could explain, someone whose every move was determined or programmed. Would reducing and explaining such a child successfully remove the penumbra of mystery that surrounds her?

Suppose further that we have determined what the child's essential nature is, as some propose to do. Having written our summary, are we then no longer able to be surprised when he then acts or speaks? Or suppose that we have made room for all the circumstances that "determine" his actions: Would he then be predictable and controllable? Commonsense approaches color the observations of even rigorous materialists, and conventional wisdom serves us well here. It frames discussion of the child of whatever genetic makeup as we observe him dealing with his complex natural and social environment, his circumstance – that which stands around the child and will also confront the senior in nature and history, in all that is possible and all that occurs. These circumstances change with the locales, seasons, and events, but few of them occasion more experiences that manifest the mystery of the child than formal development itself, the various phases and stages through which he moves in his early years, and soon after. Whoever might peddle an encyclopedic view of the child at birth or at age three or five or seven will have sold something that is out of date for the same child at four and six and eight. Still, the effort to understand these passages in life can be of some help both for interpreting the child and for penetrating more of his mystery.

Each Distinctive Child Receives Differently

With that kind of experience in mind, I have chosen to speak more often of the child than of children, using "he" and "she" in turn. To focus on the mysterious distinctives of the particular child does not mean that there is nothing to learn from the problem-oriented references that point to common and general features. It does mean that the fathomless and mysterious way of regarding the child serves particular purposes and that these deserve attention.

We inevitably do some classifying whenever we attempt to interpret something. I plead guilty for having done some classifying in two broad categories, two ways of looking at the child: as problem and as mystery. There is not much chance that we can understand "*this* child" without locating some aspects of her existence in a classification, a catalogue. To throw light on a single African-American child, a middle-class suburban youngster, one's own middle offspring, a child born to privilege or in poverty, inevitably elicits some typifying and calls for the observer to keep an eye on particular environments and responses. Each individual child, however, if given a voice, would resist being classified, hoping that we would see in this resistance a plea to have the mysterious dimensions of her existence honored. Classically, philosopher and psychologist William James spoke in ways that we can appropriately relate to children in his *Varieties of Religious Experience.* Arguing that notice must be paid to each individual, he agreed that in order to study anything one must do *some* classifying, *some* typifying. However, James warned, the observer dare not think that labeling someone has done justice to her. Thus, he illustrated in ironic fashion: "Probably a crab would be filled with a sense of personal outrage if it could hear us class it without ado or apology as a crustacean, and thus dispose of it." Instead: "'I am no such thing,' it would say; 'I am MYSELF, MYSELF alone.'"[3]

Observers and those who provide care for the problem child know of this complexity about children and make allowance for the limits with which they must work. To compensate, specialists among them may concentrate in an article or a book on a particular child, such as *this* autistic child or *this* Asian-American musical prodigy. The same observers know that they cannot spend a lifetime studying more than a few of the couple of billion children and still make much of a contribution to knowledge or to care. So they typify.

From the other angle, books that concentrate on the mystery of the child cannot do justice to the subject without treating problems that come with the mysterious character of each, or even with the problems that the approach-through-mystery may exacerbate. Being engrossed with the problems of the problem child or of those who surround him often can stifle the imagination and creativity. Isolating "mystery" can lead to frivolous and irresponsible treatment. One may be tempted to stand in awe of the wonder of the child, but it does no child a favor to ignore what dire things bad diets, overscheduling, underfunded schooling, racial prejudice, or religion-based abuse can do to kill the aura and the inner character of mystery. The caregiver who contemplates all the contingencies is instead likely to turn humble, to do anything but convey a sense of cocksureness or make efforts to gain total control. Although the ap-

3. William James, *The Varieties of Religious Experience: A Study in Human Nature* (1902; New York: Penguin, 1982), 9.

proach that reckons with mystery by its very nature allows for more scope, more good and bad guesses, fresh pedagogies, or enlivening poems than does the problem-centered approach, it also needs the dose of realism that the orientation posed by problem-solvers brings.

This mystery begins with birth, when the factor of receptivity is most evident. Admittedly, the mystery that goes with conception, the child's experience and nurture in the womb, and the medical, ethical, philosophical, and nurturing themes associated with embryonic and fetal existence have a bearing on much that follows. Beginning with birth instead of conception as we are doing is not a choice born of cowardice, an attempt to avoid the intense debates over methods of birth control, *in vitro* fertilization, and abortion. Instead this choice is made in no small measure with efficiency and competences in mind. Dealing with developmental issues before birth calls forth another whole range of ethical and metaphysical questions. They demand different kinds of expertise and displays of political finesse than does the story of the born child.

Our concentration is on the born child, who is available for observation and care. The infant emerging from between his mother's thighs is a tangible sign of the mystery of childhood. He must be touched, held, cradled, supported, and carried. Thus the newborn has at once entered the world of finitude, contingency, and transience. He is dependent upon physicians, nurses, midwives, parents, and other adults who themselves embody the awareness, as the newborn cannot do yet, that he will die, that accidents will happen, and that all traces of his existence on earth will eventually pass. What will the adults make of this child? What will they teach? How will these grown-ups be changed by this new presence — especially if they are to change and become "like" him? More questions present themselves: What new awareness, responsibilities, and concepts will result from the adult encounter with this mysterious subject? Circumstances change; so does the child, in limitless numbers of interactions with those circumstances.

The Capabilities in Their Place among Generations

Because psychology and related sciences have so much to offer on this subject, the research that experts in those fields undertake deserves the attention and favor often shown them. It is in no way a call to slow down or to put a damper on problem-centered research to say that curiosities related to the mystery of the child and the fathomlessness of her possibilities creatively complement inquiries into problems, or at least expose them in another light. In fact, it is illuminating to see how those who deal with problems themselves inform the contemplation of mystery.

Instead of thinking in universal and generic terms, responsible caregivers face what is before them: a particular child in a particular time and place. Their care naturally will differ at each stage of childhood. The agents of care may well be responsive to signals from the surrounding community, especially a community that offers religious prescriptions for care. Because we will be talking about overlapping phases of childhood and maturation more than about clearly separated and successfully left-behind "stages," it is not possible or necessary to be precise about the end of the childhood we discuss here – especially because we are determined to anticipate the fate of the mystery of childhood that is part of the person through life. Adolescence represents the ill-defined temporal zone between the experience of the child and that of the young adult. Young adulthood itself is already beyond our focus. Then a whole different set of thinkers, poets, scientists, and sociologists come on the scene to train their eye on adults.

Our concern is for the receptivity of the little child, the openness and responsiveness to "ideas, impressions, or suggestions," as the dictionary puts it, and also for reception, "the act or action or an instance of receiving." How an individual receives will depend to some extent on the signals each receives from his or her surroundings within a particular generation. One way caregivers and analysts of culture alike make sense of the stages of growth is to locate the child in a skein of such generations, each of which has distinctive experiences. Various philosophers offer their own reckonings of how humans in these generations intersect and overlap. For one example, we will turn again to Ortega y Gasset and, now, his disciple Julían Marías, who are among the twentieth century's more provocative speculators about generations.

Ortega offered his musings about generations as "suggestions," and we shall pick them up. "Each transformation of the world and its horizon brings a change in the structure of life's drama."[4] The child is born into a world made by her parents and the generations before them. It is the young one's task or gift to grasp what is around her in the culture they share. These expectations differ, depending upon who is interacting with her. From what generation do these others come: Are they tiny peers, ma-

4. Ortega, quoted by Karl J. Weintraub, *Visions of Culture* (Chicago: University of Chicago Press, 1966), 275.

ture providers of care, or old grandparents? Change occurs in a wild variety of forms as generations interact. This interaction has never meant that all of the agency comes from the dominating senior groups. The child has her own weaponry in the form of tantrums, tears, smiles, arguments, and responses to bribes or threats. She will by all means not always appear to be receptive. And she does not only receive. She in turn teaches the adult through the pictures she draws, the dreams she expounds, and the tales she tells. Interactions across the generations change the members of each generation, while many aspects of the mystery of the child are freshly exposed to view.

Ortega's concept of generations – and what they experience, embody, and project – depended upon observations that are as old as Aristotle, who distinguished among the children who mature into a world, the adults who rule in the world and keep developing it, and the older generation, whose members were most responsible for the world into which the child grows. They all coexist, and they interact across the boundaries of generations and ages.[5] Each individual personalizes the "fit" into his generation just as he effects some change within it.

Ortega spoke of the "date zone," during which in each case a particular vital function occurred. "Age is not a datum but a 'date zone.'"[6] Zones are usually related to space, but here they describe times of life and situations in cultures. One can make use of this observation by Ortega in the study of child-care manuals, to whose generational history we have already given attention. Some adults were born in and shaped by the "Dr. Spock" date zone, and others that of B. F. Skinner. What is useful about the zone is its paradoxical mix of definiteness and indefiniteness. A driver entering a particular part of a city confronts signs asking for traffic to be silent because the road passes through a "Hospital Zone." There is no particular eight-foot stretch that marks the transition, and, in my observation, one is rarely if ever notified that the zone now lies behind. "Start Honking Again" or "Turn Your Boombox Back Up" are not signs one sees at the indeterminate end of a zone. So it is with the global zones: Does one know the instant or the mile when the ship is passing from the temperate to the torrid zone? So in the stages and phases of childhood: the boundaries are indistinct, but the passages across them are decisive.

Into the sequence of generations a child is born. The original providers of care, notably parents and other family members, begin to share the oversight of the child's development. Sooner or later, nowadays sooner,

5. Ortega, in Weintraub, *Visions of Culture,* 278.

the child participates in preschool or kindergarten activities, where a new set of providers, notably teachers, takes over some of the responsibilities. Each child is a stranger to each teacher, so the teacher must quickly assess the child's capabilities, heritage, identity, and context. Characteristically, the engaged adults have to wrestle with expressions that inspire the familiar impulse to control. At each stage of childhood development different assessments and strategies will be needed, and each can lead adults to render them all in the category of problems and neglect the promise of dealing with the mystery of the child.

At once, questions about institutions relating to care come up — agencies such as Sunday or Sabbath school, nursery, preschool, and kindergarten, daycare, and the most intimate institution, the family. Those parents and other providers of care who work to ensure the freedom of their child may grow suspicious of many institutions, not least among them in many cases religious agencies, because many have the reputation of being too controlling. Or, in some cases, parents perceiving chaos or license in traditional settings invent new institutions, such as "alternative schools." Unfortunately, many in the movement to offer such alternatives believe that the only way for adults to bring up children is to assert strong control. Thus some justify the reinvention of homeschooling because it can provide rigor, discipline, and control. They find the gentler and more relaxed models of schooling to be too soft, too yielding, and thus to be contributors to waywardness and spoiling.

Rather than being gentle and relaxed forms, many institutions and styles of schooling are framed and staffed by people who are obsessed with the issue of control. Reformers have to attack them, as did John Holt, who called most education of our time in most forms "the ugly and anti-human business of people-shaping." He urged contemporaries to "let people shape themselves." This champion of free school movements charged: "We adults destroy most of the intellectual and creative capacity of children by the things we do to them or make them do. We destroy this capacity above all by making them afraid, afraid of not doing what other people want, of not pleasing, of making mistakes, of failing, of being *wrong*."[7] It pains me to think how often the religious impulse in school is designed precisely to issue in control and to produce fear. In such cases the adults stifle the child's receptivity and limit his powers of reception.

6. Ortega, in Weintraub, *Visions of Culture,* 279.

7. John Holt, *How Children Fail* (New York: Pitman, 1964), 35-36.

Developing "Ideas, Impressions, or Suggestions" of God

In few areas will issues of control be more evident than in contexts where adults deal with the deepest mysteries, many of which are focused on profound themes with which children grapple. Those providers of care who have the spiritual interests of children at heart in any institutional context pay attention to the ways in which children develop their religious or spiritual concepts. Those who cherish the mystery of the child find good reason to cheer the elusiveness of children who evade and escape the strictures of those who wish to measure, systematize, and objectify everything that children have to say, for example, on the most decisive issue, the character of God. Religiously self-assured adults often display great confidence in their ability to define God, outline the attributes of God, know and declare precisely what God is doing or what the will of God is in various circumstances. They do this with more definition than do the often ambiguous and, yes, mysterious texts that themselves inspire the religious traditions and institutions. Psychologists and educators who follow children through their development may feel called to help them clarify their concepts and images of God but then often give up in frustration – usually because they had in mind too precise prescriptions for the children in their care. Most children will and must live with some mutually contradictory images with which they express their relation to God. The world of children is so full of hard-to-pin-down understandings that one should not be surprised when many of them turn out to be heterodox or heretical when pressed to be concrete about their handling of the abstraction "God."

Not being an educator or a survey researcher, I depend upon the research of others who bring a variety of commitments to their inquiries and then use their findings as raw material for assessing aspects of the mystery of the child who is confronting the mystery of God. Little conformity to adult expectations is evident among children studied in free and relatively open learning circumstances. Kenneth Hyde, a helpful and balanced assessor of the scenes where psychologists of religion turn in their reports, himself confesses to some bewilderment or bafflement when he hears what children say about God and how their elders interpret the gap between what the little ones say and what presumably they are going to be encouraged or even "allowed" to believe when they become adults.

Hyde does not lose his analytic cool as he does his fair summarizing and reporting, but taken only slightly out of context, he sounds almost judgmental. The children he studied had difficulty producing a one-size-fits-all developmental norm and then finding the doctrines to match each at each stage. However, what might frustrate the systematizer of theology enthralls the observer of the mystery of the child as she confronts the mystery of God. Hyde fortunately is realistic in his appraisal of adults and properly acknowledges that "the variety of ideas of God held by children must be set in the context of the great complexity and diversity of belief held by mature believers."[8]

Hyde's students analyzed young children's descriptions in one group and found ninety-one adjectives that children used to picture God. These included ideas that relate to impersonal concepts of God, as in the image of God as the watchmaker who creates and winds a clock and then goes off the scene and has become inaccessible. Other children dwelt on the eternality of God or responded to the complexity of claims about God's self-disclosure. Still others wanted to find what they were told by adults to find. Some spontaneously came up with words they thought described divine kindliness, "omni-ness," and "wrathfulness."[9]

After reviewing the work of two surveyors of the literature,[10] Hyde related the various children's concepts of God to stage theories of development. The littlest ones, ages two and three, were able to connect God with nature, churches, heaven, and magic. In a phrase that echoes the writing in the Gospels themselves, he said that most "expressed little more than a simple belief in God and a trust that he cared for them." By ages four and five they surmised the existence of a powerful God, who, in the imagining of many children, was watching over people and punishing wrongdoing: the children who spoke of this wisely wanted to know and please this God. In their next two years some of them witnessed to the fact that they were satisfyingly close to God and that they recognized the orderliness of God's activity, though — and we hear a note of condescension here — their thought was "still dominated by anthropomorphic terms."

Only the front-rank children among them, Hyde found, were beginning to show traces of being at home with abstract concepts. By the time they reached age eight or nine, God for them was taking on the outlines of a loving father and was seen to be Spirit, one who inspired a sense of responsibility, as in the cases where children enjoyed church activities that

8. Kenneth E. Hyde, *Religion in Childhood and Adolescence: A Comprehensive Review of the Research* (Birmingham, AL: Religious Education Press, 1990), 64.

9. R. L. Gorsuch, quoted by Hyde, *Religion in Childhood and Adolescence,* 65.

10. H. D. Wright and W. A. Koppe, in Hyde, *Religion in Childhood and Adolescence,* 65.

advanced their understanding. Doubt was allowed to creep in during their second decade, and "finally," the scholars say, children's predilection for anthropomorphic reference ended when they entered their teens. Now, says the report, they became more responsible and eager to serve in the church, where they would learn more about God. A few then in more studied and profound ways looked for meaning but faulted God for some troubles in the world. By mid-teens the ranks of the children being studied were dividing, with some holding firm beliefs and others veering off into doubt. Children up to adolescence were seldom restrained in their imaginings unless adults on the scene – parents, teachers, pastors – wrote them off for having expressed unorthodox or even heretical themes even as they tried to build up faith.

Spontaneity begins to be hard to discern, say the survey-takers, when children approach high school: "Over-socialization by church and family inhibited many spontaneous religious ideas, and the effect of the media and television was very strong." It was the media that provided and legitimated anthropomorphic images of God.[11] For some, parochial school completed the process, as within it "the children saw God less in personal terms and more as the God of the Bible and the catechism – all knowing, all powerful, forgiving repentant sinners, but a watcher who was not too close to mankind. Theological qualities of God tended to be confused." Throughout, parents were normally at the same time the agents of confusion and clarity.[12]

As children pass from stage to stage, a divide among them widens. On one side are those who display expressive "religiousness,"[13] usually evidencing some tie to a visible body of believers. There tends to be among them considerable spiritual continuity, while the disaffiliated contemporaries begin to be engaged in a constant set of changes, in which each change tends to conflict with or replace its predecessor. But all along, says Hyde, those who pay attention to them find that children have been wrestling with the themes that animate and agitate the souls of religious adults. At first, most children were, consciously or not, unable to give much meaning to the words they were taught to say and sing and believe. But as they grew, they acquired a sense of meaning and could build on it. Many held ideas that God is another person, albeit bigger, older than, and wearing clothes different from those worn by the adults whom they knew.

11. Hyde, *Religion in Childhood and Adolescence,* 73.
12. Hyde, *Religion in Childhood and Adolescence,* 65.
13. Hyde, *Religion in Childhood and Adolescence,* 115.

These concepts and impressions get transferred from vague anthropomorphisms to formally religious ideas. At every stage and in every expression, somehow the mystery of God colored their responses. Gradually the meaningless words children first learned seemed to take on meaning; the concrete concepts turned into abstract ones and often took on a universal character. Yet, even into their twelfth year, as Hyde observes them, "confusion remains about many religious ideas and doctrines."[14] As if adults do not or should not express themselves with such confusion! As growing children learn to understand what religious institutions affirm and employ to connect God with humans, including instruments such as the sacraments and rituals, some express doubt about these while others show that they are moving toward adult versions of the stories they first learned when young. As in other contexts, the dichotomy observed on this subject is less one between girls and boys or rich and poor and more between those who have a story on which to hang their symbolic hats and those who are relating to disparate experiences that lead them either to or from religious participation.

Further, a team of scholars who devote themselves to this theme report on changing concepts. Some of them pay attention to the letters children write to God in order to ascertain what concepts the younger ones carry. Most researchers find that children image God in human terms, perhaps because only thus can the activity of God mirror what the child experiences in the family and the close-up world. The youngest children studied were less devoted to anthropomorphism than were those slightly older, who did not need to picture all expressions of God in terms of the human body, mind, and soul. Preschoolers in many cultures — as in one studied case, the Scandinavian — were found to have some clear concepts when they stated that God is in heaven, but they also showed an awareness of limits when they commented that heaven is a hard place to find. At the same time, in many studies, God is also "up close" to children, as perceived among 80 percent of the preschoolers. How, some ask, can God be far *and* close? The researchers found that children had pondered this dilemma, but there was very little stereotyping in their answers. One wonders whether any segment of the adult population would do this better if they were not pressed into conformity with preconceived or imposed ideals.[15]

Those who bracket their personal predilections and commitments

14. Hyde, *Religion in Childhood and Adolescence,* 115.

15. *Handbook of Preschool Religious Education,* ed. Donald Ratcliff (Birmingham, AL: Religious Education Press, 1988), 63-64.

as they listen and observe find that the freedom of the child, the opportunities for his growth, and the works of imagination prosper in such circumstances. Imposing dogma, be it of a psychological or philosophical orientation, will only help some adults master and control children, forcing them to be interpreted through denominational stereotypes and syndromes. Providers of care who focus on the imagination of children will find less reason to force limitations on the children than will the self-assured. Limits and boundaries are evident at each stage, but those who see the child as problem, not mystery, tend to set these boundaries rigidly, demonstrating too much adult self-confidence about their endeavor. Along the way, something of the mystery of the child then gets suppressed if not dispelled, and the child grows ever less receptive.

"Ideas, Impressions, or Suggestions" about Behavior and Discipline

The reception of "ideas, impressions, or suggestions" occurs within the dialectic between openness and boundaries, freedom and control, imagination and discipline. Thus William Crain in *Reclaiming Childhood* says that the top priority for elders should not be to promote their own goals and ambitions for children, goals that demand strict boundary setting. "Instead," he counsels, "we should give the greatest weight to the capacities that children are naturally motivated to develop at their present phase of development." He cites Søren Kierkegaard, who offered the most appropriate implied advice: "It is the art to be constantly present, and yet not be present." This is anything but an incitement to exert control. The child who grows under such circumstances, having a long life ahead, is free to revisit, appropriate, and reject some aspects of being a child through to the near end of life.[16]

Over the course of a child's life, responsible providers of care inevitably become involved with questions of behavior and discipline. Regulating behavior and imposing discipline are the first two topics in books or classes that teach adults how to control children in various environments and stages or phases of development. Promise that at the end of the course or the book for which they have paid they will be assured that the children in their care will behave better, and you will have expectant

16. William Crain, *Reclaiming Childhood: Letting Children Be Children in Our Achievement-Oriented Society* (New York: Holt, 2003), 27-28.

customers. Insist that an advertised pattern of discipline will lead to improved conduct, while all others will leave adults feeling responsible for having produced either bratty and spoiled children or repressed and abused ones, and you will have success. Flatter responsible adults by assuring them that the children in their range are angels and those who are not are, if not devils, at least threats to the good, and your name will be made as a social critic.

Offer an alternative set of contentions, however, notices that despite all efforts to improve a child, much can go wrong, or that without being disciplined in an advertised way the child can still turn out all right, and you are likely to turn people off. It is natural for providers of care to want to be in control of every step that moves a child toward her destiny. Suggest that there is not much anyone can do to ensure continued control, and you may as well turn off the classroom lights or pack up the books.

On the assumption that adults need all the help they can get when treating youngsters, we would not be critical of those who with intelligence and good will offer concerns and plans. What most of these advisers have in common is the impulse to see the child as a problem to be solved. Begin interpreting and acting with the concept of mystery in mind, and you will find yourself going in very different directions. Before that beginning, however, thoughtful adults will have to think about what counts for "good" and "bad" in the case of children — and how to regard the children in the light of this reckoning. When formulated as a problem, the issue is how to define and deal with a duality that shows up colloquially in the opposing pair, "good kids" versus "bad kids." The children in question, then, will be labeled, classified, and thus dispensed with or treated categorically and their mystery rejected. Recall what William James taught: classifying is necessary if one is to understand, but classifying is dangerous because it can overlook the individuals. The child defined as a bad kid or a good kid will tend to find a home in the category and snuggle away into a cozy corner, far from the zone where she is to be responsible in either case. The good kid then has nothing to learn, and the bad kid has no reason to learn.

Of course we see abundant evidence of the apparent good in some children and a burden of the bad in others. The frequently abrupt mental judgment separating infants into two camps inspires quick commitments to specific therapies, punishments, or dismissals. Thus the approach to the *problem* of the child commits the observer — whether parent, teacher, counselor, psychologist, or researcher — to early sorting and classifying of children. The bad kids show up very quickly in most studies, because scholarly work and most popular advice concerns itself with the bad. In these cases the child is not taken as he would have it, as the "MYSELF, MYSELF" about whom William James spoke. Instead he is in, and is expected to live into, his described and sometimes prescribed slot. He is classified as a misbehaver, liar, cheat, temper-tantrum-thrower, and the like. His actions may inspire questions: Where in the evolutionary process did his kind come from? Is he a mutation? Did he come from "the bad seed," as a book and film title had it? Is he a genetic receiver and then carrier of evil? Have family experiences, usually covered up, played their part? Is the child denominated as bad because he was the victim of abuse, parental neglect, the influence of bad peers, or all of the above? Adults huddle and ask themselves, Where problems of children termed bad are glaring, they demand immediate attention, but of what kind and degree? Should one step back to gain perspective and simply let things take their course? When the situation is not acute, the acts of labeling a child bad, seeing everything about her pejoratively, and treating her harshly can limit her future by causing caregivers to hover, to control, to be overly preoccupied with reining her in.

Following this problem-centered orientation, when adults hear about the existence somewhere of large numbers of children called good, they will be suspicious and will ask questions: Have such favored children been misdescribed by "soft" seniors? There are reasons for being suspicious and for asking: Is the caregiver or analyst someone who puts on wine-tinted spectacles and reads only books about how positive thinkers will deal with a child? Have such researchers ever met *real* children, the kind we skeptics know so well, young people who are anything but receptive, who disrupt family life, disturb the peace, and are ceaseless engineers of rebellions? Have those who admire them and who give them a long leash so they can roam spent too much time reading utopian works in which everything will come out perfectly, or have they believed those child-guidance manuals that promise the impossible? Are they in denial, refusing to see and reckon with the bad in the child? Worse, for our present purposes, does shifting the accent from the problem to the mystery of the child give those who care about children license to be full of wonder but incapable of disciplining?

"Where Do All the Good Kids Come from?"

The reader can see that I am not at home with simply labeling a child good or bad but am instead a historian who observes cultures that label children in varieties of contradictory ways. A story might provide background for my inquiries. On thirteen Monday afternoons in the academic year 2003-2004, I was privileged to codirect seminars with nineteen Emory University professors who were dealing with "the child in religion, law, and society." I liked to begin three-hour sessions with the jostling question, "Where do all the *good* kids come from?" Most participants in the seminar were busy with problems of the child and could not load up their hypotheses and inquiries with ancillary burdens. To divert the scholars from inquiries that grew out of their expertise and in most cases out of their compassionate concerns for justice and care would have been irresponsible. When I asked the question about the sources of "good kids," my intention was to find a way to amplify the sets of concerns we had all brought to the table.

"Where do all the good kids come from?" Asking that question in mixed company can elicit flippant and cynical remarks. Some will blurt out that there are no good kids, so why bother to look for them? However, the majority of participants will entertain the question, muse about it, and add other questions to deepen the discussion. One of the most urgent is, "Who is defining the good?"

Professionals do agree with the public that this question is weighty. Thus professor of experimental psychology Jerome Kagan, in his influential *The Nature of the Child,* includes a section titled "The Meanings of Good and Bad" in his chapter "Establishing a Morality":

> The capacity to evaluate the actions of self and others as good or bad is one of the psychological qualities that most distinguishes *Homo sapiens* from the higher apes. Chimpanzees are capable of symbolic communication, even though their talent falls far short of the language ability of the human three-year-old, and they behave as if fear, joy, and sadness were within their experience. But there is not the slimmest shred of evidence to suggest that these animals possess the ideas of good and bad and apply these categories to their actions or those of others.

Kagan relates ideas of good and bad to science, particularly psychology, and immediately connects his search with the experience of children:

> Admission of the idea of standard into the working vocabulary of psychology is based on the fact that some ideas and actions are classified as good or bad, and each evaluation is related to specific feeling states. Children will readily acknowledge that "hitting another" is bad, but look puzzled if asked whether "eating potatoes" is bad. They will re-

> gard "hitting a home run" as good but not know how to evaluate "opening a door." The fact that evaluative language is selectively applied to thoughts and acts that can provoke anxiety, shame, guilt, or pride implies the existence of a special class of ideas. I call this class a *standard*, with the understanding that membership in this class can be temporary.[17]

In my hearing, this second question – the one that almost always follows "Where do all the good kids come from?" and the recognition that there *are* "good kids" – is connected to Kagan's issue of standards: "What do you mean by good?" That question is so provocative and promising that it can stimulate immediate conversation or debate. It will inspire fresh observation and inquiry and may even charter some new research.

So picture the conversation beginning. One person asks, "By good, do you mean nice?" or "Do you mean a child who is solicitous, eager to please adults, unquestioning in response?" "Do you mean what white middle-class parents call good?" "Does 'good' mean simply obedient, obsequious, ready to bow low and carry out commands, never causing trouble?"

Those who have leisure or passion for parlor games can find that dropping the question "Where do all the good kids come from?" will prompt lively philosophical discussion. One school of theological thought says that children come with an original blessing and thus are all essentially good. Their counterparts, often invoking themes such as original sin or total depravity, say that children come with an original blight and thus are all essentially bad. Some participants will offer a template for the good child that relies on the classic virtues of honesty, courage, loyalty, and honor. Others in our culture reach for those that match the patterns and prescriptions in the Gospels, which include the virtues of being humble, having perspective on the self, being generous and forgiving, and the like. These they see as factors that go into the making of the good child or into the expressions of the child who is called good. Behind such classical and, in this religious case, Christian, definitions of the sources and norms of the good will stand figures like Aristotle and Jesus.

At once it will be evident that the expressions and outcomes of classical and Christian virtues, of counsels based in Aristotle or Jesus, are not in conflict with each other at all points. They and other systems – such as religious visions derived from Buddhism, Hinduism, Islam, and, of course, Judaism – provide definitions of the good that can serve for ob-

17. Jerome Kagan, *The Nature of the Child* (New York: Basic, 1984), 112.

serving and plumbing the mystery of the particular child and of children, as they interact with others who draw on other value systems.

Religions' Accountings of the Good and Bad

Specific religious communities give various accountings of the prospects for various behaviors in the child. The traditions are seldom perfectly formulated because of the mystery of good and evil, whether in individuals or not. The issues the various faiths raise are seldom settled. In the context of the majority faith communities in the West, that is, the Christian, the accounting of the bad often derives from the assent by believers to doctrines or adherence to the meanings of stories. These characteristically deal with the origin and expression of the good and the bad. The code name for many of these accountings through many centuries has been the unfortunately named "original sin." In the biblical Genesis story, humans are described as descendants not from simian strains but from a pair, Adam and Eve, made in the image of God and thus good. But in the New Testament this pair is regarded as fallen, and all their heirs are seen as in need of redemption. The writers assume and charge that all children, viewed from one prospect, do evil because they are evil. Recipes and directions for addressing the evil are specific, often centering in Christian baptism, which for most but by no means all Christians can be administered long before children reach the age of reason.

Judaism, interestingly, does not hold the child accountable so early, because he becomes responsible first when he is old enough to be instructed in the divine laws. Judaism has nothing to do with the concept of original sin. This is also the case with Islam. Thus in one manual, *The Child in Islam,* author Norma Tarazi is emphatic:

> Islam teaches that the human being's original fitrah, or nature, is pure and uncorrupted. Consequently, each newborn baby comes into this world in an absolutely pure state, untainted by anything such as "original sin," which is an alien concept in Islam. Its emotions and temperament are given to it by Allah, an inseparable part of its being. Like every other thing created by Allah, it is *muslim* with a small "m" in the sense that its original nature submits to its Lord.[18]

18. Norma Tarazi, *The Child in Islam: A Muslim Parent's Handbook* (Plainfield, IN: American Trust Publications, 1995), 11.

It is the fact of living where the doctrine of original sin was taught and had force that necessitates comment here. Mary Ann Hinsdale helpfully retraces original sin in Karl Rahner's influential writings, and they deserve attention here because his thought bears on many concepts in this book. Those who are not moved or guided by Catholic Christian argument can work out analogies to other religious viewpoints. In "Toward a Theology of Childhood," which we have cited extensively, Rahner did speak of original sin when he connected it with the "bad," as in "bad child," in the context of universal human conditions. He regretted, however, that the concept or teaching of original sin had become frozen as "a catechism truth," and he observed that in characteristic practice people who were instructed in the faith conventionally received a lesson on the topic as a doctrine, but then the theme was usually dropped and they moved on to various ways of addressing the behavior of the child.

Refreshingly for our purposes, Rahner taught that original sin was not "sin" in the ordinary sense of an individual's wrongdoing but in an analogous sense. I like very much and would like to plant in readers' minds for the rest of this chapter his formulation that instead of speaking of original sin we would do better simply to say that here is something "that should not be." In that sense it *is* sin. Hinsdale's apt condensation of this teaching informs our talk of the mystery of the child, this time from Rahner's explicitly Christian angle. The Muslim and the Jew reckon that in the world we encounter something "that should not be" and address the implications for this in the world of children and the providers of their care. Back to the Christian instance:

> The doctrine of original sin is an attempt to express the role that sin plays in a human life *prior* to one's exercise of freedom. In this sense, every human being is "situated" in a condition of prior human sinfulness that affects his or her free decisions. . . . [E]very human person is born into the world under the influence of two competing forces: the power of God's redeeming love in Christ and the power of sin opposed to Christ. However, although these two forces are fundamental, they are not equal. . . . [T]hey are two "existentials" of the human situation with regard to salvation which at all times determine human existence. . . . [T]he lack of the sanctifying Spirit is a *lack which ought not to exist* [so it] is sin only in an analogous sense, as the "state of what ought not to be."[19]

19. Mary Ann Hinsdale, "'Infinite Openness to the Infinite': Karl Rahner's Contribu-

I would lift from those difficult lines a functional definition of what goes wrong or has gone wrong with all children, be they good or bad in the descriptions of others. They have entered an existence that, inexplicably or at least never fully accountably, is a "state of what ought not to be." Do we need more accounting than that? Once more: "a state of what ought not to be" characterizes some dimensions of the life of every person, every child, the receptive and the nonreceptive, the responsive and the nonresponsive alike. Bringing out and sustaining the evidences of receptivity in the child is a major feature in concerns for development and education.

Saint Augustine and Human Understandings

Long before Rahner wrote, the great commentator on human existence, favored by some as a realist and dismissed by others as a gloomy blighter, was Saint Augustine. Paying more attention to him than to modern theorists of human behavior and childhood development may strike some as a parochial, sectarian, or traditionalist choice. But Augustine deserves notice because he receives so much credit and blame for having influenced Western Christianity and thus Western culture for fifteen centuries. The intrinsic power of his thinking and writing comes across even when it is excerpted but briefly.

Martha Ellen Stortz has revisited Augustine's thought in order to relate it to some current understandings of the human. Her inquiry necessarily began with and repeatedly led her to the early Christian's great *Confessions.* He did not have anything to observe or say about the child's presumed innocence, which in any case was not at issue in the Gospel stories as was receptivity. In his *Confessions* Augustine converses with God:

> Who reminds me of the sin of my infancy? For "none is pure from sin before you, not even an infant of one day upon the earth" (Job 14:4-5 LXX [in the Septuagint]). Who reminds me? Any tiny child now, for I see in that child what I do not remember in myself. . . . So the feebleness of infant limbs is innocent, not the infant's mind.[20]

---

tion to Modern Catholic Thought on the Child," in *The Child in Christian Thought,* ed. Marcia J. Bunge (Grand Rapids: Eerdmans, 2001), 429-30.

20. Martha Ellen Stortz, "'Where or When Was Your Servant Innocent?' Augustine on Childhood," in Bunge, ed., *The Child in Christian Thought,* 78.

Sophisticated and adept at psychological understanding, especially when he held the mirror up to himself, Augustine was wise enough to know that many children born outside the circle of his faith lived observably good lives. He knew from himself and from observation that the baptized "good" children were often bad. He drew his views of childhood from his own memories and his view of infants from his observations as an adult. The ancient saint and scholar is of help here for one consistency that his writings reveal: he helps us sort out the distinction between receptivity and moral innocence, seeing that the latter was not the quality of the child that Jesus was heard praising. Children were vulnerable, marginalized, easily victimized and misled, and dependent – but they were in any case receivers of gifts and receptive persons. Change and become like them was Jesus' command.

Observing families with children in his role as bishop, Augustine came to a conclusion voiced in a question: "I ask you, my God, I ask, Lord, where and when your servant was innocent?" Contrary to many depictions, however, he did not reach for the opposite and teach the "innate depravity" of children. His view, in modern terms, would be that the child was simply, in Stortz's appropriate if inelegant coinage, non-innocent. Etymologically, for the ancient saint and the modern scholar, innocence comes from *in-nocens,* which means "not harming." The child was innocent in the physical sense: infants were too weak to do harm. It was when they grew older that they could do harm and had to become more accountable and responsible.

From Augustine's time into our own, the questions of accountability and responsibility change as the child progresses through different phases of life. From writings of his time one can draw a conventional picture, which featured six phases. We will look at the first two.

The first, *infancy,* the one that concerns us most in the present context, lasted from the moment of birth until the child acquired language abilities, and it was "the most treacherous and the most transparent stage in all of human life." Lacking language, the child was an object of both terror and beauty. Augustine was charmed by the smile of a baby and awed by her rage.

In the second stage, *childhood,* which was marked by speech, more was expected, as the child moved "more deeply into the stormy society of human life" and was now for the first time vulnerable to punishment by adults. Still, Augustine confessed that he smarted from having been punished as a child. He did not sanction the many beatings that were commonplace in his time and place. Stortz enjoys the saint's powers of observation and analysis: "He archly observed that both adults and children played games, yet children were the ones who got punished for playing them." I cannot resist quoting further, for something of the boy remained in this man often dismissed as dour, and his insight should still inform caregivers in nursery, home, and school alike. Augustine confessed and observed further: "But we loved to play, and punishments were imposed on us by those who were engaged in adult games. For 'the amusements of adults is called business.' But when boys play such games they are punished by adults, and no one feels sorry either for the children or for the adults or indeed for both of them." The important observation followed, one that relates to adults who controlled children and children who had to be the passive victims: "The schoolmaster who caned me was behaving no better than I was."[21]

Not surprisingly, Augustine resorted to biblical stories to help account for the non-innocence and then for the failures that take the form of evil after the child has become accountable. Adam, of course, was central in this narrative, and evil was transmitted through his semen. Augustine would have been better off resorting to mystery at the beginning of one conversation instead of at the end. I refer to his unsatisfying attempt to account for Isaac's treatment of his twin sons in the Genesis story about Jacob and Esau. Cornered by an antagonist who wanted him to account for why Jacob, not a "good kid," was favored over Esau, Augustine took refuge in the sense of mystery now evidenced simply as puzzlement because of ignorance. He quoted Romans 11:33 to cover his own ignorance or inability to make something good of the explanation that he had started to make: "O the depth of the riches and wisdom and knowledge of God! How unsearchable are his judgments and how inscrutable his ways!"

Augustine would have spared himself and served his legacy better had he more often admitted that he did not know how to account metaphysically or rationally for the good and bad outcomes in such lives, in all life. Stortz calls his understanding of human nature "somatic determinism," which Stortz, herself a Christian, admits "repulses us today." He was more fascinated by evil than by good. Almost wearied by her inquiries into the Augustinian search for the good, his modern interpreter Stortz signs off with questions: "How can we attend to children in a world that is driven by adult concerns? How shall we understand and nurture the moral lives of children? How can we educate for virtue? . . . How can we

21. Stortz, "'Where or When Was Your Servant Innocent?'" 84-85.

tend and nourish the lives of children?"[22] Concepts of original sin and depravity may be satisfying as doctrines to some, but they are easily misunderstood and tend to be of little use for pedagogy or child care.

Greeting the Good

Over against this Augustinian part of the tradition, people in various particular heritages, and again in this case the Christian, offer a variety of ways to recognize the good child or recognize goodness in the child as it emerges and is to be sustained. Receptivity and responsiveness have to be the grounding of the good, according to the Gospel picture of what Jesus saw in the child and wanted to see in adults who changed to become like the child. Of course, a person can and too often will be receptive and responsive to evil signals and appeals. Augustine was sure that these were often stronger than the allure of the good. He also had to do what contemporaries still must: he had to discuss ways of evoking, prompting, or producing good in the child and, hence, in a way, producing the good child.

Infant baptism was and is perceived by many millions of believers to be a response to a divine command and a reliance on divine intervention. The baptized child may still be predisposed to do evil, but in this witness, that same child is also seen by God as good, redeemed, saved, and ready to represent the ways and works of a good God and as in line to be forgiven where there are lapses — forgiveness being the first step toward the good life. This turn toward the good is accompanied by disciplines and instruction. Though Aristotle pictured that the good was to be produced in the form of conduct that is habitual, the Christian pictured the good as obedience to God in joyful response to divine grace. As before, we contend that these do not have to be in conflict with each other.

Other traditions bracket the question of human nature and instead concentrate on the human not in essence but in history. This may today be a better approach to child development among providers of care, because good and evil emerge not as static qualities but as part of the living drama of every life. One can achieve more and effect change more through such drama than by perceiving fixed states. These traditions stress the development of the good through discipline, example, mentoring, and the instilling of habit and good conduct, congruent with the factor of recep-

22. Stortz, "'Where or When Was Your Servant Innocent?'" 100, 102.

tivity in the child. Or the child will go further with the Jesus of the Gospels and be moved by love to live out the vocations to effect change, to embody justice and mercy. In all this, emotional development plays its part and has to be noticed by those who provide care for children. Jerome Kagan advances this discussion on humanist grounds:

> Morality will always be a critical human concern because humans want to believe there is a more and a less virtuous outcome in a situation of choice, and therefore insist on criteria for action. The fact that two-year-olds are concerned with the correctness or the incorrectness of an action implies the primacy of this theme. Humans are driven to invent moral criteria, as newly hatched turtles move toward water and moths toward light.

So it is that moral discrimination in this humanist view is a social construction, but naming it thus does not reduce its complexity or dissolve the mystery of moral aspiration and failure. Kagan continues:

> The conditions for moral virtue in modern society – the state that one seeks to attain in order to reassure oneself of one's goodness – include pleasure, wealth, fame, power, autonomy, mastery, nurturance, kindness, love, honesty, work, sincerity, and belief in one's freedom. Each is a construction built over time, though traceable to universal affects. The relative prominence of each of these values is not an inevitable product of the human genome, but stems rather from the capacity for empathy with another's distress, shame and guilt over violating standards, and preparedness to inhibit actions that provoke disapproval.

If this seems to imply inconsistency in the debate over the roles of biology versus experience, Kagan is untroubled and would leave us similarly free:

> These are not inconsistent views. The young child is prepared by his biology to become attached to his parents; yet Western culture insists that he eventually develop autonomy and independence from them and be able to cope with distress in their absence – qualities that not only require subjugation of the earlier natural disposition but also ones that are probably not biologically inevitable. The moral sense of children is highly canalized because of a capacity for evaluation and the experience of certain emotions, but the surface ethics of a specific community are built from a web of social facts embedded in folk the-

> ory. Although humans do not seem to be specially programmed for a particular profile of moral missions, they are prepared to invent and believe in some ethical mission.[23]

He even adds a light-hearted religious twist: "[Novelist] Pär Lagerkvist had God reply to a question regarding His intention in creating human beings with, 'I only intended that you need never be content with nothing.'" Gnomic though that illustration is, it helps reinforce the observation that the psychologist who uses humanistic and naturalistic approaches still verges on mystery. This, once again, is not a mystery that marks where knowledge ends and ignorance begins but points instead to enduring fathomlessness.

Religious Narrative, Natural Law, and Divine Revelation

The problems of children and the problem child remain to shadow the existence of all children. Affirming the mystery of the child, however, takes off some of the pressure, relieves the adult impulse always to control the child, to insist on management and mastery, and to claim too much credit in accounting for the development of the good child. Discipline remains necessary, but how one effects discipline when control and repression are not at the base of most strategies is a more open question, not to be solved but always to be addressed.

Failing to solve metaphysical and ontological problems about the essence and being of the child does not mean that nothing can be learned or taught to inform relations with children. To suggest some of the options being presented in contemporary America, a pluralistic society in which most children are educated in public schools, I am going to reach for a "tract for the times," a convenient and fair-minded appraisal of the main options offered by Raymond R. Roberts in *Whose Kids Are They, Anyway?* Most of the writers relate to public education as a problem, but some are compatible with the conception of the child as mystery, as someone receptive to imaginative calls.

First, and consistent with our interest in the history, drama, experience, and development of the child, are the proposals of those who, with educator Charles L. Glenn, accent "religious narrative" as an aid in shaping

23. Kagan, *Nature of the Child,* 52.

the child or letting the child find a shape.[24] Like philosopher Alasdair MacIntyre and theologian Stanley Hauerwas, Glenn works with the assumption that everyone, and this includes every child, is somehow religious. This does not mean being a member of a religious community by personal conscious choice or intelligibly professing a clarified creed. It does mean that thinking persons – and children do think! – cannot function unless they live with and inside a narrative that helps them make sense of themselves and the world around them. Religion then is the main and most satisfying provider of a "framework of meaning," a "map of reality," and a "context of meanings." From these the child acquires "a symbolic universe," "a coherent interpretation of reality" that is necessary for life within a culture.

Although the need for meaning is a human universal, Glenn observes that individuals and groups live in particular worlds that are framed by particular narratives. This relation to story is a powerful address to the situation and one consistent with our observations of the mysterious character of the child. The character of individuals and groups issues in no small part from their encounter with special stories, which are mediated through particular communities. In our understanding, because these stories are so apparently idiosyncratic in the eyes of those who are not of the community, they cannot provide universal definitions of the good. Questions about why this is so, why stories work as they do, and how communities develop around them and issue in such narratives throw one into the company of those who speak expansively of the child as mystery rather than of those who concentrate on the problems of disciplining and shaping the child. This approach is clear and strong, but the public school setting makes it difficult to follow.

Intending to deal more realistically with the pluralist scene is a typical "natural law" approach, here associated with the work of Thomas Lickona, an energetic contributor to the debate. He represents the large company of those who want schools to develop good children whose morality is not based on particular religious beliefs.[25] Critics would say that the natural law approach has a metaphysical base itself that turns it into a virtual religion, but Lickona believes that because all children can reason and can discern groundings and goals in their natural capacity, they develop in ways that are congruent with those of their neighbors.

24. This discussion of Glenn draws on Raymond R. Roberts, *Whose Kids Are They Anyway?* (Cleveland: Pilgrim, 2002), 36-39.

25. This condensation of Lickona's main themes also draws on Roberts, *Whose Kids Are They Anyway?* 39-42.

Though many advocates say that only particular religious narratives and communities can provide this base, Lickona, himself a religious Catholic, believes that the nonreligious can also follow reason and natural law apart from religion and toward good ends. "People do not construct moral values; they discover them." The caregiver or teacher and, implicitly, the child, he thinks, do not depend on moral values or moral reason that is "embedded in incommensurable narratives." Lickona thus contends that the revealed religions have commensurable features because they match natural law. Therefore the good child is to be formed through education in "one universal natural moral law 'recognized by all civilized people . . . and taught by all enlightened creeds.'"

He pays little attention to particular moral cultures – for example, those that are Hindu versus those that are Christian. For him the good child relates more to universal norms of the good, values that Lickona says "bind everyone and reflect the obligations of the universal moral law." On these terms the goal of discipline and education is to produce not guiding narratives but consistent character. Character, he argues (as I do not), does not depend on stories or on the interactions among members of communities of character, but instead it "consists of operative values, values in action." Roberts summarizes for Lickona: "Good character involves knowing, desiring, and doing the moral law. These three dimensions of character (the intellect, the affections, and the will) interact in moral thinking, moral feeling, and moral acting." With Glenn, Lickona believes that religion supplements these by offering visions, purpose, and reasons for leading morally good lives.

We think of the arena for child care that is the family, a sphere that in isolation can be as destructive as it can be constructive. Parents and other adults are constantly in the business of doing what Leland Howe, another participant in our mini-symposium, asks for: they help children connect to values that may not be innate but that result from accidents of cultural history. His is the familiar approach through what is often called "values clarification." Among the originators of values are families as they engage in rituals, express generosity, or make choices.

If narratives are too subjective, if natural reason is not as natural or universal as its advocates suggest, and if the construction of values is seen as too relativistic, some in Roberts's book are antagonists of all these, among them televangelist Pat Robertson. Robertson is there located as an advocate for an absolutist approach based on religious insights, which he claims are grounded in divine revelation. Children, for Robertson, are bad because "sin prevents them from finding" divine communion. Instead, it leads them to rebel against God, create false gods, and sanction base desires. Christianity is for him the only true and universal religion, so from his perspective the truly good child can be produced only by such religion, Christianity of a special sort. No other sources of moral authority than those contained in the Bible can be productive of the good. Robertson on his own grounds also pushes toward the universal. "The Christian perspective is for everyone, not just for Christians. Those who believe that all truth is relative are simply wrong," he charges, and all other secular and religious perspectives he sees as "deviations from the universally true religion" and "evidence of sin." As such, they cannot contribute to the production of the good child.[26]

Still another approach to accounting for the bad child and producing the good child comes from David Purpel, whose approach can also be heard at many school board, curriculum, or Parent-Teacher Association meetings. He claims only that "the myths, stories, and tenets of religion provide an imaginative construction of the universe and one's place in it. Religion explains fundamental human questions of human origin and destiny" and "instructs people in the meaning of life and elevates what is truly important."[27] Unlike MacIntyre, Hauerwas, and Glenn, however, he believes that mythic constructs are not related to particular ways of looking at the world. Instead, they reach toward that which is universal and can guide anyone who would help develop the good child. Purpel, being American, turns to American myths that are traditional and religious, drawing on them to produce a framework of "civil religion" for eliciting the good and dismissing the bad, in culture, in people, in the child.

Some of the figures Roberts cites, notably MacIntyre and Hauerwas, are well-established public philosophers, while the others tend to be advocates of particular strategies in education and society or popular figures who draw on sustained and profound traditions to reinforce their cases. They serve well to suggest the complexity of debates over the bad child and the good child, as well as over what produces both of these and how one addresses change among them. Haunting all these venturers, as we have made clear, is religious pluralism. Roberts follows the implications of their thought in a society that they all agree is religiously pluralist, though some of them — Robertson in particular — wish it were not and want to make it less so. "It seems remarkable," Roberts adds, "that each

26. Robertson, in Roberts, *Whose Kids Are They Anyway?* 73-75.

27. Purpel, in Roberts, *Whose Kids Are They Anyway?* 43.

writer can note the pluralism of this time and yet draw such different conclusions as to its significance."[28]

Among them all, Purpel deserves more attention than we have given him because he addresses the specific issue before us. He offers an "educational credo," which Roberts summarizes, and with most of which we agree in our approach to the mystery and wonder of the child. This credo urges teachers to work with their students to nurture and develop (1) wonder and awe, (2) meaning making, (3) an awareness of the oneness of nature and humanity, (4) a cultural mythos, (5) the traditions of democratic principles, and (6) attitudes of outrage and responsibility" where they are appropriate. Students – and here we can include little children – are able on the bases of these to engage the surrounding culture.[29]

The Receptiveness of the Special Child

Eventually talk of good and bad children is shadowed by the question of what it means when a child is called "special" and is situated where regular norms do not fully apply, where responsibility does not develop in ways that society calls normal. Although such a child belongs to a minority, she deserves special notice in an examination of the mystery of her existence and bearing. In fact, many caregivers and observers would say that the mystery of the child is most manifest where the child does not fit into the groove and is special.

Evaluating and appraising the development of such a child becomes a prime occupation of those who give her care or study her. The presence of children who are described as having "special needs" throws the question of good kids and bad kids into a different and illuminating context. The whole reckoning with Kagan's canon of conditions for developing moral virtue in modern society[30] turns out to be overrationalized in the case of the special child. Yes, her condition may include features that display "pleasure, wealth, fame, power, autonomy, mastery, nurturance, kindness, love, honesty, work, sincerity, and belief in one's freedom," but these features take distinctive forms in the various special and nonspecial situations. These forms merit attention since understandings of these and strategies for dealing with them will illumine some features of "Everychild."

28. Roberts, *Whose Kids Are They Anyway?* 50-52.
29. Roberts, *Whose Kids Are They Anyway?* 79-80.
30. Kagan, *Nature of the Child,* 152.

In this context the question comes: Are all children to be evaluated and appraised in the context of the normal? I like to imagine that in the Gospel story, most of the children are what we would call "special," not straight-A students or high-achieving little athletes. Sally Patton, in writing a "guidebook for faith communities," states the case for an approach characterized more by the idea of "welcoming" than by evaluating and appraising. The epigraph to her preface sets the tone with a quotation from Trena Tremblay. Her *You Will Dream New Dreams,* addressed to caregivers with special children, urges them to learn from the child and his situation and not to apply conventional standards in encounters:

> Never, ever forget that you have been chosen for this very special journey. It matters not what the challenges may be; what matters is that you open your heart to this child. For as difficult as things may get, you will discover that this soul, wrapped in this precious little package, has much to give and volumes to teach you about yourself – if you are willing to learn.[31]

Patton, a liberal religious thinker, begins autobiographically:

> Although I did not realize it at the time, the diagnosis of my five-year-old son, Tyler, as severely dyslexic would launch me on a spiritual journey of discovery and healing that continues today. Back then I was, I suppose, an agnostic. Today, I believe we are all manifestations of God. (p. ix)

That reference may not qualify as orthodox, but it does show how the confrontation with the special-needs child immediately lifts one above the political conventions and calculations about how one inculcates morality in public school children in a pluralist society. It shows how limited are the usual ways of rigidly accounting for moral resources in reference to biological nature – "*This* is how humans are packaged!" – or historical experience – "*This* is the normal course of a child's life." It opened the author to mystery. Patton says at once that a "journey to this vision of the wonder of life and the spiritual connectedness of all living things was not an easy one." She confesses to a bias that, she writes, "concerns how our culture has defined what is acceptable behavior, what is in-

31. Sally Patton, *Welcoming Children with Special Needs: A Guidebook for Faith Communities* (Boston: Unitarian Universalist Association, 2004), ix. Subsequent page references to Patton's book will be given parenthetically in the text.

telligence, and what we should believe about related issues," because such definitions are quite narrow. "Any person who deviates from these normative definitions," she complains, may be labeled "disabled or disordered" (p. xi). The child with special needs, being receptive, in a way moves the labeling issue – note this well! – "beyond good and evil" and calls for an enlargement of the otherwise confining categories by means of which contemporary cultures conventionally measure growth and development.

Verging on the romantic in her expression, based on observation that is grounded in realism, Patton sees the mystery of the child with special needs in terms that educator Thomas Armstrong called the "radiant child," certainly a special embodiment of the mystery of the child.

> This is the essence of the radiant child. Belonging to both heaven and earth, the radiant child dances into our lives as a bridge between dark and light, body and spirit, ego and Self, the individual and God. The radiant child spans and sings this wholeness in every fiber. We would all be wise to listen. Even better to sing and dance along. (p. 2)

If asked what to "do" about this radiant child, those who have defined him would advocate ritualizing and dramatizing "difference" in the special-needs case. Doing so can open a community or an individual to the experience of wonder in the face of the nonspecial ones, who can also in other ways be "radiant."

The realistic view of the child to which we remain committed does not permit anyone to be carried away by this vision of radiance. This radiant child also lives a tortured existence, often behaves badly, gets described as disruptive and, in a way, even as being evil. Richard Lavoie, an expert on learning disabilities and the creator of a "behavior management" program, takes the observer behind the scenes or facades into the mind and situation of such a child, into a context that does not reduce explanations only to the circumstance surrounding each. At the same time, he will not let circumstance and culture be dismissed. Before she quotes Lavoie on this subject, Patton emphasizes: *"The hurt that troubled children and youth cause is never greater than the pain they feel."*

> Children who are experiencing trouble at home or at school often feel powerless and hurt. Their response to these feelings is often inappropriate. . . . They become disruptive and disrespectful. The parent and professional must remain mindful that this behavior is rooted in the pain of rejection, isolation, and fear that they are experiencing. There-

> fore, the most effective strategy is to attempt to eliminate the causes of these feelings . . . not to attempt to simply modify the behavior. (p. 41)

Such counsel ought to inform adults who are called to discipline children even where "special needs" have not produced acute reactions. Patton allows an adult who "was" such a child to speak for others in her book. The careful listener should see how hard it is to fit this child into understandings of being good or bad.

> I think that when I was born, I was put in a rocket ship and taken to another planet earth. I never felt that I was like anyone else here. From the time I was five, I can recall feeling like an outsider. I first remember feeling like an alien when I tried to communicate. People would raise their eyebrows and make other facial expressions of confusion when I tried to express myself. . . . Constant rejection created feelings of isolation and isolation created anger and anger created self-defeat. (p. 75)

Patton quotes testimony that will color approaches to caregiving in these instances, from L. Tobin, who wrote *What Do You Do with a Child Like This?* which is another attempt to get behind the scenes of disapproved behavior:

> I've yet to meet a troubled child who wasn't, above all else, terribly lonely. I presume loneliness even before I see the child. The misbehavior of troubled children is seldom what it first appears to be. Understanding this, I believe, is the only place to start. No child has a need to create a life of conflict. Think about it – what need is the child trying to express? (p. 156)

Patton draws once more on Richard Lavoie. He makes an important point that helps explain why discussion of the boundary-crossings in behavior by children with special needs belongs in a chapter on good kids and bad kids. In Patton's words, this observation implies counsel:

> *A child would rather be viewed as bad than dumb.* Most children, especially adolescents, would prefer to be viewed as disruptive, disobedient, or disrespectful rather than incompetent or incapable. Children with disabilities are routinely seen as incompetent and incapable. Be aware of creating any circumstance in which a child will appear stupid in

> front of his or her peers. That child may automatically become disruptive and prefer to deal with the teacher's anger rather than feel humiliated in front of his or her peers. (p. 40)

As I read such observations and counsels in this and other books on children with special needs, I was struck by how well-advised the larger community would be to approach other children with understandings gained from paying attention to the special ones. The special child more than anyone except perhaps the newborn displays what we mean by the mystery of the child and the situation of receptivity.

Dealing with the Child Who Is Doing Bad

When the child with special needs, or any child, for that matter, reacts against isolation, loneliness, or disdain in such ways that produce bad behavior, many frustrated adults, dealing with children they would wish to be "good" but who remain "bad," resort to punishment. Religious forces in the Western world historically offered their own accountings of the reasons for the need to punish, the rationales for modes and motives of punishment, and descriptions of what all this had to do with children being or becoming bad and good.

It remains for us to observe what happens in religion and culture when a child is bad, does bad things, or is at least perceived by adults as doing bad. What happens, from the adults' point of view, can mean little or nothing. They may ignore the behavior. More often, punishment occurs. The adult feels or knows that she must gain and remain in control. The literature on that subject is vast, but among us historians one book of recent decades has had influence beyond most others. Philip Greven, in the eyes of many critics, overstated the case he was making in *Spare the Child,* but he helpfully addressed the policies of chastening as he probed the topic of his subtitle: *The Religious Roots of Punishment and the Psychological Impact of Physical Abuse.* Heavily psychological in his orientation, Greven shows how religiously rooted concepts of evil that is seen to merit punishment are worked out through American religious history. He is most interesting when he shows or suggests that much "secular" punishment in mainstream culture has religious roots. He reviews instances of violent punishment that had been defended by punishers as efforts to convert bad children into good ones, or at least to show that errant behavior would not go unpunished. His collection of early Christian writings on the subject does not show preoccupation with severe physical punishment as a means of disciplining. To review the case that leads to this conclusion:

> Corporal punishment is not and cannot be grounded in words ascribed either to Jesus or to Paul. In the New Testament, only two unknown men – one the author of Hebrews, the other the author of Revelation, can be cited by even the most literal-minded Christians (who believe that the Bible is the inerrant word of God) as justification for corporal punishment of children. The practice thus rests upon only the most fragile New Testament foundation. Why, then, has physical punishment been considered "Christian" at all?[32]

His answer to his own question takes up much of his book. Rather than pursue it through religious sources, we will look only to the way these sources may have influenced secular ones. In the larger culture, the various legitimations of physical punishment are often as controversial and as frequently asserted as they are in religious traditions. The ancient and contemporary religious manuals that Greven quotes have to be described as brutal. Their literalist interpretations of some biblical authorizations of punishment will appall many readers, but they also explain some justifications offered by those who welcome support for the idea that they should beat bad children.

First, in "Judicial Justifications" Greven chronicles the ways in which American jurisprudential expressions often endure and even thrive in the long shadows of biblical interpretation concerning what to do about "bad kids." Punishing beatings in school or at home remain so egregious and are now so widely publicized that they work their way into and up the judicial system. Greven judges: "Secular, legal rationales for violence against children are no less consequential than the rationales rooted in the Bible and in religious convictions, nor are they any less deplorable" (p. 108). Many of them may well have been influenced by the Bible.

More striking is his section "Behaviorist Arguments," given the contentions of many in the modern secular spheres that, independent of biblical and other religious sources, punishment is merited. This is the case because of extreme circumstances, various philosophical commitments, inherited custom and habit, psychological assessments, and still, in

32. Philip Greven, *Spare the Child: The Religious Roots of Punishment and the Psychological Impact of Physical Abuse* (New York: Random House, 1952), 54. Subsequent page references in Greven's book will be given parenthetically in the text.

shrouded ways, biblical traditions. It is more difficult to cite such traditions blithely and regularly than it was before religious pluralism came to be so rich. It is appropriate to ask: Did the move to secular reasoning in so many sectors of life in this nation serve to lessen the appeals to punishment? Greven makes his account clear:

> Modern behaviorism has made punishment into a science. Punishment has been embedded in the behavioral sciences just as it has been in schools and the law, and arguments for pain and suffering are as much a part of behavioral psychologists' languages as of educators', lawyers', and judges'. (p. 108)

He argues that the empiricism and scientific rationality or the abstract and intentionally distancing and "objective" language of the behaviorists disguises the religious and personal roots of the interest in physical punishment.

Instance A for him in the secular company was B. F. Skinner, the most notable of the radical behaviorists of the time. In his autobiography Skinner was explicit about the way his own childhood, colored and shadowed by Calvinist theology as it was, preconditioned him to deal with the question of inflicting punishment on children. "Hell cast its shadow over the behavioral sciences just as it has over the religious convictions of fundamentalists and other Christians who ardently advocate physical punishments" (p. 108). As the story of the behaviorists unfolds, it reveals that they came along with commitments analogous to the belief in original sin and that sin merited punishment found in the circles of conservative Christians.

An illuminating example cited by Greven is Ron Van Houton, another prominent behaviorist and disciplinarian, who seemed certain that, as Greven puts it, "human beings are naturally violent and aggressive, prone to kicking, punching, and biting policemen as a matter of course if they have not first been taught, by being assaulted themselves in childhood, to avoid such aggressive behavior: here are 'echoes of original sin and human depravity,' and the physical punishment called for is 'as inevitable and necessary from this perspective as it is from that of punishment advocates among Protestants, past and present'" (p. 114). Greven does suggest that the pendulum has begun to swing away from the consistent behaviorists, both in their analysis of natural human evil and in their emphasis on necessary physical punishment to produce something of good in the child. Yet in one important section of his book he also points to outcomes of such understandings and actions. Because these consequences are not our theme, I will do no more than list the subheadings in the section "Consequences." The reader can take it from there in imagination; there is nothing mysterious here, nothing that throws light on the mystery of the child, whose devastations, occasional recoveries, and subsequent deliberations are measurable. The subheadings are:

Anxiety and Fear
Anger and Hate
Empathy[33] and Apathy
Melancholy and Depression
Obsessiveness and Rigidity
Ambivalence: Protect and Destroy
Dissociation
Paranoias
Sadomasochism
Domestic Violence
Aggression and Delinquency
Authoritarianism
The Apocalyptic Impulse

Lest I give the impression that, as Greven revisited the horrors of the religious, he revealed his own impulse to punish, it must be said that he posed "Choices" in another section. These are some alternatives to that one diagnosis of original sin and then the actual sin that warrants or even demands punishment. Proposing nonviolent methods of child rearing, he first quotes Larry Christiansen, a rather fierce Christian advocate of physical punishment: "Fear acts as a catalyst for love" (p. 218). Greven curtly reminds readers that the author of the First Epistle of John in the New Testament "says the opposite" in the observation that "There is no fear in love, but perfect love casts out fear." The biblical author refined this saying as if to let us find a match for Greven's thesis: for "fear has to do with punishment, and he who fears is not perfected in love." When a father says to his son, "You know how much I love you, but when you don't obey, Jesus teaches that you must receive the rod," Greven's gloss is: "We need to remember that Jesus never taught any such thing."

33. Greven, *Spare the Child,* 127. *Empathy,* a positive feature, seems to break the parallelism. Greven, without explaining why he does it this way, enlarges upon that one word and speaks of "the stifling of empathy."

In the second-to-last line of his book Greven points to what leads to the possibility of the "good kid" emerging on a "good earth," a child as full of complexity, ambiguity, and ambivalence as parents may be: "Love and nurture, empathy and understanding – not fear, not hate, not anger, and not revenge – must be our goal" (p. 222). Regarding what is good and what is bad in the being and expression of the child takes on one cast when the bad is only a problem. It takes on another when, along with its opposite, the good, it is seen as a mystery of being – never static, always developing.

Beyond Good and Evil: Receptivity in All of Life

So we come to the point in our exploration of the mystery of the child where we turn, for just a few pages, to what that mystery can mean for the rest of life. Though the content of those pages could well be the subject for a future book, brief mention here can at least be a test of the seriousness with which we take the witness to mystery in the child. Whatever else it has meant, we must certainly note these observations:

- *Reducing* the child to "nothing but" this or that kind of problem or explanation violates the presence of mystery and narrows the range of options among providers of care.
- Seeing the child first of all as someone whom the adult must *control* instead of being a subject and object of wonder limits the freedom of the child to emerge as a free adult who is herself capable of responding in awe and delight, before and as she faces difficulties in life.
- Picturing the child as a representative of all who are *receptive* because they are vulnerable, marginalized, powerless, and subject to being made a victim – and then as a representative of those to whom "the Kingdom of God" belongs – situates the child and adults who share their character and circumstances in a place where change can occur, for their, and society's, benefit.
- Hearing the "terrifying" word that calls for adults to *change* and become like a little child has to imply that some version of that change is also possible, that there are resources for effecting it.

So in the concluding chapter we pull back the curtain on later acts in life or turn pages to what is being filled out in the albums, diaries, and memoirs of people at all stages of life – stages that are also rich in mystery and capable of inspiring wonder.

10. The Abyss of Mystery: Postscript and Prescript

> The righteous flourish. . .
> In old age they still produce fruit;
> they are always green and full of sap. . . .
>
> PSALM 92:14

Readers of a book titled *The Mystery of the Child* have no reason to expect it to end with reference to aging and aged people. Such a conclusion should not occasion surprise, however, because I have consistently argued that something about the being of the child keeps unfolding through all the years in healthy humans. The call for adults to change and become like little children makes no sense if such adults are in no way able to respond.

Connecting the Child with All the Ages of Life

Talk about old people risks losing the interest of some to whom this book is aimed: parents, mid-career teachers, clinicians, and other providers of care in their many callings. The risk is worthwhile, I argue, because if this plot continues to interest them even into this final chapter, it will have performed a service. If humans are what Martin Heidegger called them, "beings toward death," they are also "beings toward old age," which is a kind of dress rehearsal for death itself. These sundry sorts of caregivers live in a time of life that is supposed to be as intrinsically valuable as are all other stages of human existence. The well-motivated among them will be anticipating what it will mean to grow old themselves. Those who have entered the late phases of life can also gain perspective on their final years from a vision of what it meant and means to be a child.

People in their middle or later years may be tempted to succumb to feelings of loss when reference to the being of the child is mentioned as relating to them. To hear celebrations of the dependent character of infant life as a positive feature can sound defeating to older people who may be in the process of surrendering some of their own hard-achieved independence. They must grudgingly rely again on the care of others, whether friends, relatives, or professionals who serve them through agencies. Looking back, anyone who has not lived a life consistent with that of the child as here described has lost good years. Squandered opportunities can never be retrieved after their time has passed. The vivid learning potential in a child who is beginning to speak, to build a vocabulary, and to find language skills has diminished among the aged. The ability to pick up new things for the sake of invention and adventure has atrophied. It is not creative, however, for anyone to hear these words about change as causes for regret or envy. The voice of regret would whisper to the soul: "If only I had practiced how to be like a child when I was younger, back when I had my own children or had known children of others close to me . . ." Or such a voice would prompt a person to think or say: "If only I had taken lessons in personality development and self-esteem when I was younger and mentally more supple, so that I could nurture relations with others, I would not be passive or paralyzed today." Least productive of all would be the circumstance in which the reader of the biblical text, upon awakening to its meaning, might say, "If only I had let those terrifying words soak in sooner, I would not now have the terror of concern about whether I am too late to follow this course or am predestined instead to fall short. If I am, I will have failed to be swept up in the kingdom [or humanistic equivalents of the fulfilling life]."

"Why was I not told to change and become like a child?" In the case of many, one has to say, you *were* told. That act of telling was the point of the command in the biblical story in which Jesus is heard speaking presumably to parents and certainly to his followers. Those hearers or readers who have cared about being allowed to "enter the kingdom" or about reaching some other apparently impossible goal have had many occasions to learn to live in positive relations to others and with an openness that does not allow for the atrophy of imagination, confidence, or awe. Since the age of the people in the Gospel story is unspecified, we are free to picture Jesus saying his words to great-grandparents along with parents.

No Second Childhood

With that in mind, it is jolting to hear again the stark words that have informed all these pages: "And he said, 'I tell you the truth, unless you change and become like children, you will never enter the kingdom of heaven.'" What if the story were retold with Jesus setting seniors in front of a group and saying: "Because these *have* changed and become like children, they *have* begun to enter the kingdom of heaven." Would this mean that they had regressed into an infantile state? Not at all. Colloquial diagnostic terms such as "entering second childhood" are condescending and even destructive. They offer no help in answering questions about how to live and what to think. Even to take up the subject of the oldest generation in a book on the youngest is very risky. It does no good to pretend that no deprivation or – chilling word! – decrepitude has occurred during aging. Realistic appraisal suggests that some aspects associated with childhood can surface as people age. The observer in such cases notes that the biological cycle seems to double back on itself and that old people can manifest unattractive aspects of the childhood they left behind seven or eight decades earlier. When such reversals occur, they are more often than not occasions of chagrin to self-conscious seniors and inconveniences or embarrassments to those who must cover for them or tend to their needs.

Whoever has provided care for the dependent aged or who has lived among them can testify that most signs of openness or positive relationships, unless attended to, will decline and eventually disappear. When attended to, however, they can continue to be present and, in some form or other, to prosper. Realism gets mixed with hope in their consciousness. Those who minister to the terminally ill, for instance in hospices, often testify that even those who have suffered loss of health have not abandoned hope, which does not mean hope that life will simply be prolonged. The pain they suffer is for many an incentive not to invest too much hope in such an extension of life. They may be designated *patients*, a word that relates to the Latin word for suffering. Yet even as patients it is possible for them to manifest generosity of spirit of the sort described in the chapter "The Generosity of the Ill" in sociologist Arthur Frank's book *The Renewal of Generosity: Illness, Medicine, and How to Live.*[1] Just as some who are ill are aware that they share a fellowship with others who are ill, so are

1. Arthur Frank, *The Renewal of Generosity: Illness, Medicine, and How to Live* (Chicago: University of Chicago Press, 2004).

many who are weakened by aging freshly open to relations with others who share their situation.

Frank quotes European physician and organist Albert Schweitzer, who served in a clinic in Africa. Schweitzer at one point had been seriously ill, but in the course of time he learned from his experience, just as very senior and often weak people keep learning. Schweitzer spoke of

> the Fellowship of those who bear the Mark of Pain. Who are the members of this Fellowship? Those who have learnt by experience what physical pain and bodily anguish mean, belong together all the world over; they are united by a secret bond. One and all they know the horrors of suffering to which man can be exposed, and one and all they know the longing to be free from pain. He who has been delivered from pain must not think he is now free again, and at liberty to take life up just as it was before, entirely forgetful of the past. He is now a "man whose eyes are open" with regard to pain and anguish, and he must help to overcome those two enemies (so far as human power can control them) and to bring to others the deliverance which he has himself enjoyed.[2]

Frank calls in another witness, writer Nancy Mairs, who testified even as her physical situation worsened. "I can't become a 'hopeless cripple,'" she wrote as her multiple sclerosis advanced, "without risking moral paralysis." Her medium for relating to others, her body, was "in trouble." Giving voice to what many old people fear, she added: "I have visions of enduring life at the hands of strangers: refused food or drink, shoved roughly into bed, allowed to slip from my wheelchair and abandoned in a puddle of my own urine." Yet she feared moral paralysis most:

> If I don't want to be reduced to a constellation of problems, I must imagine my body as something other than problematic: a vehicle for enmeshing the life I have been given into the lives of others. Easy enough to say. But to do? Who will have me? And on what terms?
>
> Beyond cheerfulness and patience, people don't generally expect much of a cripple's character. And certainly they presume that care, which I have placed at the heart of moral experience, flows in one direction, "downward": as from adult to child, so from well to ill, from whole to maimed.[3]

2. Albert Schweitzer, *The Primeval Forest* (Baltimore: Johns Hopkins University Press, 1998), 128; quoted in Frank, *The Renewal of Generosity,* 55-56.

3. Nancy Mairs, *Waist-High in the World: A Life among the Nondisabled* (Boston: Beacon, 1966), 60, 42, 56, 62; quoted in Frank, *The Renewal of Generosity,* 64-66.

Schweitzer's and Mairs's illnesses here are metaphors for processes of aging when those changes are radical enough that they necessitate dependence on the part of the formerly independent. Ethicist William F. May shows how middle-aged people take lessons as they observe many of the aged:

> What the middle aged fear . . . is not merely physical decay, the loss of beauty, and the failure of vitality, but the humiliation of dependency. Americans have historically taken pride in themselves as an independent people. . . . The dark side of this aspiration to self-reliance is an abhorrence of dependence. . . . The North American compulsion to be independent intensifies the threat of old age. The middle aged do not want the elderly to encumber them, and the elderly do not want to lapse into a burden.[4]

Citing them here serves to remind readers that talk about the abyss of mystery near the end of life is not all cheerful and cheering. People in perfect mental and moderate physical health who seek to follow what they receive as divine commands also do not naturally want to take up the agenda to experience change "and become like children." Like the autistic child of whom I wrote in an earlier chapter, they want to be taken seriously to the end. "Become like children": the abrupt words of the implicit command do not sound like a casual observation about human possibility. They are not ideal slogans to be preserved in the form of wall mottoes in senior suites, on greeting cards in a home or classroom, or as sentimental features in personal advice columns in newspapers. They are not presented as recommendations, secondings of the motion by a teacher of virtue. Two verbs in the short line rule out such teasing but finally compromising possibilities.

Unless the hearers and readers *change,* they cannot become part of the kingdom. That first word is both a measure or marker and a command: you adults can and must change. The idea that one can indeed change, as this line advises, belongs to the mystery of faith, but it also relates to good general and healthy humanistic counsel.

Become: that other word charges those who hear it to undertake or experience a shift. You can no longer be what you are; you can no longer

4. William F. May, "Who Cares for the Elderly?" *Hastings Center Report* 12 (December 1982): 32; quoted in Stephen Sapp, *Full of Years: Aging and the Elderly in the Bible and Today* (Nashville: Abingdon, 1987), 139-40. I recommend Sapp's book to those who wish to give more attention to the aged than we can give in this book on the child.

be living and calculating about decisions in life the way you do now. You have to undergo a reversal and enact a reaching: you must "become like children."

It is immediately clear that those words, commands that include warnings, have nothing to do with a "second childhood." That stigmatizing concept is a superficial and absurd misreading and misnaming of what childhood is about in the first place. It does not spell out what an old person's biological and psychological losses can mean in a presumed second place and time. Shakespeare's sad Jaques in *As You Like It* chronicles poetically the natural way to look at five ages of life and then describes the last two:

> . . . The sixth age shifts
> Into the lean and slippered pantaloon,
> With spectacles on nose and pouch on side,
> His youthful hose well saved, a world too wide
> For his shrunk shank; and his big manly voice,
> Turning again toward childish treble, pipes
> And whistles in his sound. Last scene of all,
> That ends this strange eventful history,
> Is second childishness, and mere oblivion,
> Sans teeth, sans eyes, sans taste, sans everything.
>
> (Act 2, scene 7)

What Jesus and counselors in his tradition commend is not a life "sans" but rather a life *with* "everything." Jesus promised the kingdom and "all" other things to be added to it. The reader or viewer of *As You Like It* can presume that spectacles, pouch, hose, and all can adorn also the older adult who *has* changed and *has* become like a child. Costumes and accessories are externals, not central to the case. Such a materially deprived person will, in the natural course of things, be nearer the end of "this strange eventful history" than to his "first" childhood. Until that end comes, the portent of "mere oblivion," while it may shadow daily living, does not blot out all other perceptions.

Shakespeare's lines have never been of help to anyone seeking a more humane and promising set of descriptive terms for the later years. Our language currently lacks a positive word for what our biblical text implies. The first one that comes to mind in our culture is to be pushed furthest away of all: "childishness" will not do. Taking refuge in another term, simply, *child,* assuming one could *become* a child, represents an impossible regression. The third option comes closer: *childlikeness.* Because the suffix "-ness" can represent a quality, one sometimes hears the word *childness,* which is working its way into dictionaries to connote what is associated with "child." It comes closer to the meaning to which we are pointing than do the others.

Because *childness* is a rarely used word, I decided not to use it in a chapter subheading. However, it connotes exactly what remains to be said. The suffix "-ness" refers to a condition or a quality. Childness is a condition that is not to be monopolized by infants and little children. Childness is a quality that people of any age can embody, so long as they remain in positive relation to others. When applied to senior people, the concept of childness illustrates and illumines "the mystery of the child."

The Gospel stories that provoke our response do not suggest that some people naturally have a personality that qualifies them for being childlike, while others naturally do not. Natural endowments differ among people, so natural childlikeness cannot have been the ideal of all in the audience as described by the writers of the Gospels. Some people, it is true, are predisposed to bear personality marks or to undertake acts that display childlikeness. The word here, however, does not say "some of you do not need to change because you are instinctively gifted with the qualities of childness." Such "naturals" would not have to change because they are already where they are urged to be. Instead, here is a universal call, broadcast to anyone and everyone: "Unless you change and become other than what you now are, you will not enter the kingdom."

We have all along been showing little interest in what some call "the *essential* child," the child whose nature foredooms her to a particular destiny shared by all children. Instead, we have focused on the child in history, the one living out the drama of a child's life. So it is fortunately impossible to specify exactly what "becoming like children" will mean to each person at each moment. Any particular senior on whom the camera focuses could be found at work or at play, in agony or in ecstasy, in action or in repose, in indecision or in resolve, in the face of incredible odds or with wind at her back, differing from all other aged persons who are in similar but never truly duplicate circumstances. Despite the fact that no single clear set of rules and no portrait of such a person will precisely apply to others, many thinkers who have pondered such texts through years of experience provide some deductions and clues about how childness might look in the mature and aged person.

As with regret, so with the equally unproductive, even destructive counterpart, envy. If envy dominated, the soul would hear: "Some people have a knack for embodying and displaying personality features that qualify as childlike. I envy them, but I am not one of them. I've gone through too much in life; I've been bruised too often and challenged or inspired too little to match the example of the virtuosos of childlikeness. I don't even know how to define *childlikeness,* but I know it when I see it in others, and I know I can't find it in me, unless I am given counsel and aid."

Continuity and the Mystery of Change

Gerontological education, as practiced by experts, includes many ideas and techniques that encourage change. Although people at seventy cannot be expected to be as physically and intellectually supple as they had been at seven or seventeen, many older people do come to adopt a worldview that permits them to be liberated from static ways of life. Let me give a personal instance, chosen from a great number of similar experiences. I once spent a morning at a senior home where a saxophonist-composer had asked a large number of participants to bring noise-making tools and musical instruments such as harmonicas or drums. Then he evoked from them rhythmic patterns to accompany his playing. The result was almost worthy of an Igor Stravinksy or a John Cage. These older people brought forth new sounds while entertaining and educating themselves with a freedom that college music majors are less likely to allow themselves. It would be foolish to argue on the basis of one illustration that senior adults who experienced creative moments one morning will be set on a new course for life. Instead, we take glimpses such as this one to note how many old people, inhibited or lacking self-esteem as they may be, have potentials for being imaginative, open to ideas and experiences and to other people.

"Where am I to be found among the passages of my life, my time? The behavior and self-concepts of older people are often influenced by whether they perceive themselves as being 'on time' or not." That is the argument of Jackie C. Lanum and James E. Birren.[5] The notion of being on time in developmental processes is precisely what the Gospel word of Jesus challenges. It was designed to upset the crowd of mature adults whom he asked to become like children. It is, of course, only natural that as peo-

5. Jackie C. Lanum and James E. Birren, "Adult Development Theories and Concepts," in *Aging, Spirituality, and Religion: A Handbook,* ed. Melvin A. Kimble, Susan H. McFadden, James W. Ellor, and James J. Seeber (Minneapolis: Fortress, 1995), 521.

ple age, they seek some measure of continuity, even as they are called to be creative about change and newness. Not a few observers of children's behavior find many of them already to be seeking such measures themselves. Robert C. Atchley spells out how adults seek such continuity and shows how it can be a healthy element for adapting and coping:

> The central thesis of continuity theory is that in adapting to aging, people attempt to preserve and maintain the long-standing patterns of living and coping that they identify as being uniquely them. They tend to use familiar ideas and coping strategies in familiar environments, activities, and social relationships. Thus, adaptation takes place in ways that preserve the continuity of character, setting, and plot. Change is designed and redefined to be integrated with one's prior history and anticipated future.
>
> Individuals have goals for their developmental direction. Continuity theory assumes that individuals actively seek to achieve their hoped-for selves and avoid their feared selves. They actively construe their future and organize their choices based on concepts of what has worked for them in the past and where they want to be in the future. As individuals age, their life experiences tend to teach them what aspirations are realistic for them. Therefore, in later life the hoped-for, ideal self tends to be more realistic and, because the gap between the ideal and the real is smaller compared to earlier in life, self-esteem tends to be higher. Accordingly, specific changes occur in a context that includes ideas about continuing identity and evolutionary direction.[6]

That identity and direction are never static, so old people are not left to be simply resistant to new ideas and means of acting on them. The Gospel narrative lets readers and hearers presume that people of parental and grandparental age are helping to make up Jesus' audience. He disrupts their sense of continuity by provocatively lifting up the child as model. What does that action do to the realistic mature person who has healthy self-esteem? Disrupting the old pattern and then opening up to the new tend to occur through what in religious vocabulary is called *metanoia,* repentance, making "about face" turnarounds, or experiencing some kind of conversion. Atchley and the colleagues he quotes recognize some limits: "Of course, continuity theory is not designed to explain religious conversion experiences, particularly those that result in a fundamental re-

6. Robert C. Atchley, "The Continuity of the Spiritual Self," in Kimble et al., *Aging, Spirituality, and Religion,* 69.

structuring of the self that endures over the remainder of a lifetime. To understand these, another kind of theory would be needed."[7]

Some of that theory could relate to the narrative in which Jesus speaks not only to certain castes and types of people. He gives an implicitly universal saying when he asserts that whoever changes and becomes like a child is in range of the kingdom. Whoever does not change and refuses or fails to become like children is out of range. There is here evidently a human universal, something ontological — having to do with the being of the human — that is not just the outcome of pedagogy and obedience. For believers, there is to be read into and out of this some sort of parable of what God is like or what God does. This can be the case, at least, if humans do not work strenuously to block the divine motion toward them. In the Gospel pictures, hearers do this blocking, for instance, by seeing themselves as being completely mature or by choosing to be jaded or cynical.

Crispation: The Drying Up of Life at Any Age

This book could just as well have been titled "the mystery of the adolescent" or "the mystery of the middle-aged," had we wanted to take up the thesis about change and receptivity and address all the other ages of life. The child, however, as exemplified in Jesus' words, allows for a purer approach to this aspect of the mystery of human existence. We have carried over observations from preadolescents to people that Shakespeare's Jaques says are near the end of "this strange eventful history." Older people represent the extreme case and are the most obvious laboratory. One least expects change or childlikeness where the soul has been shriveled to match the changing body.

The French-based word for this shriveling or drying up is *crispation,* which is the same word in French and English. Joe McCown discusses the concept as developed by Gabriel Marcel, who based it on the image of a leaf in autumn.[8] Such an image matches what the Psalmist speaks of as the sap that has dried up. It does not appear to be possible to see such a leaf become fresh again. So in the eyes of many, the very old person is presumed to be on the verge of crispation and thus will be a harder case for

7. Atchley, "The Continuity of the Spiritual Self," 71.

8. Joe McCown, *Availability: Gabriel Marcel and the Phenomenology of Human Openness* (Missoula, MT: Scholars, 1978), 12-13.

change than would be an adolescent, a youth, or a young adult, all of whom have a longer future in prospect and enjoy more fluidity and agility in the present. However, the Psalmist sets no term limits: "In old age they still produce fruit; they are always green and full of sap" (Psalm 92:14). If change was possible among the elderly people of the Psalmist's day, then it was possible among the people presumed to be of early-parent age in the Gospel story. We are speaking here again of human universals.

To explore this, we double back to the observations and promise of Karl Rahner, as voiced in Chapter 5 in this book. He referred to the biologically young child. Now the words can apply to the old man or woman. We revisit them in this new context: "Childhood," he elaborates, "is not a state which only applies to the first phase of our lives in the biological sense. Rather it is a basic condition which is always appropriate to a life that is lived aright." That condition of childness can match what Jesus' words in the Gospel of Matthew describe as becoming like children. "All the stages of life have an equally immediate relationship to God." Of course, a life does advance through "a series of stages," but if childhood were not a basic condition, the principle could not be upheld. If our existence is to be sound and redeemed, Rahner writes, "childhood must be an intrinsic element in it," a living and effective force if we are to "endure even in the depths of the mystery."[9]

Then the aged thinker spells out some markers of the childlike. We cannot rehearse them too often, since they come close to condensing the plot and goal of *The Mystery of the Child.* The markers are signs that include openness, expectation, receptivity, and a hope that is still not disillusioned. Biological childhood, Rahner insisted, is "only the beginning, the prelude, the foretaste and the promise of this other childhood," as it is present in the mature person. This sentence may sound bizarre to anyone who has confined the concepts of childhood to infants and preschoolers. Then we read another shocker by Rahner: "In other words we must take childhood in this *latter* sense as the true and proper childhood, the fullness of that *former* childhood, the childhood of immaturity." Once more, this exemplifies Paul Ricoeur's theme that anything connected with the Gospel turns everything upside down. Now, in an overturning of expectations, it is the childhood of maturity that is "true and proper" and full![10]

9. Karl Rahner, "Ideas for a Theology of Childhood," chap. 3 in *Theological Investigations,* vol. 8: *Further Theology of the Spiritual Life,* trans. David Bourke (New York: Herder and Herder, 1971), 47.

10. Rahner, "Ideas for a Theology of Childhood," 47.

Rahner's ideal is that "life becomes for us a state in which our original childhood is preserved for ever; a state in which we are open to expect the unexpected, to commit ourselves to the incalculable, a state which endows us with the power still to be able to play, to recognize that the powers presiding over existence are greater than our own designs."[11] He sets out to refute the claims of those who see the stages and phases of the life course as being discontinuities. Life is not a series of phases, "each of which is exhausted and leads on to the next, the very meaning of which is to disappear into the next, to be a preparation for it, to 'exist' for the further stages beyond itself." Succession, we read, was only one part of the truth; otherwise "childhood itself disappears."[12]

The Abyss of Mystery

Another Jesuit thinker, Drew Christiansen, does further turns on the thought of Rahner, who has dealt alike with childhood and old age. The epigraph for Christiansen's chapter that treats "a Catholic perspective" is from Rahner: "The real high point of my life is still to come," he wrote at eighty. This high point, he added, means "the abyss of the mystery of God, into which one lets oneself fall in complete confidence of being caught up by God's love and mercy forever." This being caught up is far from the "mere oblivion" of which Jaques spoke in *As You Like It.* Now the whole focus is once again on mystery. The human's very grounding, says Christiansen, "lies in the abyss of mystery, which accompanies [a person] always throughout life. The only question is whether he lives with mystery willingly, obediently and trustingly, or represses it and will not admit it, 'suppressing' it."[13]

Christiansen tells why he thinks Rahner uses the word *mystery* instead of *God* in these contexts: *"Employing the word 'mystery' reminds persons that divine presence exceeds every limit they would place on it"* (italics added). Speaking of mystery rather than of God, then, is done, he insists, "to encourage individuals to encounter the wonder and the terror that a genuine encounter with God entails."[14]

11. Rahner, "Ideas for a Theology of Childhood," 42.

12. Rahner, "Ideas for a Theology of Childhood," 34.

13. Drew Christiansen, SJ, "A Catholic Perspective," in Kimble et al., *Aging, Spirituality, and Religion,* 403.

14. Christiansen, "A Catholic Perspective," 404. Christiansen is quoting Karl Rahner, "Mystery," in *Sacramentum Mundi: An Encyclopedia of Theology,* vol. 4 (New York: Herder, 1969), 135.

The turn of which thinkers like Marcel, Rahner, and Ricoeur speak can be well represented through some word play, a rearrangement of two Latin words. Thomas R. Cole, a historian of aging, offers them in his humanist analogue to the conversion called for in the Gospel narrative and in Rahner's comments. Cole writes: "When my father died at the age of twenty-seven, I was immediately transformed into an aged four-year-old, a *senex puer,* an aged boy." He continues: "For many years, I carried a burden of guilt and depression, punctuated by primal flashes of wisdom. The sequence of generations in my life had been broken. I could not live childhood's innocence and exuberance and felt that I too would die young." The ideal for Cole later in life was to be instead *puer senex,* the senior person who bore within him the character of the boy, the child. Cole relates this to theological thinking in the Middle Ages:

> Theologians . . . did acknowledge the possibility of transcending one's bodily age and reaching a more advanced spiritual age. By a miracle of grace, a rare child (a *puer senex* or *puella senecta*) might possess the wisdom and virtue that could not ordinarily develop in the natural order until old age. Or an older person might display the virtues of *infantia spiritualis,* the simplicity and purity of a small child.

Cole adopts the mode of Rahner and observes it in a specific culture:

> Anglo-Saxon literature shows a clear preference for the wisdom of old age over the innocence of childhood — for young people achieving the spiritual condition of old age rather than older people achieving the virtues of childhood or the powers of youth. In a culture that valued eternal life rather than eternal youth, this preference is not surprising. Transcending one's age allowed a person to triumph over secular time, to enter into the timeless world of eternity.[15]

In the modern world, in which many may devalue the eternal, we find abundant examples of very old people who counsel being young all one's life — not in the sense of denying bodily debility or supporting a cult of youthful beauty, but in outlook on life. Among these, for example, was Pablo Casals, who was still playing the cello in concerts in his nineties. For him, resolve played a bigger part than conversion and awakening. He spoke to young musicians about the paradox of his life: "I am perhaps the

15. Thomas R. Cole, *The Journey of Life: A Cultural History of Aging in America* (Cambridge: Cambridge University Press, 1992), xv, 7-8.

oldest musician in the world! I am an old man but in many senses a very young man. And this is what I want you to be — young, young all your life, and to say things to the world that are true."[16]

For Rahner, however, being young is not so much an act of discipline and resolution as an attitude of openness and expectation, as in the Gospel stories of children. One does not have to be mature, heroic, or disciplined to be in range of childness. A reader can cull from the many authors cited and from my own pages some of the characteristics of the mystery of the child pointed to in the Gospel story. This child, and now in some appropriate ways an adult, is *receptive, responsive, amenable, simple, teachable, unspoiled; someone who is observed to be or who can acknowledge being relatively helpless, insignificant, unimposing, lacking status, dependent.* Yes, "of such is the kingdom of God." That sequence of words summarizes the plot of this book because it illustrates something of the surprise, the imagination, the creativity, the wonder — yes, the mystery — of the child.

A Personal Afterword on the Abyss of Mystery

This book did not begin with a foreword, because I was eager to focus from the beginning on "the mystery of the child," stopping only long enough to explain why I was writing a book on the child. Now I will forget about academic conventions and personalize this parting word with unembarrassed use of the word *I.* I hope that using this device will help seal the plot and fulfill the intent of the book. All along I have been guided by impulses condensed in a quotation from Marcus Aurelius: "You've wandered all over and finally realized that you never found what you were after: how to live."[17] I still seek and shall always seek "how to live," now not in childhood but near the other end of the course of life, facing what Rahner called "the abyss of mystery."

With the end of life in mind, sometimes along the way of writing it occurred to me that critics might find many experiences of children slighted. Do the experts and thinkers who make their appearance here too often have in mind the middle-class child in a prosperous society? I hope that I have given enough attention to children in unfortunate circumstances to counter that criticism. For that matter, middle-class existence

16. Casals's comment appears in numerous books of quotations about music and aging; I have not been able to trace it to an original source.

17. Quoted as the epigraph by Arthur Frank, *The Renewal of Generosity,* 1.

in prosperity can be an unfortunate circumstance! Now there is the hazard that this last chapter may inspire some to think that I am picturing the later stages of the aging process as a time when it is easy to relish and manifest childness.

When you read this book, I will be entering my ninth decade, having lived beyond the life expectancy for males born when I was. This means that the years ahead are "borrowed time." It is true that, except for the trauma of living with the death of my first wife and resuming life without her, my biography to this date suggests that mainly good things have happened, and my faith and hope may suggest to me that mainly good things are ahead. How long that "ahead" is, one cannot know. I learned from theologian Dietrich Bonhoeffer, martyr to the Nazis, to live *sub conditione Iacobi,* which means to be aware of the conditions of finitude, contingency, and transience set forth by the apostle James: "You do not even know what tomorrow will bring. What is your life? For you are a mist that appears for a little while and then vanishes. Instead you ought to say, 'If the Lord wishes, we will live and do this or that'" (James 4:14-15). It is wearying to "say" that every day, but one can internalize it, think it, and live.

Living now can mean taking long walks in our downtown Chicago neighborhood with my second wife, Harriet, and coming to a conclusion with her that we often ponder: "Retirement times? These are the best years. The only downside is that there are not many of them left." As our contemporaries suffer illness or – here's that unlovely but realistic word again – decrepitude, we have to know that such can be our fate. Yet, having tried to learn the lessons from Albert Schweitzer when he was ill and from Nancy Mairs when she was desperately declining, we are very much aware with them that we are part of a company. That company includes not only the ill and the declining but people of all ages, beginning with children. I would not have written this book had not love for and interest in them been such a part of my life. Now as we relate to three great-grandchildren and to so many children of others, we can take some lessons about childness from them. Admittedly, it may not be so easy to do any of that if we are at some point confined to home or "a home," and it will be most difficult to do if terminal illness comes and the provision of care finally means the hospice.

In spite of all, if childness is a spiritual reach and not only the natural endowment that it is for the child herself, that which we have connected with the mystery of the child can continue to represent aspirations and, sometimes, realizations in any circumstance. "Unless you change, and become like children . . ." (Matthew 18:3).

If that means being *receptive and responsive,* it remains a possibility and can be realized. We have seen it in people of all ages, including old age. Throughout this book I have stressed how important it is not to make control of the child or of others or of circumstances the highest ideal, but to find ways other than controlling to relate to others. The temptation to control still comes to aged people in weakened circumstances, who can use their situation to make demands on those who provide care for them.

If being receptive means being *teachable,* we can point to the millions of seniors who flock to lectures, films, and concerts; who use radio and television and libraries well; or who learn from the people they teach and whom they serve in volunteer capacities. Among them learning never stops, and I have observed a special beauty among those who learn for learning's sake, not to improve their careers. Their careers are far behind them. Now all they have left is their vocations, their callings, which do not need to include professional life.

Being *relatively helpless, insignificant, unimposing, lacking status, dependent?* Yes, these fit. As people of all ages but especially most old people have to learn, they will often find themselves relatively helpless in the face of health-care bureaucracies, stripped and lightly robed, defenseless in a hospital. We often observe that a person is regarded as significant, imposing, and of high status during the years when she is productive, being the boss or the high-achiever. Being aged, however, provides lessons in becoming insignificant to all but those who will be given the task of writing works of semifiction that we call obituaries.

Love is stronger than death, and death does not have the last word to the person of faith. I like to paraphrase Martin Luther, who said that under the old dispensation we used to say, "in the midst of life we are in death." In the new, however, we say, "in the midst of death we are in life."

So in the years ahead we hope to do "such and such," as the book of James speaks of anything and everything, but to do so *sub conditione Iacobi,* bidding others of our company and strangers along the way to enjoy doing the same. We will be receiving the gift of each new day, and with that gift the presence of children in our midst, mirrors of the divine mystery that represents both an abyss and a promise.

Index of Subjects and Names

Index of Scripture References